Science for English Language Learners

Developing Academic Language Through Inquiry-Based Instruction

Authors
Dolores Beltran, Ph.D.
Lilia E. Sarmiento, Ph.D.
Eugenia Mora-Flores, Ed.D.

Foreword
Alan J. McCormack, Ph.D.

SHELL EDUCATION

Publishing Credits

Dona Herweck Rice, *Editor-in-Chief*; Robin Erickson, *Production Director*;
Lee Aucoin, *Creative Director*; Timothy J. Bradley, *Illustration Manager*;
Sara Johnson, M.S.Ed., *Senior Editor*; Aubrie Nielsen, M.S.Ed., *Associate Education Editor*;
Grace Alba, *Designer*; Stephanie Reid, *Photo Editor*; Corinne Burton, M.A.Ed., *Publisher*

Shell Education
5301 Oceanus Drive
Huntington Beach, CA 92649-1030
http://www.shelleducation.com
ISBN 978-1-4258-0859-4
© 2013 Shell Educational Publishing, Inc.

Table of Contents

Foreword

The motto of the United States, *e pluribus Unum*, loosely translates as "one from many." Though this originally referred to the melding of the thirteen colonies into a single and independent nation, it now reflects the rich mosaic of our land of immigrants, nowhere better represented than in schools. More than 5.5 million students in U.S. schools are identified as English language learners (ELLs) and they represent more than 11 percent of the total public school population.

The National Science Teachers Association (NSTA) formulated a position statement regarding science instruction for English language learners (2009). In this comprehensive statement, the NSTA proposes that the science instruction of ELLs be standards-based, anchored to science investigations that promote hands-on inquiry, incorporate literacy skills (reading, writing, speaking, listening, viewing, and representing), and capitalize on the linguistic and cultural experiences that ELLs bring from their home and cultural environments. It also charges teachers to incorporate instructional strategies that enable ELLs to access their prior knowledge, learn science content, and communicate science ideas by using multiple modes of representation (gestural, oral, pictorial, graphic, and textual). Science for English language learners should involve a meaningful learning environment in which to develop fluency in oral and written English as well as in the discourse of science.

The authors of *Science for English Language Learners* are firm and enthusiastic supporters of the NSTA principles. They remind us that curiosity abounds in *all* children—everyday sights and sounds of the world are enticing. And, children are not afraid to act on their queries; they are ready to bend, spindle, manipulate, smell, and explore materials in every way imaginable. They are natural scientists. Just as actual scientists construct explanations for natural events, children construct personal explanations for their experiences with objects they encounter in their environments.

Beltran, Sarmiento, and Mora-Flores have proposed that science education will ideally parallel what scientists do when they "do" science. This approach to science-paralleled learning is rightly called "constructivist learning." In philosophy of science education, students are assumed to arrive at any lesson with an arsenal of prior knowledge related to the lesson topic. Students are challenged to bring their current understandings forward to a conscious level and participate in a variety of experiences to test, connect, and reform their understandings, thus *constructing* meaning for themselves. Our authors promote "doing" exciting, hands-on science based on curiosity-provoking tangible materials. To facilitate this classroom adventure, they suggest myriad wonderful techniques for making both English language and science content attainable for ELLs.

One of the best ways to approach implementation of the NSTA principles for ELL science education is to adopt the 5E Learning Cycle as described in Chapters 4–8. The theoretical "glue" that binds this into a workable approach to helping ELLs improve in both English language *and* understanding of science is the *Talk, Thought*, and *Interaction* framework for English language development proposed by the authors.

I sincerely hope you enjoy your 5E journey facilitated by *Talk, Thought*, and *Interaction*. I know I have.

—Alan J. McCormack, Ph.D.
Professor of Science Education, San Diego State University
Past President, National Science Teachers Association

Acknowledgements

The work behind this book required a large supporting group, to whom we are indebted for their knowledge, their ideas, and the courage to teach in front of others on behalf of all students. Through their efforts, we developed greater science-content knowledge and better understanding of the intricacies of teaching both English language development and science.

For this, we are most grateful to the leadership at the Montebello Unified School District for inviting us to take part in a project through the California Postsecondary Education Commission (CPEC) Improving Teacher Quality State Grant. We thank Deborah De La Torre, Interim Assistant Superintendent, Instructional Services Division; John Myers, Administrative Consultant; and Patricia Alvarez, ITQ/CPEC Grant Project Director. We also wish to thank Program Specialists Arturo Navar, Teresa Granados, Christina Cortez, and Silvia Lezama, as well as Maria Gonzalez, Senior Office Assistant.

Thank you, Gudiel Crosthwaite, James Sams, Margie Rodriguez, Robert Cornejo, and Leo Gallegos, principals at Bell Gardens, Montebello Park, Rosewood Park, and Wilcox elementary schools. We especially thank the teachers at these sites who provided us with the richness of their multifaceted perspectives. As we listened to their planning and debrief sessions and watched them teach and reteach, we derived valuable insights as they struggled to make sense of complex science content and looked deeper into the language needs of their students.

A special thank-you to the site facilitators for their support: Diana Bixler, Gloria Cunningham, Veronica Alatorre-Perea, María Hernandez, Gloria Guerrero, Martha Cervantes, Feliciano Rodriguez, Ricardo Ramirez, Esperanza Flores-Sandoval, Araceli Caldera, Leslie Hiatt, and Yvonne Andrade. In particular, we thank María Hernandez,

Martha Cervantes, and Silvia Lezama, who allowed us to videotape their teaching. We learned much from our professional collaboration and dialogue about what matters most for English language learners.

Our inspiration thrived through the observations of interactive science and language practices. A most sincere thank-you goes to our core scenario teacher, Christina Cortez. Early in the project, you enlightened us about what it takes to be an effective teacher of science while integrating the language needs of students. You were relentless in seeking out resources and taking risks in your teaching.

Another heartfelt thank-you goes to Leslie Hiatt. You demonstrated for us what can be possible when you teach a group of students for three years. Your passion for teaching, and in particular, the teaching of science, was contagious. Anytime we visited your classroom or videotaped your lessons, you practiced what an effective teacher does: you reflected on your teaching and asked for feedback. You never let us walk away without giving you suggestions on how to make it better. You never said *no,* and for that, we are very, very grateful. Your energy when teaching and the sincere love you have for your students is an inspiration for all. You confirmed our belief that the teaching of ELD through science is possible.

We are most appreciative to our science colleagues: Jo Topps, Susan Zwiep, Bill Straits, Myra Pasquier, Jackie Gallaway, and especially Gladys Garcia, who introduced us to the 5E model and demonstrated quality science instruction in countless ways. Your foundational work with professional development in science education served as a platform for us to build upon and eventually led to the writing of this book. A thank-you also goes to Leena Furtado, who collaborated with us early in the project.

And finally, a huge *gracias* to our collective families. Their patience, love, and encouragement made it possible for us to craft this contribution to the field. We love you all!

—Dolores, Lilia, and Eugenia

Managing and Maximizing Language Development Through Inquiry-Based Science

The integration of inquiry-based science and English language development provides students with optimal opportunities to learn content, develop rich academic language, and enjoy learning about the world around them.

Remember the days when classrooms came alive as students hovered around erupting volcanoes, or stood awestruck as they generated electricity from a piece of wire, a lightbulb, and a battery? Where have those days gone? We repeatedly hear from teachers that the challenge is *time*. With the mandated time blocks for language arts, mathematics, and English language development (ELD), little time is left for social studies, science, art, music, drama, dance, and physical education. One way to approach the challenge of time is integration. In our work, we have found what we call a successful marriage of ELD and science, which affords students the opportunity to experience science daily and develop high levels of academic language.

We have come a long way in our work around ELD science. We began years ago with a focus on English language development. Through thoughtful research, planning, and critical discussions, we landed upon a solid understanding of English language development. We felt that to move the work forward, we needed to have a common language around some key questions: What is ELD? What does it mean to facilitate language for diverse English-language-learner populations? Our work was shared with hundreds of teachers working with English language learners in diverse contexts. We gathered data and teacher reflections as they too began to understand ELD and see a shift in their students' language development. We were excited about the impact we were making but knew there was more to learn and share, which led to over eight years of providing professional development in English language development. Though we worked in various districts, the main focus of our work was in a large urban district with high numbers of English language learners. This district afforded us many opportunities to learn alongside teachers and students, which led us to our new focus on the integration of ELD and inquiry-based science instruction.

Through collaboration with the K–12 Alliance, West Ed, and California State University, Long Beach, a grant was awarded to the district to provide strong professional development and school-based support in the area of ELD science. As the three ELD consultants, we were committed to finding an effective and practical way for teachers to truly facilitate ELD through science. We helped teachers see how each phase of a 5E inquiry-based model could support ELLs to use, learn, and apply language through authentic, highly engaging science instruction. Each elementary school we worked with had originally demonstrated low performance on the California statewide language arts exams, in addition to having a large population of English language learners. An instructional leader at each school site supported the work. The model featured a 10-day Facilitator Academy and an 11-day Teaching Learning Collaborative Academy (TLC) for each year. The TLC included five days of science content in the summer, and six days of an extended academy during the school year. Each year, the content academy focused on either Earth, physical, or life science as well as pedagogical skills to teach young learners. In addition, all teachers received side-by-side support and professional development on the role of language in the 5E model.

This book is our attempt to share what we brought to the project as well as what we learned from it. We contributed our years of work and expertise in the area of ELD to the project, and provided a strong theoretical and instructional framework for helping English language learners access, use, and develop language. That framework includes *talk*, *thought*, and *interaction*.

A Thinking, Doing, and Talking ELD Framework

Our framework for English language development is based on three overlapping and interacting dimensions: talk, thought, and interaction. Our work with teachers of English language learners emphasizes understanding and actualizing these dimensions within the teaching and learning they design and implement.

The dimension of *talk* in instructional decision making for ELLs refers to emphasizing the creation of meaning-laden tasks that support the attainment of academic language proficiency through the modeling, practice, and use of specific content-related language. Embedded within this aspect of our framework are a focus on the vocabulary, forms, and functions of language; a rich multisensory learning environment; and authentic purposes for using language.

When students are using both language and thinking to learn new content, they are engaged in the *thought* dimension of our framework. A cognitive emphasis for planning ELD science instruction means that teachers design tasks that require students to explore phenomena in order to stimulate inquiry, uncover relationships, make inferences, and draw conclusions as they synthesize and analyze information. The reward of providing cognitively stimulating learning experiences is that they become wellsprings for language practice and use, as students are compelled to share their thinking and developing understanding with others. A thinking-and-doing curriculum while acquiring language is a critical aspect for the second-language development of ELLs.

Interaction is a key dynamic within our framework. Because we believe that social interaction is essential for English language development, this dimension emphasizes that any instructional task for ELLs must ensure the exchange of ideas and language between students as well as teachers and students. With a focus on the mediated exchange between models and users of the language, teachers continuously monitor student understanding until the student is capable of independent expression and application.

Inquiry-Based Learning

When approaching the learning of science through a framework of talk, thought, and interaction embedded in inquiry-based science, students engage in self-discovery. Inquiry approaches allow students to get their minds around something, to look closely at it, and to think deeply about their learning. They have time to explore concrete concepts and apply them to abstract ones in order to understand the learning process and apply their learning in new contexts.

As adapted from the work of Bybee et al. (1989) we came to understand the 5E process as *Engage, Explore, Explain, Extend,* and *Evaluate.* Throughout each stage of the 5E learning cycle, we can identify optimal language learning opportunities. "Inquiry-science instruction engages students in the exploration of scientific phenomena, and language activities are explicitly linked to objects, processes, hands-on experimentation, and naturally occurring events in the environment; i.e., they are contextualized … and they can communicate their understanding in a variety of formats, for example, writing, orally, drawing, creating tables and graphs" (Stoddart et al. 2002, 666). The purpose of the 5E lesson plan model is twofold: to share an effective model for developing content knowledge and critical thinking skills while developing high levels of academic language. Through a careful analysis of each stage of the 5E model, we help teachers understand academic language development.

The integration of our ELD framework of *Talk, Thought,* and *Interaction* made its way into the 5E inquiry-based science model through careful attention to language at each stage of the 5E model. What we learned from our work through the CPEC grant was that the integration of ELD and science is not only possible but also successful. We were excited to see classrooms buzzing with excitement around science. Teachers were excited to see their students enjoying science and improving their language. In the end, we also saw great gains in the students' standardized statewide exam scores.

We were excited not only about the success of our work but also about the possibility of reaching so many more teachers and students. We wanted to bring this joy of learning, the rediscovery of great science instruction, and a successful approach to ELD to more classrooms. This book is filled with the knowledge we shared with the teachers with whom we worked, and also with the voices of their students in various classroom scenarios.

Navigating the Text

This book highlights the language-development opportunities available at each phase of the 5Es as well as how language is connected across the 5Es. Our hope is that teachers never lose sight of the language-development opportunities they have throughout their day, and in this case, with science education.

Chapter 1 gives an overview of language development. It features information about how we can understand the complexity and layers of language that English language learners must navigate through as they reach high levels of academic success. This chapter serves as a foundation to better understand how we talk about language throughout the book as well as how to listen for and understand language development.

In Chapter 2, we look further at how to take what we know about language and instruction for English language learners and apply it to our own work with ELLs. This chapter highlights principles for ELD instruction and revisits our sociocognitive framework of *Talk*, *Thought*, and *Interaction*.

Chapter 3 provides a comprehensive overview of assessing English language learners within inquiry-based science. It discusses factors that influence ELL assessment and examines best practices. The chapter also positions the science notebook as a vehicle for assessment of English language learners within the 5E model, giving light to its merits and showing examples of student work.

In Chapters 4–8, we provide an in-depth look at each phase of the 5E process. Each chapter begins with questions that will focus your reading and initiate your own inquiry process. These chapters provide essential features for each stage of the 5E inquiry cycle. It also includes classroom scenarios that help make the connection between theory and practice with an explanation of how the scenario further represents a clear focus on language by both the teacher and the students. A variety of instructional strategies that are effective at each phase of the 5Es are further presented in each of these chapters with a quick step-by-step guide on how to use them in your classroom. And, though each of these chapters speaks particularly to one of the five Es, all of them are connected through a core scenario that builds from one chapter to the next. The purpose of this is to show that, though each phase of the 5Es has distinguishable goals and objectives in science and language, they build upon one another.

The Afterword contains our concluding thoughts, and we end the book with a look at the effectiveness of connecting science to academic language development. Our hope is that we communicate clearly that this work is not only possible but it is also powerful in supporting English language learners in ways that can lead to a lifetime of curiosity and inquiry.

What continues to excite us about this work is watching students take control of their learning. Students are talking, and they are talking about academic content. Students are demonstrating confidence in their use of academic language because they are provided with opportunities to observe, explore, think, and comprehend before having to use language to explain and reflect on their thinking. Through the 5E inquiry-based model for science, students are provided powerful opportunities for *talk, thought,* and *interaction.*

CHAPTER 1

Understanding Academic Language Proficiency for English Language Learners

You May Wonder:

- What must a teacher of English language learners understand about academic language proficiency?

- What is the framework for developing academic language through inquiry-based instruction?

Since 1979, the population of English language learners in United States schools has nearly doubled (Federal Interagency Forum on Child and Family Statistics 2005), representing nearly 10 percent of students nationally (NCELA 2011). Expectations are that the number of ELLs in U.S. classrooms will continue to increase (Passel 2007).

Because of the No Child Left Behind (NCLB) legislation of 2001, a focus on the mathematics and reading achievement of subgroups such as ELLs was brought to light. As a result, realities of the current education of such populations became a critical conversation among educators across the country. More than ever before, districts, schools, and teachers began to focus attention and resources on meeting the needs of English language learners. In 2011, President Barack Obama released the blueprint for the reauthorization of the Elementary and Secondary Education Act. Part of the blueprint focused on the need to improve the education of English language learners, stating that education should "[f]ocus on developing promising practices and scaling up effective practices for improving the instruction of English Learners and for preparing and developing effective teachers of English Learners" (U.S. Department of Education 2010, 41).

The teachers who are featured in this book hold many beliefs about how to provide the language acquisition and development modifications that English language learners need in order to achieve second-language literacy and academic English language proficiency. The foundations for their beliefs and practices emanate from a strong theory and research base in second-language learning and ELD instruction. As effective teachers, they view it as their responsibility "to choose the best of what others have experimented with and adapt those insights" to their own situations (Brown 1994, 15). A reality that they must grapple with is the complexity inherent in the English language learners they encounter in their classrooms and the challenge they face as teachers to ensure that these ELLs develop English academic-language proficiency. For educators to grasp the complexity of educating English language learners, they must focus intensely on language development and academic learning in a second language through the lens of best practices illuminated by research—the best of what the field knows at any given time. This chapter will discuss the predominant theoretical foundations and research that all teachers of English language learners must understand and rely upon for their instructional decisions. The theoretical framework that stems from this research has served as the basis for our work in inquiry-based teaching and learning.

English Language Learners Are Complex

The English language learners who attend our schools are culturally, linguistically, and academically diverse. Speaking more than 400 languages, the racial/ethnic composition of the 2.7 million limited-English speaking students in the United States in 2005 was 70 percent Hispanic, 13 percent Asian/Pacific Islander, 12 percent non-Hispanic white, and 4 percent non-Hispanic black. Over a third of the limited-English speaking students resided in poverty (35 percent), in comparison to a poverty rate of 19 percent among public school students who were not limited-English speakers (Federal Interagency Forum on Child and Family Statistics 2005; NCES 2006; Passel 2007).

English language learners come to U.S. schools with many and varied resources for academic achievement, including linguistic resources in their native languages. At the same time, ELLs also represent a wide range of need in English language development, English literacy, and subject-matter knowledge in English in order to become academically successful in American schools. The diversity within the ELL student population presents significant features that impact their instruction and achievement.

Migration patterns among immigrant families result in English language learners entering our schools at different ages and grade levels. Since research indicates that certain aspects of second language and literacy development are related to general cognitive maturity (August and Shanahan 2006; Genesee et al. 2006), age of entry and academic history are factors for teachers' instructional planning. Older English language learners acquire academic language proficiency in English more rapidly because cognitive academic language proficiency is more developed in their first language (Cummins 1981), and they may be learning a language that is very similar to the one they already know (Lightbown and Spada 2006). For example, a recent synthesis of the research on English language learners finds that phonological awareness skills and awareness of shared cognates in both languages are found to be a more well-developed resource for older second-language learners (Genesee et al. 2006). However, similar levels of awareness and development are not as likely for primary-age English language learners. But, Lightbown and Spada (2006) call attention to a prepubescent *critical period* in language learning in which younger language learners are favored by certain innate capacities, time to devote to language learning, and a greater acceptance of trial and error in language use.

Variations in educational background also pose particular issues for classroom teachers (Garcia and Curry-Rodriguez 2000; Olsen and Jaramillo 1999). Some ELLs enter U.S. schools with strong academic preparation in their countries of origin. In addition to strong academic skills, students who have been successful in their native countries may bring well-developed study skills and confidence in their abilities as learners. Other English language learners enter school with limited or interrupted formal schooling, requiring additional time to become accustomed to school routines and expectations. These students find themselves in "catch-up" situations in which they start behind their native English-speaking peers in language development as well as academic development.

In addition to the implications of the amount and quality of schooling in an English language learner's native country, researchers have similarly identified the amount and quality of schooling in the United States as a critical factor for instruction and achievement (Genesee et al. 2006). Some English language learners are native-born U.S. citizens even though they enroll in school with limited-English proficiency. Because of detrimental factors in schooling—inappropriate curriculum and pedagogy, inconsistent instructional programs, high transiency rates, and unprepared teachers—many native-born ELLs lag in both linguistic and academic progress. These students can become long-term English learners trapped by the failure of schools and districts to respond to their unique needs (Olsen and Jaramillo 1999; Valdés 2001).

Sociocultural variables associated with family, expectations, and economic circumstances contribute critical factors for the teaching and learning of English language learners. For example, research shows that family literacy experiences and opportunities, including parent education, are generally associated with superior literacy outcomes (August and Shanahan 2006). However, the literature also finds that schools often underestimate and underutilize parents' interest, motivation, and potential contributions.

Communities are often conflicted by attitudes toward immigrants and poverty, resulting in misinformation, the inequitable distribution of resources, and lowered expectations for ELL achievement. How students feel about themselves as learners and schooling in general are influenced by the attitudes of their teachers and their schools. Social dynamics and power relationships associated with identity, ethnic group affiliation, and learner beliefs influence how students approach language learning (Lightbown and Spada 2006). Decades of research has documented the breakdown of quality and equitable instruction for ELLs (Cummins 1986, 1996, 2000; Freeman and Freeman 1998; García and Curry-Rodriguez 2000; Housman and Martinez 2002; Klesmer 1994; Olsen and Jaramillo 1999; Valdés 2001). Reports about the high dropout rate among English language learners and the growing achievement gap between white and Asian students and Latino and African-American students clearly point to the disconnect between schooling and their needs (Freeman, Freeman, and Mercuri 2002; Fry 2007). These statistics highlight the need for concerted efforts from all sectors of the community to meet myriad linguistic and academic needs.

Because English language learners make up a student population with a wide range of abilities and needs, teachers must view these students as complex learners requiring a complex linguistic, cultural, cognitive, and academic instructional response. The caution for teachers is not to reduce their English language learners' instructional needs to any single component, but to expand their teaching to meet a compendium of multiple and varied needs in order to help students achieve academic language proficiency in English.

The Complexity of Academic Language Proficiency

Academic language proficiency refers to the ability to successfully use language for reading and writing and for accessing information in content areas. Current legislation and policy favoring English-immersion instruction is based on a flawed assumption that students learning English as a second language will become fully fluent quickly, in a matter of one to two years. Such perceptions demonstrate a lack of understanding of the challenge inherent in the complexity of developing academic language proficiency. Communicative competencies such as using complete sentences, expanded vocabulary, and conditional tenses are requisite skills for academic language proficiency. Native English speakers naturally take these language competencies for granted. English language learners must acquire these assumed competencies prior to or at the same time as they master English language arts and content-area standards. They must also apply their limited language competencies to learn challenging grade-level content with equal success as their native English-speaking peers. In most cases, it takes English language learners as long as five to seven years to develop the same level of depth and breadth of language and academic skills as their native English-speaking peers (Collier and Thomas 1999; Cummins 1989).

Much of what we understand about what it means to become proficient in a second language comes from the extensive work of Jim Cummins (1981, 1986, 1989, 1994a, 1994b, 1996, 2000, 2001, 2003, 2005). Cummins (2005, 7–9) describes language proficiency in terms of three dimensions: conversational fluency, discrete language skills, and academic language proficiency. He views the development of these dimensions as a dynamic, interconnected process:

> They [the three dimensions] develop concurrently, and at various stages of development will correlate with one another. However, they also behave differently from one another—with respect to when they reach a developmental

plateau, to the kinds of experiences and instruction that promote each dimension, to the communicative contexts in which they are likely to be exhibited, and to the components of language on which they rely.

Conversational English Fluency

Conversational fluency is the ability to have a meaningful conversation with a native speaker in a social setting. It is often viewed simplistically as interpersonal casual talk (e.g., talking with a friend, playing a game in the schoolyard, or sharing what you did over the weekend) embedded in meaningful and immediate contexts. In English conversation, extralinguistic cues like facial expressions, gestures, and intonation along with authentic social purposes help second-language learners understand what is being communicated. Participants actively negotiate meaning directly through feedback to one another (Genesee and Riches 2006). General consensus has held that relatively high levels of conversational fluency, or social language, can be acquired in one to two years. However, recent synthesis of research examining rates of language development indicates that ELLs on average require several years to develop oral-English proficiency (Saunders and O'Brien 2006). Additionally, findings indicate that ELLs tend to make more rapid progress from lower to middle levels of proficiency (e.g., from level 1 to level 3), and slower progress as they move to higher levels.

Nevertheless, when considering the ability to engage in a conversation in a second language, we must challenge ourselves to understand the complexity of social discourse. In order to communicate their experiences, needs, opinions, and emotions, conversational fluency must develop in sophistication and complexity as ELLs acquire greater communicative competence and achieve greater cognitive maturity. Conversational fluency continues to develop as students work toward academic language proficiency.

Discrete Language Skills

Cummins describes *discrete language skills* as "specific phonological, literacy, and grammatical knowledge that students acquire as a result of direct instruction and both formal and informal practice" primarily through literacy instruction (2005, 7). Discrete language skills such as sound/symbol correspondence can be learned by English language learners relatively early in English language acquisition as ELLs are developing their conversational fluency. A characteristic of these skills is that they can be learned in isolation from the development of more sophisticated aspects of vocabulary understanding and the comprehension of text. For example, an ELL student can be considered a "fluent" reader (decoder) but have limited understanding of what was read.

Academic Language Proficiency

The most complex element of the three dimensions referenced by Cummins is academic language proficiency. Cummins explains that academic language proficiency "includes knowledge of the less-frequent vocabulary of English as well as the ability to interpret and produce increasingly complex written (and oral) language" (2005, 8–9). Guerrero helps further illuminate our understanding of academic language proficiency when he states: "[A]cademic language proficiency is more than mere lexical representations associated with different aspects of the curriculum. It is an internalization and automatization of dealing with cognitively complex decontextualized language at the level of discourse. This discourse is subject to pragmatic conventions, that are embellished with kinesic nuances, specific subject-area characteristics, and sociocultural references. Academic language, in any language, requires time to develop and theoretically has no finite boundaries" (1997, 68).

The level of proficiency needed to successfully read social studies texts for conceptual understanding, to discuss character motive, to solve mathematical word problems, or to report conclusions based on a scientific experiment can take five to seven years to develop

(Collier 1987, Hakuta 2001). As English language learners acquire and develop English, they accumulate certain language competencies. They become increasingly less dependent on explicit instruction to handle complex tasks. They are increasingly better able to combine a variety of extralinguistic clues (e.g., kinesic nuances, such as body language and facial expressions, jargon, and culture) in addition to the language itself, to think critically, to apply previous learning, and to express complex thinking using complex language (Guerrero 1997). However, attaining academic language proficiency is never complete; it is a lifelong process.

Defining *Proficiency*

The term *proficiency* is used today in many contexts, especially within the No Child Left Behind (NCLB) environment. Most state-level English-proficiency assessments focus only on oral language and discrete language skills and not on the application of these skills to academic contexts. Certainly, students should not be considered proficient until they can competently use the language with some consistency in academic contexts. English-language proficiency and proficiency with academic content standards, such as the English language arts standards, tend to be confused with each other because of the common term *proficiency*. The two concepts are not the same.

Evidence suggests that the academic uses of language are associated with higher levels of oral language proficiency and with literacy achievement (Saunders and O'Brien 2006). When planning instruction for English language learners, teachers must understand language proficiency as multifaceted and recognize academic language proficiency as the ultimate goal. The pursuit of this goal is the only way for ELLs to reach the highest levels of English literacy. Teachers must understand that the varied elements of language proficiency do indeed "develop concurrently, and at various stages of development will correlate with one another" (Cummins 2003, 4). Even though the competencies that constitute being proficient in a language develop concurrently, they do not develop independently of one another and are essential elements that must be addressed in ELL instruction.

The Importance of the Primary Language

There is much consensus about the important role of the mother tongue, or primary language, in ELL achievement (August and Hakuta 1997; Cummins 2000; Dutro 2001; Fillmore and Snow 2000; Fitzgerald et al. 2000; Gersten and Baker 2000; Goldenberg 2008; Gutiérrez 2001; Tharp 1997). The primary language is a valuable resource that should be included in instructional planning. Pedagogy that is guided by an instructional philosophy that includes this principle can support English-literacy development along with the oral and academic English language development of all English language learners.

The relationship between the primary language and academic proficiency has been most recently corroborated by the findings of two major comprehensive syntheses of the research on English language learners' literacy development and academic achievement (August and Shanahan 2006; Genesee et al. 2006). Both reports concurred that:

- Language-minority students who are literate in their first language are likely to be advantaged in the acquisition of English literacy

- Language-minority students (elementary and secondary) instructed in their native language as well as English perform on average better on English reading measures than language-minority students instructed only in English

- Students with high levels of bilingual proficiency exhibit elevated levels of academic and cognitive functioning in comparison to students with less well-developed bilingual skills

- The educational success of ELLs is positively related to sustained instruction through the student's first language

A student's primary language is not only the most important medium for literacy in their native language but it can also support their English literacy and their oral and academic English language acquisition. English language learners' understanding of concepts established in their primary language facilitates their understanding of these same concepts in English (Cummins 1981). The common underlying proficiency between languages ensures that once knowledge and abilities are developed in one language, they are potentially available for the development of another. For example, once a child has learned to read in his or her primary language, the child then has many components of reading available to help him or her learn to read in a second language.

English language learners' primary language is an essential and foundational element in their education. Teachers must treat the primary language as a resource that will assist students in reaching the highest-possible levels of English literacy and academic language proficiency. The challenge facing teachers of ELLs is to understand the role of the primary language and to optimize this role as a resource in ELL instruction regardless of program mandates. While full primary language development is relegated to bilingual program models, Gersten and Baker cite the potential and need for a "strategic" use of the mother tongue in English-only immersion program settings (2000, 13).

Teachers who recognize the primary language as an asset employ varied strategies regardless of their instructional program. If they are able, they use the primary language to frontload important concepts for teaching content in English and use the primary language to clarify when needed. They design lessons that emphasize the similarities in cognates and contrast structures of the primary language to teach English-language structures. They maintain clear, distinct, and meaning-enriched contexts for each language during instruction, and they facilitate cross-cultural interactions by organizing instruction to help students understand and respect themselves and their own culture as well as the cultures of the broader society. In the absence of a full primary-language literacy-development pathway in either a dual language or transitional bilingual program, a student's primary language must still be treated as a resource that contributes to their academic success.

Developing Second-Language Proficiency

Throughout the 5E inquiry-based model presented in this book, teachers provide students with opportunities to learn from previous knowledge and use their primary language in early stages of the learning process as a vehicle for learning English as well as learning science content.

Educators who serve English language learners have further shared a basic understanding that a second language is acquired in much the same way as the first language is acquired (Fillmore and Snow 2000). In second-language acquisition, the beginning English language learner receives English-language input from the language resources within the classroom environment, including teachers, classmates, objects, visuals, and texts. As the input from the new language becomes comprehensible—that is, meaningful—the English language learner demonstrates understanding by gesturing and by uttering one- or two-word responses. In the initial stages of the 5E inquiry-based model, *Engage* and *Explore*, students are presented content in a meaningful and highly engaging manner. The level of input is high for ELLs because the content is visible. They are experiencing and engaging directly with the content. This helps students in the language-learning process when they reach the *Explain* stage of the 5Es. At this point, they are explicitly presented the language of science that explains their learning.

As the second language continues to develop, the English language learner expresses understanding and meets his or her social and academic needs in a progression from simple vocabulary embedded within simple phrases and sentences to more grammatically complex sentences using expanded and descriptive vocabulary within extended discourse.

However, this basic understanding belies our evolving understanding that learning a second language is much more complex than we have understood, and therefore, the complexity of acquiring a second language requires attention to multiple essential factors and conditions. Brown reminds us of the rich and varied foundations of language learning and teaching when he states that its cumulative history "has taught us to appreciate the value of 'doing' language interactively, of the emotional (as well as cognitive) side of learning, of absorbing language automatically and of consciously analyzing it, and of pointing learners to the real world out there where they will use English communicatively" (2007, 34). Science provides students with these language-rich experiences. Attention to language development while "doing" science enhances the language-learning process.

Theoretical Perspectives on Learning a Second Language

There are several key perspectives on learning a second language that merit attention because of their significance for ensuring the development of social and academic language proficiency. These include sociocognitive, functionalist, and sociocultural perspectives.

A Sociocognitive Lens

The Natural Approach to teaching and learning a second language was given prominence by the research of Stephen Krashen in the early 1980s. Krashen's work has left a legacy of essential elements for English language development. According to Krashen (1982) and his colleague Tracy Terrell (1981), the conditions that foster the acquisition of a second language in classrooms are based on the understanding of a receptive period of language that precedes language production within a supportive, risk-free and language-rich environment. Krashen's Monitor Model is the theory of second-language acquisition that is the most familiar to practitioners. Figure 1.1 provides a summary of the Monitor Model hypotheses (1994).

Figure 1.1 Krashen's Monitor Model

Five Hypotheses of the Monitor Model	
Acquisition-Learning Hypothesis	Language acquisition is the informal, unconscious awareness of correct and appropriate usage through modeling and practice, not the overt correction that is part of the conscious drill and practice of formal language learning.
Natural Order Hypothesis	There is a universal order (represented as levels or stages) to learning a second language that is similar to that of a first language.
Monitor Hypothesis	As an individual learns and internalizes rules of the second language, an internal monitor edits errors before or after an utterance.
Input Hypothesis	Language is acquired when input is received that is comprehensible and just beyond the current level of competence.
Affective Filter Hypothesis	An environment that reduces anxiety, increases motivation, and promotes self-confidence establishes a low affective filter that enhances language acquisition.

As a result of Krashen's influence, instructional approaches to language acquisition have been imprinted with core features that support a nurturing language-learning environment, value language models, encourage gestures as legitimate demonstrations of language comprehension, use visuals and realia to support meaning, organize resources around themes or thematic topics, and promote real-life, or authentic, purposes for using language.

Since the 1980s, the work of Jim Cummins has contributed greatly to an understanding of the multidimensionality of language and its implications for second-language instruction. As has been discussed previously in this chapter, Cummins's early research (1981, 1994b) emphasized the social and academic dimensions of language and their relationship to contexts of language use and second-language development. Cummins distinguished social language as basic interpersonal communication skills (BICS) in contrast to academic language, which he identified in early writings as cognitive academic language proficiency (CALP). He plotted language characteristics along continuums of cognitive demand and embedded context to demonstrate how increasing the meaning of language through context (i.e., concrete, tangible representations) can support students' understanding of more abstract, or cognitively demanding, language.

Cummins's research has impacted effective second-language practice by helping educators understand what must be added to instruction to make it comprehensible to English language learners and by demonstrating how instruction can be differentiated for their social and academic language proficiency. As an outgrowth of his work, we understand that the development of language and the mastery of content for English learners are most effective when students are challenged cognitively while provided with the contextual and linguistic scaffolds required by the curriculum.

The work of Cummins and Krashen has provided a basis for the differentiation of teacher talk, language-development strategies, and instructional resources according to language-proficiency levels as well as what the grade-level content demands. The academic discipline of science provides rich content for language learning. Though the content is challenging and involves complex concepts, its real-world relevance makes it ripe for language development. Through an inquiry-based model, students get the opportunity to experience science in the classroom.

A Functionalist Lens

Another theory that is essential to our understanding of second-language development is provided by Halliday's (1978) focus on the functions, or purposes, of language, which provide impetus for students' communicative competence. Communicative competence depends on the integration of acquired language knowledge with the proficient use of forms appropriate to functions. English language learners must be able to employ "a dynamic system of linguistic choices...to accomplish a wide variety of social, academic, and political goals in and out of school" (Gebhard, Harman, and Seger 2007, 421).

Building on the functionalist perspective, Dutro and Moran (2003) have demonstrated that effective approaches to second-language instruction begin with instructional planning that includes a careful analysis of the specific language forms, or structures, and vocabulary related to the function, or purposes, for using the new language. We use language to accomplish something in formal or informal settings and for social and academic purposes. Functions are the basis for the cognitive tasks that drive us to connect thought and language. The instructional design must include strategies for introducing and reinforcing the newly acquired language as well as provide opportunities for practice and for developing fluency.

A Sociocultural Lens

There are a number of researchers who emphasize the importance of social interaction as a catalyst for the complex dynamic of learning a second language (Brown 1994; Ellis 1994; Gibbons 1991; Skutnabb-Kangas and Cummins 1988; Van Lier 1996). These researchers help us understand that it is not enough for children to be immersed in language input with access to good language models. To develop language competence, children also need to use language in interaction with other children and adults. For students' acquisition of English, Swain (1993, 1995a) emphasizes the need to optimize opportunities for language interaction contextualized within problem-solving activities or collaborative projects. McGroarty (1993) supports group work for second-language learning, finding that when a group of students talk as they work, language input is increased; that the dynamic of the task provides a compelling purpose for using the language, thus increasing language use (output); and that understanding increases as the input and output are contextualized within a meaningful group task.

In her work on scaffolding language and learning, Pauline Gibbons (1991, 2002) emphasizes a sociocultural perspective for second-language teaching and learning that draws on the work of Vygotsky (1978, 1986). Gibbons offers a model that foregrounds the collaborative nature of learning and language development between individuals, the interrelatedness of the role of teacher and learner, and the active roles of both in the learning process (2002). Vygotskian theory points to the significance of interaction in learning and views dialogue as constructing the resources for thinking. For second-language learners, it is through discourse in classroom-based social contexts that much linguistic and conceptual learning can occur. Hudelson (1994) posits that interactive strategies recognize and promote the acquisition of a culture of literacy. Moreover, to read with meaning requires an understanding of words and grammatical forms, which are quite different from those encountered in everyday chat about concrete experiences or from the sort of language that children may use while they are engaged in hands-on activities. Consequently, explicit attention must be given to instructional tasks within group structures that promote the conceptualization and articulation of ideas and concepts through questioning, responding, hypothesizing, analyzing, or summarizing for second-language learners. Within the dynamic of an apprenticeship with more capable language speakers— whether teachers or peers—understanding and knowledge are jointly constructed.

Gibbons warns against viewing language learning as merely a psychologically driven, or mentalist, process. Language learning is a socially embedded process, and because of this, teachers need to choose particular kinds of support, or scaffolding, that challenge English language learners to acquire language just beyond their present levels.

Theoretical Connections

The educational implications of the varied theories and research on language learning presented in this chapter promote the shaping of an ELD instructional framework that focuses on the dynamic of student talk, cognitive engagement, and the influence of social interaction as essential and interrelated elements for the acquisition and development of a second language. The instructional strategies and practices shared throughout this book hold true to what we refer to as a *Talk*, *Thought*, and *Interaction* approach to English language development.

Talk

When we refer to *talk* in ELD instruction, we focus on practices that promote academic language proficiency. These practices include an understanding of the vocabulary, functions (i.e., the purpose for using language) and forms (i.e., the manner in which words are put together in phrases and sentences that express what one knows) that comprise each content area's language (Zwiers 2008). Although disciplines share some functions of language use, for example describing and inferring, the purpose of talk in a given discipline is that it has linguistic properties that distinguish it from the language of other disciplines. Through talk, teachers model the language of thinking like a scientist; provide hands-on, manipulative tasks rich with academic-language input; and sustain opportunities for facilitated shared language output.

Thought

Cognitive engagement is a valued element of any notion we have as educators about effective instruction. Because language facilitates and illustrates thinking, cognitive engagement is widely viewed as a catalyst for language learning in second-language theory and practice (Balderrama and Diaz-Rico 2006). In English language development, cognitive engagement occurs when students are thinking about a language, using language to think, and using both language and thinking to learn new language. A cognitive emphasis for ELD instruction exposes the relationship between thinking and language in interactive social contexts. Because students are using language to negotiate meaning for the completion of a task, their thinking about language and their use of language can be extended and reinforced with strategies and tools for language learning. Teachers must make instructional decisions that ensure that students engage in rich cognitive tasks and share their language and thinking. Within our framework, thinking and doing while acquiring language is a critical aspect for the second-language development of English language learners.

Interaction

The axiom "No one knows alone" can be appropriately transformed into "No one knows *language* alone" when considering the second-language development of ELLs. An inherent feature of ELD teaching and learning is the dialogic and mediated exchange between models and users of the language. Social interaction, including exchanges between the teacher and the student(s) and exchanges between students, plays a pivotal role in second-language development. Teachers should continuously monitor their students' understanding and performance in a mediated interplay of modeling, demonstration, and feedback until the student has internalized the new learning and can apply it with self-regulation. Tasks that promote peer interaction provide English language learners with authentic and intrinsically interesting opportunities for exposure to language beyond that provided by the teacher or other adults (Enright 1991), contributing to a less anxiety-producing setting for acquisition (Johnson 1994).

The *Talk*, *Thought*, and *Interaction* Sociocultural Framework is summarized in Figure 1.2.

Figure 1.2 The *Talk*, *Thought*, and *Interaction* Sociocultural Framework

Talk

Students engage in social and academic discourse with a clear purpose for talk: vocabulary, functions, forms, and fluency.

Thought

Language events promote critical thinking and cognitive engagement with real and authentic purposes.

Interaction

Students and adults are actively involved in using language to accomplish academic tasks.

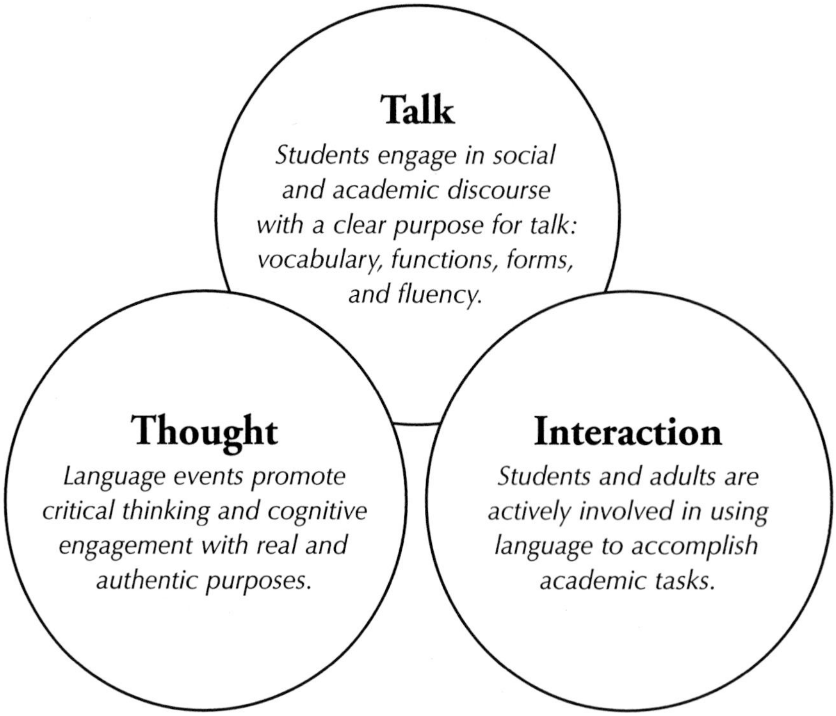

Inquiry-Based Learning

In our work, we marry the framework of *Talk*, *Thought*, and *Interaction* to an inquiry-based learning model. We have found that inquiry-based learning provides students with optimal opportunities to develop content and academic language effectively and deeply. Inquiry-based approaches allow students to get their minds around something, to look closely at it and think deeply about their learning. They have time to explore concepts ranging from concrete to abstract in order to understand the learning process and apply their learning in new contexts. Though inquiry-based teaching and learning can be employed across the curriculum, the focus of this resource is on the development of academic language through science. Approaching the learning of science through a framework of thought, talk, and interaction embedded in inquiry-based science, students engage in self-discovery and develop high levels of content knowledge and academic language development. More specifically, we follow a 5E inquiry-based planning and implementation model.

Engage

The 5E model begins with *Engage*. Students are exposed to a topic, concept, or idea in a way that stirs curiosity and captures their attention in order to get their minds around the learning at hand. The activities teachers use for *Engage* can include displaying a picture, performing an experiment, posing a question, presenting a video clip, and more. The idea is for students to make connections to their prior knowledge and begin to question what they know.

At this stage, students are encouraged to share their thinking at their level of English proficiency and to use their primary language as necessary. If the purpose of *Engage* is for students to generate prior knowledge and engage them in the thinking around science, students should be encouraged to use either English or their primary language. It is the teacher who serves as a model of language for students at this stage. Students are exposed to academic language when the teacher uses it to pose questions and introduce science content. This stage provides high levels of "comprehensible input" through the careful attention to academic language on the part of the teacher, and the opportunity to look, feel, touch, and think "science." The integration of language and content at this point comes from the personal experiences and prior knowledge the student brings to the learning environment. It meets students where they are. It is a great opportunity for teachers to informally assess students' language and make better instructional decisions about how to support ELLs throughout the remaining stages of the 5E model.

Explore

Exploration continues the inquiry process through hands-on learning. At this stage, students are involved in observation, data collection, making predictions, and hypothesizing around what they understand and are seeking to understand. During *Explore*, teachers give students an opportunity to investigate through experiments, observations, and shared inquiry. The teacher serves as a guide for the inquiry process. Through modeling, asking probing questions, and providing feedback and suggestions, students are asked to deepen their thinking.

At this stage, comprehensible input remains high as teachers elicit students' thinking and language while they are engaged in hands-on experiences. Through the level of questions posed by the teacher, students are asked to use English at higher levels. The deeper they are asked to think, the higher the level of language they will naturally use in their thinking, in their writing, and in their speaking. Once again, as students use language to engage in the thinking and doing of science, teachers can informally assess students' language and content knowledge.

Explain

By this point, students have had opportunities to think deeply and question key content and concepts. They have not been asked to produce specific academic language or content. It is in the *Explain* stage that teachers will clearly support students in understanding the content and language objectives of the lesson at hand. Through the use of read-alouds, demonstrations, direct teaching, modeling, and guided or shared reading of curricular texts, teachers guide students to find the answers to their questions. Teachers can offer alternative points of view and explanations. At this stage, misconceptions are clarified and new questions are generated. Students will be further guided through explicit vocabulary instruction of key academic terms and concepts as questions are answered and information is shared.

At this stage, there are also opportunities for explicit language instruction. As students are asked to explain their learning orally or in written form (e.g., diagrams, charts, drawings, text), they may require explicit instruction and support in the functions and forms of language needed to explain their thinking. The teacher will provide forms of language for students to use to express their thinking. These language frames will be developed based on the level of English language development that the students exhibited during the *Engage* and *Explore* portions of the lesson, and what the teacher already knows and understands about his or her students as English language learners. This careful attention to the varying levels of second-language acquisition in order to provide the appropriate frames is critical in facilitating ongoing language development.

Extend

In referring to this fourth phase of the 5Es, the words *extend*, *expand*, and *elaborate* are often used interchangeably. What they share is the understanding that students need an opportunity to put their learning into practice—to engage once again in an exploration that allows them to use what they have learned in a new context. Students get the opportunity to carry out a new project that involves the thinking and language processes they have developed to this point. Too often, students are heavily guided in their learning but are not provided enough opportunities to apply their learning. Without the chance to transfer their knowledge to new contexts, they may not come away with a deep level of understanding for long-term retention.

At this stage, students get opportunities to use the language that they have learned and developed in meaningful ways. Teachers will hear students using their newly learned vocabulary, functions, and forms in natural ways. When students practice language in meaningful, enjoyable contexts, they increase their academic language. This is also an opportunity for teachers to informally assess students' newly developed language.

Evaluate

With any lesson, students need an opportunity to reflect on their learning. Thinking about the content and language developed as part of the 5E learning cycle helps students internalize their learning and work toward developing metacognition. *Evaluate* can take the form of more formal assignments, such as final presentations, creative projects, written reflections, or formal assessments such as exams. However, *Evaluate* can also involve a quick end-of-lesson task in which students are asked to stop and think about their learning and share it through an exit card (e.g., writing down one thing they learned and one question they have) or in a discussion around their learning. What makes the *Evaluate* stage of the 5E model powerful is the time students are given to think about their learning. Often, in content-area instruction, students can feel overwhelmed by the amount of information presented. This allows them to process their learning before starting the 5E model again and continuing to build content knowledge and language development.

Sheltered Instruction

Any attention given to ELL instructional accommodations for academic content references an approach called *sheltered instruction*. Sheltered English instruction—also known as SDAIE, or Specially Designed Academic Instruction in English—refers to specifically accommodated curriculum content for English language learners who are expected to master grade-level content in English. (The terms *sheltered instruction* and *SDAIE* are used interchangeably in this resource.) SDAIE should be distinguished from ELD in two major aspects: ELD instruction focuses on language using the content themes as a medium. A SDAIE approach focuses on the development of content knowledge and skills using language strategies as support. ELD instruction targets needs along a continuum of English proficiency, while SDAIE targets grade-level content objectives. Sheltered instruction focuses on utilizing strategies that will enable ELLs to access content concepts and the academic language of the content area being taught, which can be quite a considerable load for an English learner. Content acquisition and the development of academic language proficiency are integral components in SDAIE instruction. A key construct for sheltered instruction is that the content is not diminished or watered down. The content is specially tailored through strategies that adjust the cognitive and linguistic load for ELLs but not the cognitive-level or grade-level appropriateness of the content (Northcutt and Watson 1986; Echevarria, Vogt, and Short 2004; Schifini 1985).

The framework for sheltered instruction is consistent with the research base for academic language proficiency that has been presented in this chapter. Through highly supported, or scaffolded, instruction, grade-level content can be accommodated for English language learners' linguistic, social, and academic needs.

Making Sense of It All

On any given day, teachers of English language learners must respond to a wide array of issues and needs to plan and deliver effective instruction across literacy, language development, and content curriculum. A reality they must grapple with is the complexity of their English language learners and the challenge they face to ensure that ELLs develop English academic language proficiency.

Genesee and Riches (2006) caution educators to realize that teaching English language learners requires more than employing specific techniques or methods. Gándara, Maxwell-Jolly, and Driscoll (2005) presented the alarming discovery that the prevalent instructional approaches for English language development are weakened by inconsistent delivery of theoretically driven, research-based practices and teachers' general lack of understanding of second-language learning. Teachers of ELLs must be highly cognizant of the beliefs and attitudes that underscore the instructional principles they use to guide the planning and delivery of their instruction.

The research base is clearer now than ever before about the value of ELD instruction for the academic achievement of English language learners. A comprehensive framework informed by theory and research on best instructional practices can help make sense of the complexity and challenge of developing second-language proficiency.

Tips for Thinking About Academic Language Proficiency Within Inquiry-Based Science

When thinking about academic language proficiency within inquiry-based science, consider the following:

- View the strengths and needs of ELLs as complex.

- Identify the interrelated dimensions of academic language proficiency: conversational language, discrete language skills, and academic language.

- Recognize that the primary language is a valuable resource for ELL students.

- Understand the basic elements of second-language development: comprehensible input, comprehensible output, social interaction, cognitive engagement, and focus on form.

Reflect on Wonderings

1. How do the components of *Talk, Thought,* and *Interaction* interrelate in academic language development?

2. Which of the theoretical concepts is the most relevant for your teaching?

CHAPTER 2

Developing Academic Language: A Framework for Decision Making

You May Wonder:

- What are the principles that should guide instruction for English language learners?

- What are the factors a teacher of English language learners must consider when designing instruction that promotes academic language development?

When faced with the challenge of meeting the instructional needs of English language learners, teachers must respond to a complex set of issues. The decisions teachers make are based on their experiences with English language learners, are shaped by their beliefs and attitudes about the potential of these students, and are grounded in the knowledge and skills they have acquired in preservice training and professional development. What teachers know and believe are powerful influences on instructional decision making. As has been stated previously, the various theories and research on language learning point to a framework for designing instruction that focuses on the dynamic interplay of student talk, cognitive engagement, and the influence of social interaction. *Talk*, *thought*, and *interaction* are essential and interrelated elements for the acquisition of a second language and for developing academic proficiency. To realize the optimal potential of an ELL-centered approach, principled teachers must consider the following tenets when making decisions about strategies, activities, and resources in day-to-day planning for English language learners.

Principle 1: Scaffold

A principled teacher of ELLs scaffolds language learning to make it comprehensible and relevant. *Scaffolding* has become ubiquitous in the lexicon of educators. The term *scaffolding* was first used by Wood, Bruner, and Ross (1976) in their examination of parent-child talk in the early years. As an instructional metaphor, scaffolding conjures up the activity of teachers who guide their students through learning tasks constructed with all the necessary supports students require to become independent, self-regulated learners. To help students master rigorous content standards, teachers use scaffolds in the form of instructional tools and strategies to help their students construct new knowledge until they can learn without the extra support structures. The instructional support provided by scaffolds should not be construed as simply help for the learner. Rather, scaffolds represent calculated and deliberate decision making on the part of teachers to not reduce the cognitive level of the task but to hold "the task difficulty constant, while simplifying the learners' role by means of graduated assistance from an adult or a more capable peer" (Gibbons 2002, 10).

Vygotsky's concept of the *zone of proximal development* has become a common referent for scaffolded instruction (Ellis and Worthington 2004). Vygotsky defined this zone as "... the distance between the actual development level as determined by independent problem solving under adult guidance, or in collaboration with more capable peers" (1978, 86). Instruction within the zone of proximal development involves what Ellis and Worthington refer to as "a delicate balance between diminishing teacher guidance and increasing student competence" (2004, 30). Instruction within the zone implies an expert-novice relationship in which errors are welcomed as opportunities for learning through redirection and feedback. There is also an orientation toward the future, toward getting the student to the next step in his or her formation. Building on a dialogical exchange between the teacher and the student, the teacher continuously monitors the student's understanding and performance in a mediated interplay of modeling, demonstration, and feedback until the student has internalized the new learning and takes it on as his or her own in application and self-regulation.

For teachers of English language learners, standards and assessment provide a basis for purposeful, informed decision making about the linguistic and cognitive needs of their students. When considering scaffolds as support for second-language learners, Pauline Gibbons alerts teachers of English language learners to pay close attention to "the nature of the support" for these students (1991, 12). This means that the decision about scaffolding must involve serious consideration of its purpose for the development of the English academic proficiency of English language learners. It goes beyond just identifying a task for students to participate in. This leads to the consideration of scaffolds for language and content instruction that operate on two different levels—purpose and task. The principled ELL teacher must inventory the purpose, or the nature of the support, that will be provided as a guide for the selection of any tool or strategy.

Comprehensible Input

English language learners need *comprehensible input* to develop the linguistic competence to become successful communicators and master the academic ideas and thinking skills in the content-area standards. The legacy of Krashen's influence in second-language instruction has shown educators that language is acquired in one way: when it is comprehensible, or readily understood. The implication of the concept of comprehensible input is that the instruction must be designed to make the new language understood. Furthermore, for teachers to build on the understanding of the new language toward communicative competence and academic proficiency requires a wide array of strategies and approaches.

A key feature of making new language understandable is the progression from concrete to abstract representations of its meaning. The connection of an unknown word, phrase, or sentence to a tangible object, model, or visual enhances its meaning for the language learner. An additional factor is the sensory modality for the input; a balance should be achieved for language input that is visual, auditory, or kinesthetic. The learning context must support a dynamic blend of all of the ways in which the individual gains knowledge.

Therefore, to ensure that the input is understood, the informed ELL teacher uses visuals, realia (i.e., real objects), and manipulatives as requisite concrete tools for language learning. There is evidence of the purposeful use of the visual and the concrete for language learning. The language-learning classroom is stocked with illustrated texts, posters, and picture cards. Charts with pictures and words are displayed throughout the room as the documentation of pictorial and narrative input and the interaction between the teacher and students to make meaning of the new language. Role play and dramatization are supported by puppets, props, and costumes. Developmentally and age-appropriate chants, rhymes, songs, and storytelling provide language modeling and practice. Movement, including games and dance, is integrated into instruction as it supports making meaning of English language and concepts.

As scaffolds, these tools and approaches provide English language learners with a concrete, contextualized, and multimodal basis for the input they receive on their pathway to greater proficiency. As ELLs acquire greater language proficiency, the need for these concrete scaffolds may diminish; however, they may continue to be valuable for the language demands of complex concepts and abstact terminology.

Dialogue

The prominence of dialogue is a key distinction of scaffolded instruction as teacher and student engage in a give-and-take exchange toward new understanding (Paris and Winograd 1990; Ellis and Worthington 2004). For English language learners and their language development, significant aspects of this dialogic exchange relate to the pacing of second-language instruction, to making connections to prior experience, and to the support provided by modeling and demonstrations by more mature language learners.

An important factor in making language understood within the dialogic exchange that occurs in language and content instruction for ELLs is adjusting the language of instructional delivery to enhance comprehensibility. This type of language accommodation, along with monitoring the amount of input and changing the pacing of instruction, is significant in mastering a second language. To be effective, ELL teachers must extend instruction and slow down its pace.

To accommodate for these needs, the principled ELL teacher increases opportunities to provide multiple examples of the new language, to break down oral presentations and written texts into smaller segments, and to check more frequently for comprehension. Moreover, as the Center for Applied Linguistics (1998) suggests, the principled ELL teacher assists students in their understanding by physically facing the students, pausing frequently, and paraphrasing often. The teacher thinks ahead about the complexity of the language that he or she will model to avoid the utilization of idiomatic expressions and to present and use target vocabulary and structures with the support of intonation or writing on the board. Because the teacher understands that instruction needs to be adjusted, "wait time" for students to answer is increased and the focus is on students' meaning rather than grammar. Correction occurs through restating and modeling.

Prior Knowledge

Research has found that students learn best when they can make the connection between what is to be learned and what has been learned previously (Ellis and Worthington 2004; Pressley et al. 1987; Swanson 1991). Swanson explains this process of elaboration as involving "extra ways of mediating the information" to make sense of it, such as visualizing, associating, or categorizing (1991, 134). These ways of mediating the information make the material to be learned more meaningful and personal to the learner. Moreover, as students connect to new learning through previous learning, relevancy and interest are enhanced.

The principled ELL teacher, therefore, organizes language and content instruction to build on previous learning and experiences. Working within program parameters and the realities of the daily schedule, the teacher organizes instruction thematically so that his or her English language learners can authentically use the language they are acquiring in varied academic settings. Furthermore, activities and tasks built on content themes provide the stimulating and rich contexts for language learning while emphasizing authentic purposes for using the language. For example, the language for sequencing and describing can be modeled, demonstrated, and practiced while English language learners are growing plants from seeds and documenting their ongoing observations as authentic scientists. The informed ELL teacher recognizes the value of firsthand experience, home-school connections, and culturally relevant resources. The teacher selects language content for which his or her students have background knowledge and does not assume that students lack prior experience. Whenever possible, the teacher utilizes real-life experience and community resources. For example, if the language-learning focus for English-language development and content is the life cycle of plants, the teacher visits community or home gardens or involves knowledgeable parents as experts and collaborators. Additionally, the principled teacher uses texts that represent the cultural heritage of the students in the classroom.

Graphic Organizers

A major tool in the mediation of second-language learning and academic proficiency is the graphic organizer. In mainstream research, several studies have demonstrated the efficacy of graphic organizers in promoting students' learning (Moyer et al. 1984). Gersten and Jiménez (1997) found in their presentation of the practices that promote the learning of English language learners that ELLs benefit when teachers think aloud and model strategies that mediate information, making visible the cognitive processes that are normally invisible. Laternau confirms that "ELLs benefit when teachers explain strategies and steps for tackling instructional tasks, check for student understanding before students start the task independently, and present numerous examples of concepts being taught" (2003, 286). Through the use of an established array of graphic representations or organizers, English language learners have access to a repertoire of cognitive, strategic thinking and language structures that can prove helpful to them in their English language development and beyond into their content-area mastery.

Because linguistic scaffolding ensures access to language proficiency, the principled ELL teacher uses graphic organizers and paces instruction appropriately—by breaking it down into meaningful chunks—to bridge the gap between the cognitive and linguistic demands of instruction for any given language development level. The graphic organizer becomes the scaffold upon which the teacher and students rely for language modeling, language use, and cognitive engagement. The use of graphic organizers remains constant while the language becomes more complex and sophisticated as ELLs progress in academic language proficiency. For example, the use of a basic grid of three (or six or even nine) boxes can become the language-learning and thinking tool for retelling a story. At an initial-proficiency level, the teacher carefully guides the retelling of a familiar story, filling in the boxes with illustrations labeled with words, phrases, and simple sentences as captions. The teacher's interaction with the students may focus on identifying and describing characters or developing sequencing language for beginning, middle, and end. Once students have become familiar with the organizer and have increased their language proficiency, the teacher may remove himself or herself as the key support for the interaction, and the ELLs will use the organizer, working collaboratively with other students or independently, to reinforce and expand their language fluency. Thus, after repeated use of graphic organizers as linguistic scaffolds, students feel comfortable taking risks to use new language for academic applications because they know that they will be supported and challenged at the same time.

Rituals and Routines

The principled ELL teacher recognizes the value of instructional ritual as a scaffold. He or she incorporates the repeated use of a familiar and developmentally appropriate set of instructional rituals for language learning. Whether a familiar set of ways to organize and talk about a new topic or a predictable pattern for working in collaborative groups, the knowledgeable ELL teacher makes language learning manageable and accessible for students.

Principle 2: Provide Explicit Academic Language Instruction

A principled ELL teacher supports explicit academic language instruction for authentic social and academic language purposes. In their research synthesis of effective teaching principles and instructional design for mainstream education, Ellis and Worthington (1994) identify a list of motivational, cognitive, and academic characteristics that empowered students. They conclude that among the academic skills and strategies that successful students must possess is the ability to communicate and demonstrate their academic competence.

Consequently, teachers of English language learners must understand the role that language competence plays in academic achievement as well as the essential components of the language they seek to develop. To build language competence in targeted instruction, teachers must engage in purposeful practices that focus on the language features that English language learners need as they progress toward academic proficiency. To accomplish this, the ELL teacher requires basic, fundamental knowledge about language in order to design effective instruction and to be able to access the requisite tools.

Explicit Academic Language Instruction

To support a focused approach to academic language learning, the language targets for instruction must encompass the components of vocabulary, functions, forms, and fluency (Chamot and O'Malley 1994; Dutro and Helman 2009). Targeting vocabulary instruction has long been considered an essential element of ELD instruction. ELL teachers have become adept at guiding students through naming objects and demonstrating with gestures, movement, and drawings in order to build students' understanding of verbs and descriptive adjectives. However, language is not merely a collection of isolated terminology. Vocabulary is part of a meaningful and dynamic lexicon that involves using vocabulary for a wide array of purposes within an equally varied assembly of forms in phrases and sentences.

As an example, consider an everyday shoe. When asked to name the shoe, a language-proficient adult may say *shoe* or *slipper* or *sneaker* or *high heel*. And, when asked to describe the shoe, he or she may say *brown* or *suede* or *comfortable*. Proficient speakers express themselves with basic yet varied vocabulary for these tasks. However, if asked to compare an everyday shoe to a pair one would wear to a wedding, the function or purpose of the language changes from naming/identifying and describing to comparing and contrasting. One may say *My sneakers are comfortable to walk in, but my high heels are not.* The function, or purpose of the language, changes the components of the language we use. In this example, the form of the language consists of nouns, verbs, pronouns, and adjectives strung together to communicate a specific purpose within a frame: *My _____ are _____ to _____ but my _____ are not.* If other proficient speakers were asked to make the same comparison of everyday shoes and dress shoes, they would likely provide an array of forms and frames, such as: *One is white and the other is black.* (Frame: *One is _____ and the other is _____.*); *The color is the same but the heels are different.* (Frame: *The _____ is the same but the _____ are different.*); *These cost more than the other pair.* (Frame: *These _____ more than the _____.*)

This example is a compendium of language representing a small subset of the vocabulary, functions, and forms of a proficient English speaker. The significance of presenting this array of language for a common object such as a shoe is that it points to the breadth and depth of desirable language for the English language learners we teach. Whether the topic relates to a common familiar object or an abstract academic concept, the goal is to support all English language learners in achieving the highest levels of language proficiency they are capable of. Figure 2.1 displays various language functions and forms that represent the type of academic language that is required for communicative competence in such tasks as comprehending a story, relating a sequence of events, formulating hypotheses, or making evaluative judgments.

Figure 2.1 Academic Forms and Functions

Function (purpose for using language)	Form (vocabulary, syntax)	Fluency (language in use in academic context)
Describing People, Places, and Things	The _____ is _____. The _____ has _____ and _____. There is a _____ in front of the _____.	• Presentation on physical properties of rocks • Describing the setting of a story
Describing Action	_____ is _____ the _____.	• Teaching someone to play a game • Describing the plot of a story
Comparing and Contrasting	_____ has _____ but _____ has _____. They both have _____.	• Comparing physical features of planets in the solar system • Comparing the roles and responsibilities of community helpers
Retelling Past Events	First _____, next _____, and finally _____.	• Sharing an autobiographical incident • Reporting a sequence of historical events
Making Predictions	Because I see _____, I think _____ will _____.	• Reporting next steps in plant growth • Predicting events in a story
Asking Informational Questions	Why did the _____? What is _____?	• Interviewing a partner
Expressing and Supporting Opinions	I think _____ is _____ because _____.	• Collaborating on a conservation poster
Describing Cause and Effect	As a result of _____, _____ happened.	• Summarizing the causes of the Revolutionary War

Function (purpose for using language)	Form (vocabulary, syntax)	Fluency (language in use in academic context)
Drawing Conclusions	If _____, it must mean that _____.	• Examining how polar bears survive in the Arctic • Reviewing a series of poster illustrations depicting the lifestyle of California Indians
Imagining	I wonder what would happen if _____. If I were a _____, I would _____.	• Collaborating on a group project to design a spacecraft to travel to Mars
Hypothesizing	If _____ had _____, then _____ would have _____.	• Creating a nutritional menu for the school cafeteria
Evaluating	This seems to be _____. It makes me think that _____.	• Discussing the outcome of an experiment on mixtures and solutions

Teachers of English language learners must be intentional and focused to move their English language development instruction beyond simplistic vocabulary and merely identifying or describing objects. Expectations for language embedded within the standards, such as *uses consistent grammatical forms* or *uses expanded vocabulary,* must be enhanced to involve a wider array of language components for use in authentic academic tasks. Nevertheless, the language targets must be organized and matched to the language needs of students along a continuum of language proficiency levels.

Authentic Learning Opportunities

While students are actively and dynamically engaged with peers in authentic tasks that require the use of language to make meaning, the role of the teacher is critical as an informed facilitator, active mediator, and vigilant evaluator. Through a thoughtful sequence of *directed interaction*, the instructor uses careful modeling and demonstration of the explicit forms and functions targeted in the lesson. The ELL teacher provokes the use of this explicit language by personally reinforcing the target language and by guiding its use through questioning, clarifying, and probing the students while they are engaged in language practice and application tasks. As an active participant in these exchanges, the teacher mediates language use on the spot, accommodating the changing needs of English language learners who are constantly growing in their English proficiency. The tasks themselves are designed to promote the use of stretches of language for a range of audiences and purposes and to build on scaffolds such as visuals and oral rehearsals that lead to written products.

Principle 3: Differentiate Language Instruction

A principled ELL teacher differentiates instruction in order to meet the diverse needs of English language learners. Differentiated, or responsive, teaching means that a teacher is attuned to students' varied learning needs within the context of delivering required curriculum (Tomlinson 2003; Tomlinson and McTighe 2006). A differentiated approach is predicated upon the belief that any community of learners represents a complex array of diverse factors that affect academic success. Because what matters in a differentiated approach to instruction is enabling each student to learn in a way that meets his or her needs, responsive teachers make instructional modifications in order to support the maximum amount of success for each learner.

The ELL teacher understands that English language learners do not come to the classroom in "one size." In addition to their English-language proficiency, ELLs have varied backgrounds, interests, abilities, learning styles, and primary language-proficiency levels. Within a classroom, there can be any combination of English language learners and English-only students. The English language learners in the classroom can be new immigrants with high levels of primary language proficiency, or with little or no school experience at all. Within a given classroom, ELLs can range from a beginning level of proficiency to an advanced level. Even if all English language learners were at the same proficiency level, they could represent an array of sublevels of need because their rates of second-language development will vary.

Gándara, Maxwell-Jolly, and Driscoll interviewed teachers of English learners in California and found that "teachers expressed frustration with the wide range of English language and academic levels found in their classrooms" (2005, 8). Because English language learners in today's classrooms are complex socially, linguistically, culturally, and academically (Galguera 1998), the concept of a differentiated approach is a critical component of ELD instructional decision making. The principled teacher of ELD understands the challenge inherent in student diversity, and therefore he or she makes every effort to differentiate instruction with strategies and approaches that meet the varying needs of each English language learner in the classroom.

Grouping Strategies

The organizational and management difficulties presented by delivering and facilitating instruction for varied linguistic and academic needs require an understanding of flexible grouping and techniques for making group work successful. Because of the myriad needs inherent in educating English language learners at different proficiency levels within a classroom, *flexible grouping* has become a popular recommendation for ELL teachers (Echeverria, Vogt, and Short 2000; Irujo 2007). Flexible grouping refers to the purposeful use of various grouping patterns that enable the teacher to support the level of comprehensible input and output of the language and content lesson tasks for ELLs at varied proficiency levels. In Irujo's review of the literature that supports the use of flexible grouping for ELLs, she reports that within-class grouping can be effective when it reduces a wide range of abilities. She also notes that grouping English language learners in small groups is most effective when it targets specific skills at specific times, and that the groupings must be fluid and adjusted frequently based on monitoring of need.

For ELL instruction, there are several options for grouping students to meet varied needs: whole group, pair work, small heterogeneous groups, small homogeneous groups, collaborative groups, or individual work. When working in pairs or small groups, the potential for student interaction is increased. Collaborative groups rely on student self-guided interaction to make meaning for completion of a task. In all configurations, the teacher has an active role as director, model, facilitator, or evaluator.

Small teacher-guided group instruction (six to eight students) promotes the opportunity for greater intimacy between the teacher and the English language learners, since the teacher and students can interact with each other more frequently. In small groups, students are more willing to take risks with using the second language, and the teacher has more exposure to evaluate a student's progress and provide corrective feedback. Small homogeneous groups are composed of students who are at approximately the same level of proficiency; small heterogeneous groups are intentionally made up of students who represent a range of proficiency levels, and students at low levels of language proficiency are grouped with those at higher levels.

When attempting to define the makeup of a group for differentiation, it is important for teachers to remain aware that all groupings of students are heterogeneous, "given the fact that all students are different and bring differential strengths to the classroom" (Walqui 2003, 168). Although whole-group instruction may seem the least desirable for student engagement and output, a skillful ELL teacher can engage students through active demonstrations and questioning. By arranging students heterogeneously on a rug or at desks, a teacher can break up a teacher-centered whole-group sequence by asking students to turn to a partner to discuss new information for a more dynamic exchange.

There are many possible combinations of grouping options. To make the appropriate decision, teachers must consider the following:

- Language goals

- Student need

- Instructional activities

The following section discusses three models that exemplify a flexible grouping approach for differentiating ELD instruction.

Figure 2.2 Flexible Grouping Model 1

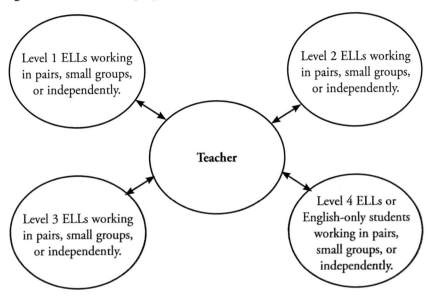

Figure 2.2 represents a familiar grouping pattern for classroom instruction. Within the context of ELD instruction, English language learners are working on a level-appropriate language task either in pairs, small collaborative groups, or individually. In this setting, the teacher either pulls students to work with him or her or joins a group of students where they are working. The teacher has the flexibility of choice to work with students based on either the need of beginning-level students for specific language support to complete the task, or the need of advanced-level students to move beyond the language requirements of the task. This format also allows for flexibility of time, since the teacher adjusts time spent with a group based on specific need. For classrooms where English-only students are part of the student population during the ELD block, this model can allow the teacher to design instruction to meet their specific needs. In order for this model to work well, careful attention must be paid to providing clear directions and to establishing expectations for the task.

Figure 2.3 Flexible Grouping Model 2

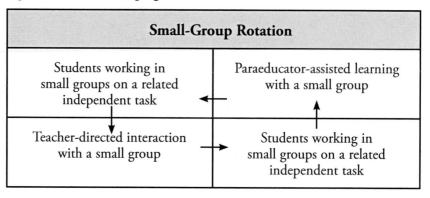

Figure 2.3 represents a rotational cycle for delivering ELD instruction. It is the most structured of the four models. However, because of its predictability, it can provide a temporary source of support for new teachers or teachers new to ELL instruction. Experienced ELL teachers may have used this model to establish rituals for ELD instruction at the beginning of a new school year before moving on to other options. Although it depicts a four-group rotation, it can be modified for three or even two groups, depending on class size and the availability of a classroom assistant or paraeducator. (If necessary, English-only students can form a group for their own instructional focus.) English language learners are grouped homogeneously according to proficiency level. The tasks in each group are directly related to the language focus and thematic content of the teacher's directed interaction with his or her small group of students. The independent small-group tasks can be designed to support language use by requiring students to work in pairs. The teacher can tailor instruction in the directed interaction group to specifically meet the needs of the group's proficiency level. Within an ELD instructional block, the teacher can rotate groups two or three times. The recommendation, however, is that the teacher spend five to 10 minutes setting up the tasks with the class and delineating instructions and expectations. Then, the teacher should spend 20 to 30 minutes with one small group. The rotation of groups can occur during the next day's instructional period.

Figure 2.4 Flexible Grouping Model 3

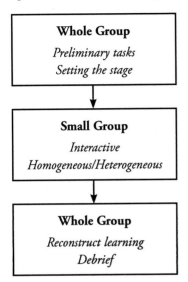

Figure 2.4 provides a blend of structure and flexibility consistent with the goals of language learning and differentiated instruction. In this model, all students begin the instructional period in a heterogeneous whole group to engage in building background and modeling the language for the language practice and application tasks. Because all levels of English language learners are together, activities such as chanting poems, participating in read-alouds, interacting with visuals, or role-playing optimize modeling and the demonstration for input. Thus, the stage is set for the language application that follows.

At the next level of Model 3, the teacher organizes the students into small groups for language practice. Groups may be organized homogeneously to address specific level-appropriate language targets. Or, students can be organized in small collaborative heterogeneous groups that engage them in using the language in a dynamic interaction with more fluent peers. As with the other models, the needs of English-only students can be served in this model if they are present in the classroom during the ELD instructional period.

The final level of this grouping model involves gathering all students back into a whole group where the teacher facilitates the use of language and student products to reconstruct and debrief the learning experience. This model may be the most time-consuming model, requiring approximately 10 minutes for whole group, 20 to 30 minutes for small-group interaction, and five to 10 minutes for reconstructing learning. But, it offers the most opportunity for guided language learning along with independent language use that is differentiated for language-proficiency levels.

Although there are strong benefits for English language learners that can be derived from employing a flexible grouping approach, there are challenges for teachers. Teachers who effectively use flexible grouping for ELL instruction provide clear instructions and model all procedural elements of tasks as well as language use. Teachers who are effective at grouping students for ELL instruction establish clear expectations for roles and responsibilities, emphasizing opportunities for language use while engaged in the tasks. They make sure all resources are provided, that there is a plan for cleanup, and that options are identified if a task is completed early. There is a system to assign students to heterogeneous or homogeneous groups quickly, such as posted lists, color-coded tags, or counting off. The effective ELL teacher recognizes the value of establishing signals for transitions, getting students' attention, and cleanup. He or she allows enough time to monitor the room, clarifying instructions and expectations while circulating through the groups so that students are engaged in tasks. The principled ELL teacher is an active agent in facilitating student language learning by providing explicit language instruction, provoking language use, or providing corrective feedback.

While flexible grouping can be viewed as an essential frame for the level of interaction during language learning, there are other aspects (e.g., comprehensive input and output, the design of the task, performance expectations, language demands of the content) that help construct a more complete view of what it means to differentiate instruction for ELLs.

Principle 4: Optimize Language Use Through Cognitive Engagement and Social Interaction

A principled ELL teacher optimizes language use through the cognitive engagement and social interaction of English language learners. In cognitive-based instruction, students are seen as co-constructors of knowledge. The role of students' prior knowledge is seen as a critical influence on the acquisition of new information. A cognitive model of learning considers learning as an active, dynamic process in which learners select, organize, connect, use, and reflect on new information (Bruner 1986; Ellis and Worthington 2004; Pressley 1990). Cognitive-based instruction embraces practices that develop higher-order thinking skills. Teachers ask challenging questions, model the learning process, and engage in interactive dialogue with students.

Vygotsky (1986) reasons that children learn to engage in higher-level thinking by first listening and then speaking. Their intellectual development is built on verbal interaction in their first language. The more children use language in social contexts within their families or in the classroom, the better they will learn to think and develop an internal and external language for thinking and learning. An implication of this perspective is that teachers must value language and thought in their instruction. They must make instructional decisions that ensure that students work collaboratively and share their language and thinking.

Because language facilitates and illustrates thinking, cognitive engagement is widely viewed as a catalyst for language learning in second-language acquisition theory and practice (Balderrama and Diaz-Rico 2006; Chamot and O'Malley 1994; Dutro and Moran 2003; Gibbons 2002; Herrell and Jordan 2004). Cognitive engagement refers to the idea that when students are thinking about language and using language to think, they are utilizing both language and thinking to learn new language. A cognitive emphasis for ELL instruction exposes the relationship between thinking and language in interactive social contexts. Because students are using language to negotiate meaning for the completion of a task, their thinking about language and use of language can be extended and reinforced with strategies and tools for language learning.

Therefore, the principled ELL teacher pays attention to cognitive engagement as an element of successful ELD instruction. He or she recognizes the role that social interaction plays in developing thinking and language. The teacher heightens the level of cognitive engagement by designing tasks that involve students in making meaning with others, all the time recognizing that cognitive potential may outpace language production. While co-constructing tasks with peers, language is tested, confirmed, and refined by recognizing patterns in repeated exposures and by making and correcting errors. If cognition leads language use and development, tasks have to allow for a range of cognitive-processing levels as well as language-proficiency levels to function.

Social Interaction

In their synthesis of research on the English oral language development of ELLs, Saunders and O'Brien (2006) report that in the studies they examined, exposure to English mattered less than the use of that exposure and the interactions that ensued. Additional findings of their analysis indicate that ELLs increase their practice and use of newly acquired language through social interactions with peers and teachers. This is significant because the increased use of the second language is associated with improved English proficiency.

Comprehensible Output

There is a body of research that provides guidance for classroom teachers as to the practical implications of promoting interactive output in ELD instruction (Gass 1997; Long and Porter 1985; Pica 1994; Pica et al. 1996; Swain 1995a, 1995b). This research confirms that input and output are multifaceted acquisition processes. Moving beyond Krashen's concept of ensuring that input is comprehensible, Swain proposes that input matters when it is *comprehended* (Swain 1995a, 1995b), therefore, shifting the emphasis to the language learner. Intake and integration are additional aspects of language input that have implications for language output (Gass 1997). The intake of the new language is integrated semantically (i.e., given meaning) as it involves a functional need to know and is used (i.e., output) syntactically in interactive, form-focused tasks (Gass 1997). Interactive contexts that encourage high levels of production compel the language learner to try out the language derived from meaning and put it together syntactically. The language learner exerts some control over the process by using an array of language-learning strategies, such as clarification requests, repetition or paraphrase, nonverbal cues, corrective feedback, hypothesis-testing, and self-correction, so that the language learner can understand and be understood. Meaningful input is increased as group members collaborate in this process and the task output becomes increasingly comprehensible (Swain 1995b).

Because the effect of conversational interaction on acquisition may be influenced in part by the task, Gass supports pedagogical approaches that "compel the learner to do something with the input" (1997, 152). In a given English language development instructional task, the language learner is aware that he or she is learning a new language and will be expected to use it. As the English language learner works through the task, attention to appropriate ways of using the language are contextualized within the need to make meaning with peers and the teacher.

The social features of peer interaction have additional benefits for second-language learners. Tasks that promote peer interaction provide English language learners with authentic and intrinsically interesting opportunities for exposure to language beyond that provided by the teacher or other adults (Enright 1991), contributing to a less anxiety-producing setting for acquisition (Johnson 1994). Working with peers encourages the development of what Ervin-Tripp (1991) refers to as *linguistic capital* for forms of language, such as negotiating, persuading, questioning, and encouraging.

Language Models

The presence of more proficient English speakers is significant for optimal conditions of second-language use (Fassler 2003; Saunders and O'Brien 2006). This idea is important for ELL teachers who have classrooms comprised entirely of English language learners, or have a majority of English language learners. Instructional design for interaction must facilitate groupings of English language learners that represent as wide a range as possible of English-language proficiency, including native English speakers. However, it is the content and quality of the language input and output event that has been found to be of equal, if not greater, importance than only exposure and use (Saunders and O'Brien 2006). There is some consensus in the interactionist literature that suggests that teachers need to create situations for peer interaction that encourage students to push one another to increase the clarity and precision in their communication (Fassler 2003; Gass 1997; Swain 1995b). Because of these factors, it may be that the role of the teacher as co-negotiator and facilitator of the language used in the collaborative interaction will be more prominent in instructional settings where native English students are not available.

Dynamic Language-Learning Tasks

Based on the analysis of how language works and the essential decision-making principles for an instructional design for English learners, the following list outlines desirable features for language-development tasks. Dynamic language-learning tasks should:

- Promote social interaction

- Require collaboration toward the completion of a product or performance

- Require the full participation of all members

- Compel students to use functionally specific, form-focused language

- Provide appropriate scaffolds

- Correlate to a curriculum theme or topic

- Be actively facilitated and monitored by the teacher

- Establish a clear awareness of its language learning purpose

- Provide multiple sequences of input and output

- Allow for language risk taking: the possibility of miscommunication and self-correction

- Integrate cognitive engagement and the negotiation of meaning

- Enable students at varied linguistic and cognitive levels to develop language

Teachers can move beyond focusing on merely acquiring a compendium of good strategies to promoting their heightened awareness of powerful, potent purposes for these strategies within language and content instruction. Any given instructional task or activity in itself is benign, inanimate, and merely an idea or words on a page. It takes passion and commitment informed by knowledge to create a high level of dynamic and complex instructional delivery. The teacher must be actively engaged in a multitude of roles to engage students, provide input, stimulate output, and monitor learning.

Principle 5: Treat Sociocultural Factors as Resources

A principled ELL teacher bridges the diverse social, cultural, and linguistic resources that English language learners bring to the classroom for optimal learning. Considerations of cultural and linguistic difference are critical for the success of English language learners in all aspects of their academic development (Thomas and Collier 1999). The principled ELL teacher seeks to bridge access to academic proficiency by empowering English language learners and valuing the diverse resources they bring to the classroom. Regardless of local policy that either restricts or provides access to their primary language, teachers of English language learners must respond to the diversity of need among young immigrant students. The impetus for ELL teachers being linguistically and culturally responsive decision makers must be their reflective practice (Au 1980).

If teachers fail to become aware of the unique needs of children of diverse linguistic and cultural backgrounds, they are certain to underestimate their abilities (Ada and Campoy 1998; Heath 1983; Moll 1992; Nieto 2003; Rueda and Mehan 1986). If teachers of English language learners privilege only mainstream language and culture and middle-class values, their classrooms serve as barriers rather than bridges to academic achievement (Trumbull et al. 2001). These classrooms fail to become the type of setting where English language learners can acquire strategies for understanding their cultural and linguistic diversity as resources and for negotiating these resources for academic proficiency (George, Raphael, and Florio-Ruane 2003; Nieto 2003). If teachers slim down the curriculum and reduce the complexity of pedagogical approaches to "one-size-fits-all" instruction when teaching English language learners, they diminish rather than optimize the available opportunities for language acquisition and academic learning. If teachers of English language learners dominate the delivery of instruction within passive, nonparticipatory, skills-based approaches, neither teacher nor student can benefit from being active co-agents in the learning process through which expertise is shared and rapport and respect flourish.

Teachers must fight against powerful influences that narrow curriculum, accept low performance, limit pedagogy, and immobilize productive practices for English language learners. Within this highly charged context in which English language learners are threatened with disempowering practices, their instructional needs can be viewed by their teachers as problematic and impossible to address (Gándara, Maxwell-Jolly, and Driscoll 2005).

As strong advocates for a quality education for English language learners, we strongly support an inquiry-based model of teaching and learning. This book shows teachers how to provide ELLs with a cognitively-demanding, language-conscious, and language-rich approach to learning. The 5E model provides ELLs with opportunities to use their diversity as an asset for learning, both for enriching their own knowledge and for enhancing the learning experiences of others.

English Language Learner Assets

It is essential for teachers to view a first language not as a problem but as an asset (Hamayan 2006). From a value-added perspective, the principled ELL teacher recognizes that English language learners bring a unique set of abilities and experiences and therefore enhance the learning environment. Because they bring a different way of approaching and interacting with their environment, their perspectives can enrich the thinking of a classroom, adding intellectual, social, and cognitive dimensions to the task of learning. Viewing English language learners as assets reinforces the belief that "all students are able to contribute, learn, and show us, and themselves, what they know" (Hamayan 2006, 26).

An additional asset teachers must be aware of is the *funds of knowledge* that are resources for English language learners and that can be exploited for their learning in school (Moll 2001; Moll and González 1997). This perspective does not view the English language learner as an empty slate. The teacher who operates from a funds-of-knowledge perspective recognizes that the cultural and social knowledge acquired through living in a household and functioning successfully in a community is valid and represents a vibrant knowledge base for the academic learning required in school. Knowledge of local economic systems, oral literacy heritages, and historical events, and knowledge derived from household apprenticeships (e.g., gardening, carpentry, sewing, or translating) are but a few examples of the cognitively and intellectually enriched knowledge bases that English language learners can draw upon. Parents and members of the community are recognized as teachers, and home and community activities are recognized as sites for teaching and learning (George, Raphael, and Florio-Ruane 2003). For optimum instructional decision making, it is critical that teachers understand that the cultural and language diversity of English language learners are additional instructional assets fostered within the home and community.

A Linguistically and Culturally Responsive Approach

The following represents a synthesis of practices that can serve as a bridge between the cultural and linguistic capital that English language learners bring to their instruction and the cultural and linguistic competence they have yet to acquire.

In order to be responsive to the cultural and linguistic needs of English language learners in language and content instruction, principled teachers of ELD must instill an appreciation of the value of diversity, use the family and community as instructional resources, use prior experience as a tool for language learning, cultivate a sense of bilingual competence, help develop strategies for navigating difference, and study the cultural and language backgrounds of English language learners.

One practical way to instill an appreciation for diversity within the ELD instructional setting is for the teacher to share personal language learning and cultural experiences from his or her own life (George, Raphael, and Florio-Ruane 2003). Within the interactive exchange of collaborative group work, the teacher can point out, or ask the students to share, examples of how having different opinions or pooling language resources were beneficial to completing the task in their instructional debriefings at the close of instruction (Cummins 1994a; Laternau 2003). Choices of thematic topics for instruction can contribute an appreciation for the contributions of diverse groups or for how diversity works within their community. For example, if the theme is immigration, the language topics can involve comparing and contrasting travel routes or different purposes for coming to America among immigrant groups. If the theme is *community*, students can explore their neighborhoods in order to acquire language for classifying resources for the types of goods and services that are available. Through the use of multicultural literature, comparisons can be made to resources for other cultural groups.

The ELL teacher can involve family and community resources in English language learners' second-language development (Cummins 1994b; Laternau 2003; Moll and González 1997). Family and community members can be brought into the classroom to demonstrate their expertise, or their places of work can provide opportunities for field trip experiences. Whether the original experience occurred in English or in another language, ELLs can reconstruct the experience in English by sequencing through retelling it, supported by photos and charted word banks. A classroom visit can involve ELLs in preparing and asking questions for interviews. The teacher can utilize these resources to provide his or her students with a sense of the language diversity that exists in the community (Moll and González 1997). Family members or members of the community can visit the classroom to share their experiences learning English (George, Raphael, and Florio-Ruane 2003). They can also work as volunteers to support language development and content mastery.

To support the development of the second language, teachers can encourage parents to play an important role by continuing to develop the primary language to the greatest possible extent (Ada and Campoy 1998; Cummins 1994a; Delgado-Gaitan 1990; George, Raphael, and Florio-Ruane 2003; Laternau 2003). Conversations and field trips within the family can expand English language learners' strategies for listening and critical thinking. Sharing good literature and engaging in in-depth discussions about meaning support the values of intellectual thought that are important in schools. The teacher can design family projects that guide parents' interactions with their children to create models or inventions from household materials. English language learners can take home an activity or project that they have completed and use English to teach their family members how to do it. The English language learner thus becomes a language expert and teacher in an authentic display of his or her developing competence.

Teachers can use the English language learners' knowledge and experiences resourcefully if they always begin and end their instruction with activities that allow students to reveal what they know. Through the use of graphic organizers, visuals, or read-alouds, the teacher can discover the concept knowledge students have as well as the language they have acquired already to communicate their understanding. Students can be encouraged to share personal experiences and therefore maximize the connection between home-language or primary-language knowledge and the school (George, Raphael, and Florio-Ruane 2003). Thus, the English language learner can start with thoughts in his or her first language to support learning in a second language (Hakuta 2001; Laternau 2003). Selecting texts or visual resources for instruction that mirror the ethnic or cultural background of English language learners also strengthens the links between home culture and school.

The final tenet of a linguistic and culturally responsive approach is exemplified by the teacher who becomes as familiar as he or she can with the cultural and linguistic backgrounds of the English language learners in the classroom. The teacher can survey the students or their parents about opportunities for second-language use in the home or in the community. The teacher can canvas the neighborhood to inventory available resources to enrich instruction. The teacher also can be accessible to parents through frequent communication or by inviting them to the classroom, recruiting translators as necessary, or even working to learn the primary language of the English language learners in his or her classroom.

This chapter has presented guiding principles for making decisions about ELL instruction. Within each principle, there are essential elements for facilitating the development of academic language within content instruction, as shown in Figure 2.5. Acting on these principles optimizes the language-learning opportunities for English language learners through a framework that promotes talk, thought, and interaction in ELL instruction. English language learners are involved in cognitively engaging instruction in which they learn (input) and use (output) academic language in meaningful and compelling interactive exchanges with their teacher and peers. Scaffolding and differentiation are approaches to instruction that enable teachers to provide students with opportunities to comprehend and acquire the language at developmentally appropriate levels. The English language development of ELLs will flourish within an approach to instruction that optimizes their cognitive, linguistic, and cultural assets. These elements comprise an enriched and multifaceted system of interrelated components that meets the complexity of developing second-language proficiency with equal complexity.

Figure 2.5 Essential Principles for Academic Language Development Instruction

Principle 1: A principled ELL teacher scaffolds language learning to make it comprehensible and relevant by • Implementing varied opportunities for comprehensible input • Maximizing the role of dialogue • Facilitating learning by building upon prior knowledge • Using an array of graphic organizers • Establishing rituals and routines
Principle 2: A principled ELL teacher supports explicit academic language instruction for authentic social and academic language purposes by • Focusing on explicit academic language for instruction • Ensuring authentic language and learning opportunities
Principle 3: A principled ELL teacher differentiates instruction in order to meet the diverse needs of English language learners by • Adapting instruction to meet the varied language and learning needs of students • Utilizing flexible grouping strategies
Principle 4: A principled ELL teacher optimizes language use through the cognitive engagement and social interaction of English language learners by • Promoting high levels of cognitive engagement and thinking • Utilizing interactive structures in dynamic learning tasks that optimize comprehensible output and access to language models
Principle 5: A principled ELL teacher bridges the diverse social, cultural, and linguistic resources that English language learners bring to the classroom for optimal learning by • Viewing sociocultural factors as resources • Recognizing and utilizing ELL assets • Employing a linguistically and culturally responsive approach to teaching and learning

Tips for Instructional Decision Making

When making decisions about instruction for English language learners, consider the following:

- Have a clear purpose and intention for ELL instruction.

- Reflect on the needs of your English language learners.

- Inventory your knowledge and skills of ELD.

- Engage in professional development.

- Embrace the principles for instructional decision making.

Reflect on Wonderings

1. How do the principles for decision making support the *Talk*, *Thought*, and *Interaction* framework for English language development?

2. Which factor is the most relevant to your teaching?

CHAPTER 3

Assessing English Language Learners Within Inquiry-Based Science

You May Wonder:

- What assessment factors and features are pertinent to the teaching and learning of ELLs within 5E inquiry-based science?

- What are practical and effective tools for assessment and informing instruction?

Certainly, assessment is an important consideration in any discussion of curriculum and instruction. The specter of assessment looms large, especially now, as accountability dominates educational discourse. In order to honor the productive role that assessment can have within instruction, it is important to understand that assessment and accountability are different. *Assessment* is the fair and reliable measurement of student abilities and progress. *Accountability* is the process of holding individuals and institutions responsible for the strengths or weaknesses detected through assessment (Vialpando, Linse, and Yedlin 2005). The main purpose of assessment is to provide appropriate placement and instruction that will result in student learning. Effective assessment both validates and informs instructional planning.

Factors That Influence ELL Assessment

The challenge of assessing ELLs has never been greater than it is today. English language learners are a unique student population within schools. Their needs embody a range of elements that influence the key educational considerations of curriculum, instruction, and assessment. Learning English in order to learn in English is a holistic, nonlinear, and constantly evolving process predicated upon multiple instructional factors that much of current assessment practice does not adequately address (Pappamihiel and Walser 2009).

The considerations required to effectively assess ELLs represent a bundle of varied aspects that include culture, language, socioeconomic status, academic achievement, bias, equity, and more. These aspects are not neatly arranged into separate compartments but rather blend complexly in each student.

Understanding English Language Learners as Complex Individuals

An effective approach for designing and delivering quality instruction for the unique ELL population rests on the ability of the teacher to know as much as possible about the resources, strengths, and needs of the ELL student. Knowing the student in complex ways moves considerations of ELL assessment deep into the educational process and into the classroom where expectations, curriculum, and instructional planning intersect. The assessment of English language learners requires an analysis of performance based on the interrelated dynamic of who each child is socially, linguistically, and academically. Because of this, ELLs require a framework of complexity that will guide the design of all facets of their education: identification, placement, curriculum, instruction, and assessment.

What does it mean to assess ELLs through a framework of complexity? Extensive research shows that no single assessment measure can be used to evaluate fairly the academic and linguistic knowledge of ELLs (Abedi 2004, 2005, 2010; Escamilla 2006; Genesee et al. 2005). In fact, the current Title III U.S. federal law governing the education of ELLs requires that multiple up-to-date, high-quality assessments of language and student achievement be implemented. As part of a framework for complexity, a multiple-measures approach to assessment can contribute a fuller and more accurate picture of primary- and secondary-language resources as well as the strengths and needs of ELLs through social, academic, and language-development lenses.

Assessment should be a measure of what students know and can do rather than a measure of what they do not know or cannot do. Within a framework of complexity, thoughtful consideration must be given to the validity and reliability of any ELL assessment. A *valid* assessment measures what it purports to measure; a *reliable* assessment is consistent over time and when used by different raters. Language forces educators to broaden expectations for ELL assessment. Providing language accommodations for English content assessment, framing the results of English tests through expectations for varied language-proficiency levels, and matching assessment to the language of delivery are important criteria for determining the validity and reliability of ELL achievement results.

Previous experience, academic background, and language matter. It is essential to gather linguistic data because students frequently have many more linguistic resources available to them than we are aware of (Gibbons 1991). All considerations of assessment and ensuing instruction must be intertwined with considerations of the resources that the ELL student brings to the classroom.

Adopting a framework of complexity for ELL assessment requires taking on a particular perspective that processes all educational considerations through a differentiated lens. As with other considerations when working with ELLs, the approach of differentiating instruction expands beyond content, process, and product to linguistic differentiation (Tomlinson 2004). In addition to making accommodations for primary-language needs, taking on a differentiation perspective for ELLs implies understanding that ELLs develop English-language proficiency in phases or stages. Differentiating instruction for ELLs involves filtering both assessment and instruction through proficiency-level expectations, along with grade-level or maturational expectations, to match student characteristics to instruction and assessment.

Because language acquisition proceeds through predictable stages, or levels, of development, the assessment of English learners needs to reflect the particular characteristics of each stage (Hamayan 1985). The emphasis in the beginning stages is placed on assessing sociolinguistic proficiency and growth reflected primarily in oral-language development and in emerging reading and writing competencies. As English language learners increase their English proficiency, more emphasis is placed on developing reading and writing competencies that demonstrate growth in formal language knowledge (Hadaway, Vardell, and Young 2002). Therefore, the assessment of English language learners should provide evidence of how students use language across a range of specific academic tasks to accomplish proficiency-level mastery in all dimensions of language—listening, speaking, reading, and writing (O'Malley and Pierce 1996).

Numerous documents for teachers have emerged across the decades that outline a developmental sequence of characteristic language performances for language acquisition. It is essential that teachers of ELLs have an understanding of the characteristic features of each language-proficiency level, from no knowledge of English to native-like speech. Terrell (1981) identified four levels of proficiency: Preproduction, Early Production, Speech Emergence, and Intermediate Fluency. The Teachers of English to Speakers of Other Languages (TESOL) Association standards (2006) identify the levels as Beginning, Intermediate, and Advanced. The California Department of Education's ELD standards (1999) have five levels: Beginning, Early Intermediate, Intermediate, Early Advanced, and

Advanced. The World-Class Instructional Design and Assessment (WIDA) Consortium's 2004 ELP standards have also identified five levels of developing language: Entering, Beginning, Developing, Expanding, and Bridging.

Regardless of the number of levels, teachers should become familiar with the proficiency levels that mark the features of language progression, which build on each other and serve as indicators for assessing and planning appropriate instruction. Matrices that summarize the essential features of each level, such as the one featured in Figure 3.1, synthesize the standards and provide teachers with a quick and easy tool to identify strategies and resources in addition to the expectations for their instruction.

Figure 3.1 English Language Development Proficiency Levels

Beginning Proficiency Level (B)
English learners at the BEGINNING level of English language proficiency demonstrate dramatic growth. They progress from having no receptive or productive English skills to possessing a basic use of English. Students at the BEGINNING level are able to comprehend high-frequency words and basic phrases in immediate, physical, concrete surroundings; produce learned words and phrases and use gestures to communicate basic needs; interact with frequently used English print in a limited fashion and demonstrate initial English print awareness; write familiar words and phrases; demonstrate understanding of familiar words, phrases, and questions drawn from content areas; follow classroom routines and schedules; express basic personal and safety needs; respond to questions with one-to-two-word answers and gestures; and demonstrate and use basic social conventions.

Early Intermediate Proficiency Level (EI)

English learners at the EARLY INTERMEDIATE level of English language proficiency respond with increasing ease to more varied communication tasks with learned material. Students at the EARLY INTERMEDIATE level are able to comprehend a sequence of information on familiar topics as presented through stories and face-to-face conversations; produce basic statements and ask questions in direct, informational exchanges on familiar and routine subjects; interact with a variety of familiar print as part of a group; recognize words and phrases from previously learned material; write basic personal information and short responses within structured contexts; use high-frequency vocabulary drawn from other content areas; express basic personal and safety needs; respond to questions and simple phrases; and participate in simple face-to-face conversations with peers and others.

Intermediate Proficiency Level (I)

English learners at the INTERMEDIATE level of English language proficiency begin to refashion learned material to meet their immediate communication and learning needs. Students at the INTERMEDIATE level are able to comprehend information on familiar topics in contextualized settings; produce sustained conversations with others on an expanding variety of general topics; interact independently with a variety of simplified print; write basic information and expanded responses in contextualized settings; comprehend main ideas and basic concepts in content areas; express a variety of personal and safety needs and respond to questions using short sentences; and initiate simple conversations with English speakers outside of school.

Early Advanced Proficiency Level (EA)

English learners at the EARLY ADVANCED level of English language proficiency begin to create with the English language in more complex, cognitively demanding situations and are able to use English as a means for learning in other academic areas. Students at the EARLY ADVANCED level are able to comprehend detailed information with fewer contextual clues on unfamiliar topics; produce, initiate and sustain personal, spontaneous language interactions using circumlocution when necessary; interact with increasingly complex written material while relying on context and prior knowledge to obtain meaning from print; write to satisfy limited social and academic needs through the recombination of learned vocabulary and structures; participate actively in all content areas; express more complex feelings, needs, and opinions using extended oral and written production; and participate actively in nonacademic settings requiring English.

Advanced Proficiency Level (A)

English learners at the ADVANCED level of English language proficiency communicate effectively with various audiences on a wide range of familiar and new topics to meet social and academic demands. In order to attain the English proficiency level of their native-English-speaking peers, further linguistic enhancement and refinement are necessary. Students at the ADVANCED level are able to comprehend concrete and abstract topics and recognize language subtleties in a variety of communicative settings; produce, initiate, and sustain extended interactions tailored to specific purposes and audiences; read grade-level material with limited comprehension difficulties; write to meet most social needs and academic demands for specific purposes and audiences; participate fully in all content areas at grade level; express and satisfy personal and safety needs in a wide variety of settings; and participate fully in nonacademic settings requiring English.

(Writing Reform Institute for Teaching Excellence 2003)

An understanding of proficiency-level expectations as provided by a corpus of well-developed ELD standards supports a clear and common focus for ELL instruction, assessment, and materials. Familiarity with the expectations of each level supports teachers in understanding what the ELL student can already do in English, thus allowing them to build on strengths. If a teacher understands the targets that the student is moving toward, he or she can reasonably challenge the student just beyond an independent level of performance to move ever closer to the next level and native-like proficiency. For example, a teacher of Early Intermediate (EI) level English language learners can use his or her understanding of the writing expectations for the EI level student to be able to *write basic personal information and short responses within structured contexts* (refer to Figure 3.1, Early Intermediate Proficiency Level) to design instruction that provides structured support for his or her English language learners' writing. Appropriate support could take the form of a word bank, cloze sentences, or language-experience approach frames. Moreover, because the teacher is familiar with the expectations at the next proficiency level (Intermediate) he or she can target instruction that will enable English language learners to *write basic information and expanded responses in contextualized settings* (refer to Figure 3.1, Intermediate Proficiency Level). The teacher can thus reduce the scaffolding structures for the English language learners as they move toward the Intermediate level with a focus on increasing open-ended written responses and expanding vocabulary beyond high-frequency or familiar words.

As teachers are able to use the standards-based expectations as markers of growth and for the establishment of new goals, the incremental flow of language and literacy development is facilitated and promoted. When groups of teachers have a common understanding of expectations for the language proficiency level of their ELLs, consistency and collaboration within grade-level planning can enhance the potential for language learning. Furthermore, the continuity of instructional quality and effectiveness as English language learners move from grade level to grade level can be supported.

What teachers say and do in ELD instruction is the catalyst for input and understanding. Therefore, the way teachers talk and the strategies they use should be adjusted to meet the needs of specific levels of English language proficiency (Herrell and Jordan 2004). Since Early Intermediate students should be able to respond by using phrases and simple sentences, the teacher's modeling and questioning should be adjusted to elicit that level of language production. For the Early Intermediate student, there is a difference in the level of challenge between answering the question *Can I buy eggs in a library or a supermarket?* and *Why did you have eggs for breakfast and not cereal?* The former example represents the level-appropriate question. Since Beginning-level students understand brief, basic, highly contextualized input with visual support, reading aloud a grade-level text without any visual support is highly inappropriate and ineffectual. Equally inappropriate is reading aloud a heavily illustrated text composed of simple phrases and sentences to Advanced-level students. Application of a differentiation perspective to assessment and instruction could involve contextualizing content through visuals, realia, simulations, or the use of the primary language; providing peer support through flexible grouping; adjusting time; leveling questions; or adapting text to match language-proficiency levels.

Educators who serve ELL populations are challenged by myriad issues and instructional considerations to become careful and proactive data gatherers and interpreters. They must employ a comprehensive assessment approach for ELL progress monitoring and curriculum design. Instructional delivery should consist of a compendium of assessment types, including multidimensional and multimodal, that encompass standardized tests (measures of academic progress and language proficiency development) and classroom-based assessments (informal, formal, authentic, performance based, formative, and summative). It is imperative that teachers of ELLs understand and critique the benefits of all assessments for their students as well as understand their limitations.

Classroom-based Assessment for English Language Learners

Current ELL literature on assessment supports the efforts in classroom-based assessment to move beyond multiple-choice testing for mastery of discrete behavioral objectives toward assessment procedures that rely heavily on focused observations and samples of student work collected during day-to-day classroom learning activities (Gottlieb 2006; Kuhlman 2005; Peregoy and Boyle 2008). There are several advantages to relying on classroom-based assessments over standardized tests: Evidence can be gathered of student mastery of the standards that is broader than that which can be obtained from a standardized test administered in a brief period of time. Also, a greater number of standards can be assessed, including those that are difficult to measure via standardized tests, and assessments can be based on a wider range of student performance. In essence, assessments can be conducted in more authentic and meaningful ways. Also, teachers have immediate access to assessment results, which they can then use to improve their instruction (Vialpando, Linse, and Yedlin 2005).

Within a classroom-based assessment system, curriculum-embedded—or program-based—assessment is yet another aspect of ELL assessment that must be analyzed for appropriate use. Curriculum-embedded assessments by nature are derived from content frameworks and mandated standards. Moreover, to ensure that ELLs can access the content concepts and skills, accommodations for these students have been embedded within curriculum frameworks. Publishers and other educational agencies produce instructional materials that are aligned to a given framework and its standards. Formal standards-based assessment tools (e.g., diagnostic assessments, chapter tests, and rubrics) are embedded within these instructional materials. Often, these tools have become benchmark assessments to monitor progress at the school and district levels and are used to initiate instructional intervention.

In spite of closer proximity to the actual processes of teaching and learning, these assessments can be just as problematic for teachers of ELLs as standardized assessments, with regard to ELL needs. The published program material measures academic growth based on general grade-level content that has been developed for a national market, or at best, a state-level market. This means that this type of assessment often does not reflect the nuances of primary- or second-language proficiency development. Without consideration to language and differentiation, a curriculum-embedded assessment may pinpoint failure over and over based on normed grade-level measures in English. Scales adjusted for language-proficiency level expectations that measure growth in smaller increments or that factor in language may offer a solution. If a teacher is looking at the results of a writing benchmark assessment that indicates ELLs consistently scoring 1 out of 3 on a rubric scale, it would be beneficial to also have a rubric scale adjusted for language-proficiency level expectations to indicate strengths and needs through a language filter. The result could be a clearer focus for the linguistic scaffolds that support writing development.

Informal assessments such as performance-based student work products, journals, checklists, and observations can be the most adaptable, relevant, and accurate tools available to teachers within a classroom-based assessment system. Informal assessments are designed to help the classroom teacher plan and modify the curriculum to meet the needs of individual learners. Through ongoing informal classroom-based assessment, teachers will notice when ELLs need extra practice to meet an objective and when they are able to tackle more challenging academic materials. Assessment can be differentiated on the spot quickly and purposefully according to varied expectations for language-proficiency levels. They will provide opportunities for students to give complex, multifaceted answers instead of simplistic responses. Results from structured, informal assessment (e.g., anecdotal records or student surveys) can be retrieved for ongoing analysis of progress or stored in portfolios for analysis of progress across longer periods of time. Portfolios of student work can provide a holistic and evolving assessment practice that matches the nonlinear process of learning a second language. Because portfolios contain work done as part of the regular curriculum, they do not take time away from the teaching and the learning process as traditional testing does (Freeman and Freeman 1998). Portfolios can involve the student in thinking about his or her language performance and progress and will provide an authentic and accessible artifact of data that can be shared with parents.

Teachers have the most direct control over informal assessment. This allows them to creatively gather varied representations of an ELL student's authentic performance in the classroom—including performance in the primary language—on an ongoing basis. It also allows them to easily differentiate assessment to meet the needs of ELLs and to match the assessment to the language of strength or the language of instruction.

In spite of the robust, positive aspects of informal assessment, there are limitations that teachers of ELLs must be aware of. As with other forms of assessment, teachers must be able to ensure the relationship between what is taught and what is assessed. Knowledge of the curriculum and ELL pedagogy is critical for informal assessment to be consistent with the goals of the content and responsive to the language needs of ELLs. Kuhlman cautions teachers that "performance-based assessment is only useful if the teacher (and student) pay attention to what students know and can do. It is easier to make guesses about that, or to rely on norm-referenced, decontextualized measures" (2005). Teachers must select assessment strategies and techniques that produce data that can be relied on for instructional planning. While much can be learned about students through firsthand observation, this form of assessment can be weakened by a lack of structure for recording observations and their periodic review. Detailed information can slip away from the teacher, resulting in subjective judgments about what students are good at and what they need to develop. Because it is difficult to standardize analysis of informal assessments, results may be very different among teachers. Without paying attention to these factors, the result can be inconsistent and inappropriate instruction.

Important Features of ELL Assessment Within Inquiry-Based Science

Authenticity, intentionality, and purposeful interaction should be principles of ELL assessment. Certain features of assessment practice ensure that the language strengths and needs of English language learners are given appropriate prominence in the 5E learning cycle for science. Each stage of the 5E model has a particular focus for its assessment. When developing English is added to the mix, each stage has particular implications for assessing language performance.

In the *Engage* stage, the preassessment of English-language proficiency can be captured through careful observation and documented in anecdotal records. Analyzing the language use of English language learners at the onset of instruction will provide insight into what students understand, the level of vocabulary students already know and use, and their ability to communicate their understanding in the appropriate grammatical forms. This initial data will aid teachers in determining the language support ELLs will need in order to maximize the acquisition of academic language through science content.

In the *Explore* stage, formative assessment is used to help teachers understand the progress students are making in understanding science concepts as well as their progress in practicing and using new language. Finding out what students struggle to express orally and in writing at this early stage helps guide the design of future instructional interventions in the remaining stages.

The goal of assessment for ELLs in the *Explain* stage is to determine whether enough academic language has been acquired to enable students to use content-related vocabulary and language forms to communicate what they know. Finding out how students express themselves orally and in writing helps teachers monitor progress along a language-proficiency continuum. Since *Explain* requires greater emphasis on focused, explicit language instruction, teachers place greater emphasis on evaluating students' language performance. There is an expectation that students will use the language they have been taught as they articulate their learning.

The role of assessment in *Extend* is to gauge how well English language learners demonstrate their ability to apply and transfer their understanding to new contexts as well as how students use formal representations of science knowledge (e.g., terms, formulas, and diagrams). The outcomes can help teachers determine what will be important to evaluate in the next phase.

The assessment of language performance in *Extend* focuses on how well English language learners demonstrate their language ability as they transfer acquired academic language to new contexts and approximate scientific discourse in oral, written, and graphic forms in the expression of their scientific understanding. For teachers of English language learners, forming opinions about student progress in English language development will be important in determining the final summative assessment steps of inquiry.

The key to ELL assessment in *Evaluate* is to ensure that language learning can be demonstrated along with content understanding. Students must understand what they have learned and how they have learned it in order to learn effectively during future instruction. Teachers must also understand what and how their students have learned to teach effectively in future instruction.

To accomplish the goals of each stage with respect to the assessment of language performance, particular practices for teachers will be elaborated upon and exemplified in each of the forthcoming 5E chapters. These practices include evaluating the authentic use of language, actively monitoring language performance, using anecdotal records, and promoting student self-reflection.

Authentic Use of Language

Using language for authentic purposes is an important feature of developing a second language. The need to communicate in order to share thoughts, information, observations, wonderings, and learnings are the real, or *authentic*, fruits that emanate from a science curriculum focused on thinking and doing. Evidence of authentic language use must be multifaceted in order to capture its use in oral, visual, or written form as students describe, explain, analyze, synthesize, report, and justify within genuine scientific practices.

Active Monitoring

Our view of active monitoring refers to a systematic process in which the teacher is frequently circulating among the students as they explore the content. The intentional purpose of this is to directly or indirectly probe or prompt students to find out what they understand and how they can communicate what they understand. This type of ongoing monitoring moves beyond the surface levels of language performance in search of the expression of scientific thinking. Adopting specific rituals or procedures for monitoring can ensure the success of a given task as well as the gathering of meaningful data.

Anecdotal Records

The use of anecdotal records has long been a widely used strategy among teaching professionals for assessing instruction. Through the English-language-development lens, compiling a retrievable record of the language of the instructional moment on sticky notes, in a notebook, or as a list ensures that observable oral language use will become part of a greater data pool of linguistic progress. Noting the language performance in words, phrases, sentences, and gestures can influence instructional decisions in the immediate context or in future instruction.

Student Self-Reflection

An essential assessment practice is ensuring that students are mindful of their role as a learner. An important aspect of the teacher's role for this practice is guiding students to develop a habit of self-reflection that moves beyond thinking about what was learned to include thinking about how it was learned. As language learners, ELLs can be guided to self-reflect on the language they have acquired to develop a meta-awareness of the skills and tools they have available to them. Self-reflection will occur across the learning cycle and involve oral and written presentations to varied audiences aside from the students themselves. English language learners benefit from having opportunities to talk about their learning with their peers, teachers, and parents.

Science Notebooks for ELL Assessment

Science educators consider the use of science notebooks in instruction as a valuable thinking tool for students (Gilbert and Kotelman 2005; Hargrove and Nesbit 2003; Klentschy 2008; Marcarelli 2010). Because students archive what is taught and learned through the integration of language arts, using notebooks is also viewed as important for the development of scientific literacy. Science notebooks are promoted as a "central place where language data and experience operate jointly to form meaning for the student" (Klentschy 2008, viii) and where students are engaged in authentic science processes (e.g., recording information, experimenting, and drawing conclusions) just like those used by professional scientists (Young 2003). They are designed to foster the formulation of scientific explanations from evidence, the analysis of various types of scientific evidence or data, and the formulation of conclusions based upon relevant evidence. In addition to their importance for student learning, science notebooks are considered an excellent ongoing assessment and feedback tool for teachers (Ruiz-Primo, Li, and Shavelson 2002).

Figure 3.2 Science Notebook Entry

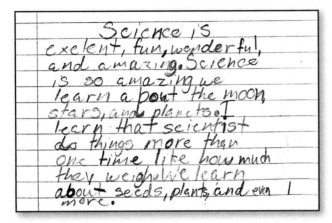

Science is
exelent, fun, wonderful,
and amazing. Science
is so amazing we
learn a bout the moon
stars, and plancts. I
learn that scientist
do things more than
one time like how much
they weigh. We learn
about seeds, plants, and even
more.

This opening science notebook entry from an ELL student communicates his passion and enthusiasm for science.

Through varied types of notebook entries such as technical drawings, graphic visuals, notes, practice problems, investigations, analyses, and reflections, students move through myriad cognitive processes. These processes include tapping into schema, observing, questioning, predicting, reporting, drawing conclusions, and reflecting.

Utilizing science notebooks is a powerful tool for evaluating the multidimensional aspects of an English language learner's learning: language use and academic content understanding. Science notebooks as formative assessment can help teachers make ongoing decisions about English-language-development instruction—in addition to content instruction—as ELLs move through the 5E process. Seeing how students use the language of science visually and in written form can help teachers determine what will be important to evaluate in the following phase.

A noteworthy feature of assessing ELLs through science notebooks is how well the notebooks capture the authentic language of scientific thinking, moving beyond simply learning academic vocabulary toward using scientific discourse to express conceptual knowledge.

Typical thinking processes that can be archived with language are observing, questioning, analyzing, predicting, summarizing, and drawing conclusions. From a language perspective, these thinking processes when articulated orally or in writing have particular language structures or forms. When drawing a conclusion, the student may write: *Since we used different materials, we found ....* When comparing rocks and minerals, another student may explain: *The difference between rocks and minerals is ....* These authentic expressions of scientific thought emerge from participation in inquiry through the 5E learning cycle. The science notebook serves as a window into how the ELL student is thinking about a particular concept as well as how he or she can use language to reflect thinking. An additional aspect to highlight is that the student-centered, learning-centered approach to using the science notebook ensures a safe place for the ELL student to practice language to communicate newly acquired understanding about science, regardless of English-language proficiency level.

Figure 3.3 Science Notebook Entry

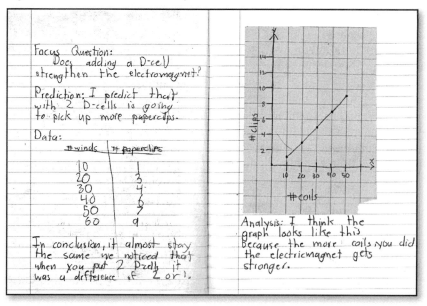

This multifaceted entry represents the levels of thinking and language—questioning, predicting, data recording, drawing conclusions, and analyzing—that English language learners can express in science notebooks.

Another aspect of implementing science notebooks for ELL assessment is that science notebooks document the English-language proficiency level of a given student, reflecting where he or she is performing in terms of language development and growth along a continuum toward increased English proficiency. As artifacts of thinking and learning, the language ELLs use becomes more complex as students are guided to deepen their scientific knowledge. A related benefit for ELLs and their teachers is that the consistent use of science notebooks as a companion to scientific inquiry across a school year results in a useful archive of language progress over time. Figures 3.4 and 3.5 depict notebook entries from the same Intermediate-level student. Figure 3.4 was part of the *Engage* stage of a 5E cycle exploring the properties of rocks and minerals. It reflects a simple sentence structure: *It is…*. Figure 3.5 occurs much later in the 5E cycle. In her entry, the student explains what she did and draws conclusions. She had just received instruction on composing complex sentences. Her authentic experiences with scientific thinking and focused language instruction have resulted in a vibrant and convincing use of academic language.

Figure 3.4 *Engage* Notebook Entry   **Figure 3.5 Science Notebook Entry**

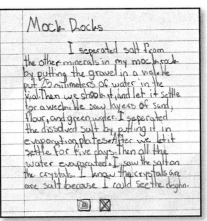

In addition to the established procedures and purposes for science notebook work, there are certain features related to language development that teachers of ELLs must consider in the design of their science notebook implementation.

- **Flexibility.** When designing the entry, consider the need to differentiate the task based on the language it will require of the English language learners in the classroom. Based on the proficiency level of the students as well as considerations of maturity and academic skills, consider the incorporation of drawings and other visual presentations like tables or graphs that will enable all levels of English language learners to communicate what they understand. Consider allowing certain students to work with a partner in order to take advantage of additional language models and supports through more proficient language peers. Figures 3.6 and 3.7 represent notebook formats that allow students with varying levels of language proficiency to use the language they have to represent the details of their understanding through the use of visuals and single words along with phrases and sentences. Note the attention to developing academic vocabulary through word study in Figure 3.7.

Figure 3.6 Science Notebook Entry

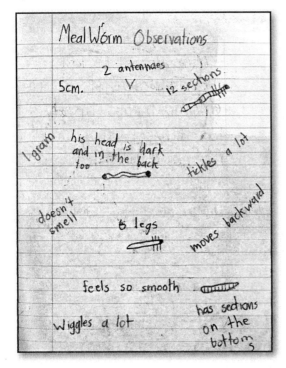

Figure 3.7 Science Notebook Entry

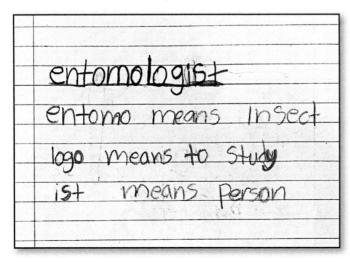

- **Oral rehearsal.** Prior to composing an individual written entry, it can be very supportive to provide an expanded period of talking and thinking for English language learners with their peers.

- **Concrete to abstract.** Keep in mind an instructional sequence of ensuring comprehensible input for language development that progresses from concrete representations of a concept to more abstract representations. If students experience instruction that guides them from comprehensible input grounded in concrete visual examples of language to tasks that involve language output in interaction with peers (such as in partners or groups), then the subsequent science notebook entry acts as the platform to link language usage to more abstract thinking about scientific phenomena.

- **Writing scaffolds.** When English language learners are at the early levels of language proficiency or are expected to write an entry for a type of thinking experience that is unfamiliar to them, use structured writing prompts or sentence frames as temporary scaffolds. Figure 3.8 represents the work of a student who is using various prompts (e.g., *In the study of ...*, *Another thing I did ...*, *After doing ...*, *As a next step ...*) to guide his reflection on mealworms. His teacher provides the prompts in a language script that serves as a temporary scaffold. It will eventually be eliminated as the student develops an understanding of the structure of a self-reflection narrative.

Figure 3.8 Science Notebook Entry

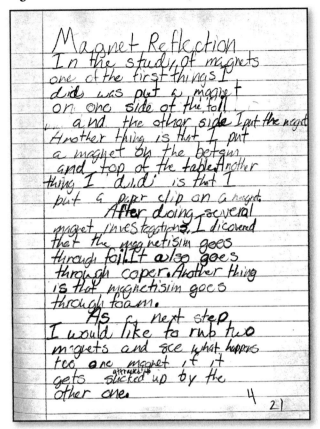

Magnet Reflection
In the study of magnets
one of the first things I
did was put a magnet
on one side of the foil
and the other side I put the magnet
Another thing is that I put
a magnet on the bottom
and top of the table. Another
thing I did is that I
put a paper clip on a magnet.
After doing several
magnet investigations, I discovered
that the magnetisim goes
through foil. It also goes
through coper. Another thing
is that magnetisim goes
through foam.
As a next step,
I would like to rub two
magnets and see what happens
too one magnet if it
gets sucked up by the
other one.

4   21

Tips for Assessing English Language Learners Within Inquiry-Based Science

When assessing English language learners within inquiry-based science, consider the following:

- Match your expectations for language performance to English language proficiency level expectations.

- Use multiple measures for assessing language and content understanding.

- Evaluate language produced both orally and in writing.

- Establish a classroom assessment system for evaluating language in ongoing instruction.

Reflect on Wonderings

1. How does assessment support the academic language development of English language learners?

2. Which factor is the most relevant for your teaching?

CHAPTER 4

Activating Language Through *Engage*

You May Wonder:

- What do I need to think about when designing an engaging science activity for English language learners?

- In what ways can I support the development and understanding of language and science in *Engage*?

- How can I assess students' language and prior knowledge?

The following chapters guide the teacher through a professional inquiry into the 5E model as a vehicle for supporting the English language development of English language learners. To that end, carefully selected classroom instructional scenarios that capture the best of teacher decision making and ELD practices are embedded in inquiry-based science instruction. Each chapter presents a stage of the 5E model through the lens of second-language development with in-depth discussion of ELD instructional features and strategies. Each chapter closes with a discussion of ELL assessment practices for the stage and a summary of tips for implementing the stage with ELLs. A final reflective section guides the reader through a series of questions that will support instructional planning for each stage.

Ms. Cortez's Class—Grade 2 Scenario
ELD Levels: Early Intermediate and Intermediate
Part A: A First Glimpse at English Language Learner
Instruction During Engage

A low buzz fills the room as the children anticipate the day's lesson. Two photographs of different earthworms in a variety of habitats lay on the tables. Each of the 20 Spanish/English bilingual students in this second-grade classroom sits side by side with a lab partner. At one side of the room, a girl wearing a pink sweater moves her head from side to side and shakes her hands in front of her. Another student sitting at the front sits on his legs and strains his neck in order to take a closer look at what is moving in and out of the pile of dirt in a bin next to the document camera. What are these students thinking as they sit at their desks anxiously awaiting the lesson of the day?

Since the beginning of the semester, the students have been engaged in a model of inquiry in which they learn by investigating through simple experiments. The teacher, Ms. Cortez, places a photograph of an earthworm under the document camera.

Ms. Cortez: *We have been studying the life cycles of animals. We have looked at the life cycles of frogs and mealworms. Today, we are going to investigate more closely what we observe about earthworms. Say the word with me:* earthworms.

What Is *Engage* for English Language Learners?

The 5E model begins with *Engage*. Students are exposed to a topic, concept, or idea in a way that stirs curiosity; it captures their attention in order to get their minds around the learning at hand. The activities teachers use for the *Engage* stage can include displaying a picture, conducting an experiment, posing a question, showing a video clip, and more. The idea is for students to make connections to their prior knowledge and begin to question what they know and what they do not know. Reasons for further exploration are established.

At this stage, English language learners are encouraged to share their thinking at the level of English proficiency that they are comfortable with and to use their primary language when applicable. Since the purpose of *Engage* is for students to generate prior knowledge and engage them in the thinking around science, English language learners should be encouraged to use either English or their primary language to talk about their thinking. It is the teacher who serves as a model of language for students at this stage. Through the academic language the teacher uses, the questions asked, and the introduction to science content, students are exposed to academic content-area language. This stage provides high levels of comprehensible input through the careful attention to academic language on the part of the teacher as well as the opportunity to look, feel, touch, and think science. The integration of language and content at this point comes from the personal experiences and prior knowledge that the ELL student brings to the learning environment. It is a great opportunity for teachers to informally assess students' English language development and make better instructional decisions about how to support ELLs throughout the remaining stages of the 5E model.

Reflecting on the opening scenario, the teacher has clearly established a motivating instructional climate filled with living earthworms and real-life photographs. These English language learners are excited and poised to engage in their new investigation.

Ms. Cortez's Class—Grade 2 Scenario
Part B: Looking Deeply into ELL Instruction During Engage

As Ms. Cortez says the word *earthworms*, she writes it on the board. She underlines the diagraph *th*.

Ms. Cortez: *The* th *may be a difficult sound to pronounce because it doesn't exist in Spanish. I want you to stick your tongue out and bite on it and blow through your teeth. Say the word with me,* earthworms.

The teacher has intentionally planned this moment of quick language practice because she understands that this sound is a new sound for her students. She wants to provide her students with opportunities to practice making this sound throughout this investigation.

Ms. Cortez: *We are going to begin our lesson by closely observing photographs with a partner and sharing what we notice about earthworms. Look at the photograph that I have projected on the whiteboard. I am going to demonstrate what you will do with your partner.* She begins to model for the students how scientists observe photographs and use language to describe what they see: *I notice that this is a photograph of an earthworm. The earthworm is long and has a curved body. I also want you to notice that the earthworm is shiny. Look at how the light is shining on its body, making the earthworm shiny.*

As the teacher shares her observations, she labels the photograph and points to specific parts of the earthworm's body. Before having the students get up to work on their own, she has each student turn to a partner and share what he or she will do in the task. The teacher knows that it is critical for the students to understand what they are going to do prior to the activity. She circulates among them to check their understanding of the task.

In partners, the students huddle shoulder-to-shoulder and begin to share what they notice about earthworms in the photographs. The teacher moves from group to group to listen to the students' conversations and to record what they are saying. At times, she leans in closer and mediates the students' language.

Robert: *Oh, look at this earthworm. It is shiny.*

Desiree: *It blue on top.*

Robert: *I notice that it is curly.*

Ms. Cortez: *Yes, it is curly. Notice how the earthworm is coiled.* (She traces the curled-up shape of the earthworm.)

As the teacher signals, students rotate from table to table. After the full rotation, each student is asked to select a word and to share one thing that he or she noticed about the photographs of the earthworms.

The teacher is satisfied that her students have had varied opportunities to think and talk about what they know about earthworms, using the language they already have. She has modeled new vocabulary and language forms. She has encouraged her students through questioning to express their thinking in the language they bring. Now, her students are ready to move on to a more complex way of thinking and talking that includes writing.

For the next step of this activity, an Inquiry Chart is placed under each photograph. It is a large sheet of construction paper divided into two sections. The right side is labeled *I notice ...* and the left side is labeled *I wonder ....*

As the students gather on the rug, the teacher demonstrates how to complete the Inquiry Charts by having a student role-play with her.

Ms. Cortez: *Let's look at this photograph. I notice that the earthworm is long. What do you notice?*

Raquel: *It has lines.*

Ms. Cortez: *Yes, you're right. As we look closer, we see that the body is divided into parts. It is* segmented. *Let's write that down. Now look at the chart. It says, "I wonder ...." What questions do you have about this earthworm? What are you wondering about?*

Raquel: *Does it have eyes?*

Ms. Cortez: *Let's use this frame: I wonder if it has eyes. Write that down on the chart.*

In partners, the students move from table to table recording their observations and questions. After 10 minutes, each set of partners moves from table to table reading all of the responses. Their initial step is to select one photograph that they found engaging. From that chart, each student selects one response under *I notice ...* to share out later in an activity called a Whip-Around. Moving from group to group, each student reads one *I notice ...* response. Then, in the same manner, students share out one response from the *I wonder ...* column.

Activating Language in *Engage*

Teachers of English language learners must develop a strong awareness of how language is used in each of the 5E stages. From a clear sense of the workings of language, teachers can determine how to maximize all opportunities for second-language development through thoughtful, purposeful instructional design. The interplay of the key language instruction dimensions of *talk*, *thought*, and *interaction* is strongly evident in *Engage*. The previous scenario provides many clear examples of intentional planning that supports the English academic language development of ELLs that will be discussed in this section.

During *Engage*, the instructional environment cognitively engages students and promotes their language development through the interaction of teacher talk and student talk, which is achieved through the features of ELL practice listed in Figure 4.1.

Figure 4.1 Essential Features for Developing Academic Language in *Engage*

- Tapping into prior knowledge
- Establishing a supportive, low-anxiety environment for language practice and use
- Selecting instructional resources, such as visuals, real objects, or texts to support second-language understanding
- Modeling language use by teacher (or peers)

Tapping Into Prior Knowledge

Whether in their primary language (L1) or their second language (L2), the hands-on experiential activities of *Engage* compel students to make connections to what they know (schema) and to formulate questions about what they want to know (inquiry). At any age, English language learners will use language to express the meaning that they are making during natural interaction with peers and adults. This language will serve as the catalyst of their inquiry process as the language they have to express their prior knowledge is brought to the forefront of the instructional experience.

Think about the scenario presented earlier in this chapter. This brief instructional sequence for *Engage* provides students with multiple opportunities to interact with photographs of worms, to think about what they are seeing, and to make connections to their previous experiences. Examining multiple photos on their own and interacting with a partner or the teacher establishes a dynamic in which ideas and knowledge are shared.

Establishing a Supportive, Low-Anxiety Environment

Because the instruction in this stage is informal and open-ended, accepting whatever the students bring to their initial experience establishes a low affective filter (Krashen 1982). English language learners feel comfortable expressing their prior knowledge and their questions in the language they have available to them. They are encouraged to comfortably interact with their peers and their teacher in authentic social interaction structures, such as small groups or pairs.

Returning to the scenario, it is apparent that language is flooding the instructional setting. Students are expressing what they know with the language they choose to use, confirming what is already known, presenting new information, and expressing wonder and observation. Students move from the support of the group on the rug to observing and conversing with a partner. Expectations are communicated clearly through modeling of the tasks. At first, the expectation is for students to look and talk, which the teacher actively facilitates as he or she moves from pair to pair. The structure is relaxed movement from table to table prompted by a signal at a comfortable interval. The added complexity of writing (recording) follows a number of opportunities for oral rehearsal.

Selecting Instructional Resources

English language learners build conceptual and linguistic understanding initially through context-embedded instructional sequences as they move along a continuum toward cognitively demanding and context-reduced learning environments (Cummins 2005). This means that teachers must thoughtfully select instructional resources that clearly depict the new target language and that will support science concept development. Photographs of actual phenomena (e.g., weather conditions) are more effective than illustrations. Authentic, concrete objects (e.g., real apples, real rocks) that can be experienced through multiple senses provide more comprehensible input than photographs or drawings. A richly illustrated book written in accessible language can promote better understanding than text read aloud without the support of visuals or realia. Photographs of animals in nature provide opportunities for observation, especially for students in urban settings. Photographs can also offer a vivid resource for conceptual understanding that serves as the basis for language.

In the second-grade scenario, the selection of real-life photos of worms is a significant element in the design of the lesson. The photographs have to grab the students' interest and engage them as well as accurately represent scientific concepts. As resources for language production, the photographs contain much detail, serving as a catalyst for rich and varied academic vocabulary.

Modeling Language Use

The teacher's use of targeted language and the facilitation of language interaction among peers is a critical part of this stage. Although not yet presented through explicit instruction, the teacher assumes the primary role of modeling the English language use she expects to target throughout the 5E sequence. The teacher is strategic about how he or she models and facilitates new language input during the *Engage* experience. The teacher explains, discusses, questions, prompts, or recasts L1 responses in English while interacting with students and encouraging them to interact with one another.

In the grade 2 scenario, Ms. Cortez is deliberate and precise about the language she uses and her facilitation of student talk. She wants to set the stage for the focused language instruction that will occur in the remaining stages. Within the meaningful context of student inquiry in *Engage*, she uses scientific terminology such as *life cycle* and *observe*. She also models more sophisticated language choices, saying *investigate* or *notice* rather than *look at,* calling the object a *photograph* rather than a *picture,* and describing the earthworm as *coiled* instead of *curly.* Ms. Cortez also explicitly provides students with new, expanded vocabulary when she says, "… the body is divided into parts. It is *segmented.*" Indirectly through her instruction, she models appropriate structures of language, including the use of sentence frames.

Thus, through intentional instructional decision making in the *Engage* stage, students give language to their thoughts as they are inspired by the excitement of a hands-on, cognitively-engaging experience. With equal intention, planning for the social interaction of students and adults compels the meaningful input and output English learners bring to learning science concepts. This sets the stage for the acquisition of the academic language that will follow in subsequent stages of the 5E process.

Figure 4.2 *Engage* **Activity**

The teaching of English requires a firsthand experience to engage students and to develop language.

Examining ELD Practices in *Engage*

In the previous section, several ELD practices that are essential for the *Engage* stage were highlighted in a second-grade classroom scenario focused on earthworms. In this section, we continue the analysis of notable practices for ELLs during *Engage* by focusing on additional scenarios from a fourth-grade study of the effects of weathering on rocks and a seventh-grade science class launching a unit on cells.

> ### *Mrs. Reyes's Class—Grade 4 Scenario*
> ### *ELD Levels: Intermediate and Advanced*
>
> As the fourth-grade students enter their classroom, they find different rocks placed on each desk. Some are as small as a quarter and others are as large as a hat. It is hard for

students not to touch the rocks as they each take their seats. The teacher, Mrs. Reyes, begins to show them the other materials that are placed at each station. She begins by telling students that today they will be working as geologists. She shows them various tools they will work with: small picks, magnifying glasses, scales, journals for notes, and a map of California. She explains that the rocks have been sent from a secret locale in California and that their job will be to identify and categorize the properties of the rocks to figure out how the rocks were formed and where they came from. In their role as geologists, the students rotate with a partner around the room and closely examine each of the rocks, using their senses and geological tools. Mrs. Reyes has explained that their look at the rocks will be quick this first time and that they will engage in deeper study later in the unit. At each station, they must record one or two findings in the tabletop journal.

Because vivid and precise descriptive vocabulary will be an important part of her language focus for this unit, Mrs. Reyes is eager to gain some insight into the language the students already have and spontaneously use. With her clipboard in hand, she actively circulates among the students during this time. She leans in to listen to two students as they pick up a rock.

Maria: *It is heavy. It is hard to break.*

Amadi: *It came from a volcano.*

Mrs. Reyes: *What makes you say that?*

Amadi: *It is black, so I think it came from a volcano.*

Mrs. Reyes takes note of this response on her clipboard and moves on. One student brings the rock up close to her nose.

Mrs. Reyes: *What does it smell like?*

Tiana:	*Like salty water.*
Juan:	*I think they found this one in the ocean because it looks like it has fish scales.*

After about 10 minutes, the teacher asks the students to call out some describing words in a Whip-Around. The teacher records their responses and then asks the students to choral-read the charted words. Afterward, she guides the students to think about what the words have in common and create basic categories that represent the rocks' physical features.

Notable ELD Practices

Like Ms. Cortez, Mrs. Reyes designs an *Engage* sequence of instruction that encourages students to share what they know, hoping to illuminate their previously acquired concepts and language. She carefully selects materials for students to explore that will interest them and trigger varied responses. She piques student interest by establishing their roles as *geologists*, simulating an authentic investigation. By sending the students to explore in pairs, she sets up a learning environment that is sure to spark an easy exchange of ideas and language. Mrs. Reyes designs the task to allow her to capture both oral examples (on the clipboard) and written examples (on the tabletop journals) of language as she actively circulates among the students. In her role as the teacher, she is doing more than just launching a unit; she has begun her own inquiry into the language needs and strengths of her students. For this purpose, Mrs. Reyes is prepared with questions and strategies that encourage students to analyze, categorize, and elaborate on the phenomena before them. The hands-on, multisensory experience provides a meaningful context for thinking and talking in which students tap into their personal, cognitive, and linguistic resources as well as the resources of their peers.

Mr. Asaad's Class—Grade 7 Scenario
ELD Levels: Early Intermediate, Intermediate, and
Early Advanced

The students sit in partners at each table facing the front of the room. Because Mr. Asaad's middle school students for this period represent a range of English-language proficiency levels (including English-only), he has seated his English language learners next to more proficient English speakers for science instruction. At a signal, the students quiet down to focus on today's introductory lesson on cells.

Mr. Asaad *Before we begin to read the next chapter in our book, I want to know what you know about cells.* Mr. Asaad displays the word *cell* on the board. *You learned about cells in third grade and in fifth grade. What do you remember?* (He accepts several responses from students before continuing.) *In our new unit, we are going deeper to build on what you have learned before. We are going to complete a K-W-L Chart as a tool to help with our inquiry into cells. I am going to demonstrate how to set up your science notebook. First, you are going to divide your notebook into three columns. At the top of the first column, write a* K; *in the middle column, write a* W; *and in the third column, write an* L. (As Mr. Asaad talks, he demonstrates each step under the document camera.) *Write the following question in the* K *column:* What do I know about the cell? *Add bullets. Write your answers in complete sentences in bullet form, not in paragraphs. In the* W *column write:* What do I want to learn about the cell? *Here, you will write some questions. Here is your chance to ask questions. After today's lesson, you will complete the* L *section, recording what you learned about* *the cell. Before writing your individual responses, let's look at these examples of cells on the screen. (Mr. Asaad shares a cluster of diagrams with basic terminology related to cells.) What do these illustrations help you remember about cells? Think. (Mr. Asaad pauses for a minute to provide wait time.) I'm going to give you two minutes to share what you remember with your table partner.*

As the students share, Mr. Asaad circulates among the students with a clipboard. As he listens to the responses of his students, he jots down notes on key points of understanding along with the language they use. Then, he shares some of the responses he heard before asking students to individually complete the *K* column in their notebooks.

After the students write in their notebooks, Mr. Asaad records the students' responses under the document camera. He uses an array of questioning techniques to probe student thinking and support their use of academic language. Figure 4.3 shows a completed K-W-L Chart from the lesson.

Mr. Asaad:	We are going to start with what you know. What do you remember about cells?
Mikayla:	Every living thing has cells.
Mr. Asaad:	Raise your hand if you wrote the same fact.

Seven hands go up.

Angelo:	There are many different types of cells.
Mr. Asaad:	Can you name at least two different types of cells?
Angelo:	Chicken and brain cells.
Mr. Asaad:	Someone else?
Alex:	Animal cells are different from plant cells.
Mr. Asaad:	Did everyone hear what Alex said? Alex, please say that again.
Alex:	Animal cells are different from plant cells.
Mr. Asaad:	How do you know that?
Alex:	I think I learned that in fifth grade.
Mr. Asaad:	What else have you learned about cells?
Tyrone:	Some cells have different shapes.
Mr. Asaad:	Do you have some examples?
Tyrone:	Brain and skin cells.
Mr. Asaad:	You're right. A brain cell that sends a signal about our environment is different from skin cells.

After recording some of the students' responses about what they know about cells, Mr. Asaad directs the students to think about what else they want to learn about cells. He displays some examples of question frames under the document camera to help students express themselves in the form of a question. He asks for a volunteer to use one of the frames to share what they want to learn about cells. Then, he asks students to take two minutes to share what they want to learn with their table partners. Mr. Asaad circulates among the students listening and taking notes on his clipboard. He asks students to fill in the *W* column in their individual notebooks.

After a few minutes, he returns to the document camera to elicit and record their questions.

Mr. Asaad: *Now we will record some of your questions.*

Tyrone: *How do cells form?*

Mr. Asaad: *If you don't have this question, please write it down.*

Samantha: *How would plant cells act in our body? What would we look like?*

Tanya: *Are there any ugly cells?*

Mr. Asaad: *Would ugly seem more like an opinion? What may be ugly to you may be beautiful to someone else. It depends on what your perception of ugly is. What are some other questions?*

Ricardo: *What do cells do?*

Mr. Asaad: *You want to know what the functions of cells are. Good.*

Phillip: *What are cells made of?*

Carina: *What do cells look like?*

Mr. Asaad: *You will be able to answer those last two questions after our lesson today.*

Figure 4.3 K-W-L Chart

K What do I Know about the cell?	W Questions that I want to learn	L What I've learned about the cell
• Every living thing has cells. • There are different types of cells. • Animal cells are different from plant cells. • Some cells have different shapes.	1. How do cells form? 2. How do plant cells act in our body? 3. What are the functions of cells? 4. What are cells made of? 5. What do cells look like?	

Recording students' responses validates what the students have to say and serves as a model of written English.

Notable ELD Practices

Because English language learners make up the majority of his middle school students for this period, Mr. Asaad designs his instruction to accommodate their language needs. He recognizes that he will need to devote some additional instructional time to integrate necessary language scaffolds. However, he understands the importance of doing this for both the language and concept development of English language learners. This initial stage in the 5E process is his first opportunity to evaluate the language needs of his students that will help guide subsequent instruction.

The scaffolds Mr. Asaad utilizes enable his students to articulate and use the language they are comfortable with. It also exposes them to the language of more capable peers and adults. Seating the students in pairs with more proficient English-speaking table partners is one way in which he establishes an instructional environment conducive to academic language practice and use. Having students talk to each other in pairs also enables him to capture some of their language as anecdotal notes on his clipboard. His use of the document camera and the K-W-L graphic organizer serve as examples of the use of visuals to stimulate and represent cognition and language as learning tools. He provides students with multiple opportunities to hear their thinking expressed aloud—serving as language models and triggers for what they remembered. Mr. Asaad is intentional and purposeful about his own language use as he restates student responses and poses questions that probe their thinking.

The practices of the teachers in each scenario exemplify key features of the *Engage* stage for supporting the English language development of English language learners. The integration of language and content at this stage comes from the personal experiences and prior knowledge that English language learners bring to the learning environment. Students are exposed to academic content language through the language models and elaboration provided by the teacher. High levels of comprehensible input are ensured because students are compelled to look, feel, touch, and think science in a supportive, language-rich environment.

Strategies for ELL Instruction During *Engage*

Engage involves the use of strategies that provide students an opportunity to generate prior knowledge that introduces them to the science concept at hand. Some of the strategies presented in the scenarios for *Engage* are described below, including:

- Natural Language

- Inquiry Charts

- Whip-Around

- K-W-L Charts

These strategies are not necessarily exclusive to this stage and can be employed effectively in other stages of the 5E model. However, they strongly support the language goals of *Engage*. Students are provided with opportunities to generate prior knowledge and explore the targeted science concepts through the use of known academic language with exposure to new language. Strategies used during Engage allow students to freely use their natural language to explore science.

Natural Language

Natural Language is the language students know, understand, and use in and out of the classroom. As a strategy, Natural Language allows students an opportunity to use this preferred, personal language development in a first or second language to learn and share their learning. With Natural Language, English language learners are able to talk about their learning by using language that is most comfortable for their level of second-language acquisition. Whether speaking in English or in a primary language other than English, they feel safe trying out their thinking. Natural Language removes the pressure on English language learners to use particular vocabulary and forms of language.

When students engage in an authentic interaction with a peer, they simply talk; they do not worry about form or function. This is the type of interaction we would see on the playground when students feel free to talk with peers. Some students interact using a primary language, while others talk at different levels of English. In an academic context, Natural Language allows students the freedom to focus on the content and not let the language get in the way of their thinking. Providing students with the opportunity to use Natural Language strengthens their engagement and thinking about a topic or concept.

During *Engage*, ELLs are asked to tap into prior knowledge and share what they know and understand about the topic of study. This gives them an opportunity to use Natural Language to demonstrate their thinking. It also allows teachers to informally assess students' knowledge of the science concepts and of language. As students talk about the content, the teacher can take note of what they know and understand. In addition, the teacher can listen for and document the vocabulary, functions, and forms of language the students use to share their thinking. Students who are often silent may be more involved during this phase because they are able to use their primary language. Even if the teacher does not understand the student's primary language, he or she can get a sense of how much a student is able to contribute. As students continue in their English language development, they will eventually start to use English as their language of choice. These informal assessment opportunities help teachers determine the appropriate next steps for developing content knowledge and language.

As students progress through the 5E model, they will be asked to use known and newly developed academic English to learn and share their learning. The use of Natural Language in *Engage* will support the language-development process students will experience as they progress through *Explore, Explain, Extend,* and *Evaluate.*

How Do You Do It?

1. The strategy of Natural Language is grounded in the interactive experience. Begin by presenting students with a clue, an image, text, a presentation, realia, a song, a demonstration, a video, etc.

2. Direct students to engage in a conversation with a peer or small group about what they are seeing or hearing. Allow students to talk freely about the learning at hand.

3. Walk around and listen as students share their thinking and language. Take note of the content and language they are using as they interact with one another.

4. Have students continue to talk with a different partner or with a small group. Providing the opportunity to use language to share their thinking in a natural and relevant interaction should be the focus of the activity.

Inquiry Charts

Originally, Inquiry Charts were developed as tools intended to stimulate students' thinking by exploring multiple sources of information (Hoffman 1992). They provided students with a framework for documenting their thinking and research as they explored a particular topic. In English language development, they can be used as a way for students to share their prior knowledge and generate further inquiries around a single source of information or experience.

Inquiry Charts build students' curiosity and help focus their learning. They are tools for documenting a student's thinking, and they serve to guide their learning. As students explore a science concept or topic, they have an opportunity to think about past learning and generate new questions or ideas about the unknown. For English language learners, Inquiry Charts provide a safe place to jot down their prior knowledge using simple language. They are not judged on their form or function but are allowed to simply write, at their level, what they see, hear, observe, or read. In addition, an Inquiry Chart provides a space for asking questions. Students know there is a great deal to learn, and a successful Inquiry Chart documents what students do not know or have questions about. It is a safe place to ask about what is unknown or unclear at this initial stage of the 5E process.

During the *Engage* stage of the 5E model, students set a focus for their learning as they tap into prior knowledge and get a glimpse of the science concepts. An Inquiry Chart provides a tool for students to document their initial thinking around content. As a language-development strategy, Inquiry Charts activate students' thinking and engagement, thereby maximizing the students' opportunities to use and record the language that is accessible to them related to the topic.

Inquiry Charts can also serve as a form of assessment. They show teachers what students have observed and documented about an object or source of information as well as the written language students use to represent their thinking. In the case of Inquiry Charts, students demonstrate the language functions of description, explanation, and generating questions. Teachers can then build upon the content and language students bring to the learning experience.

How Do You Do It?

1. Provide students with a sheet of paper. Ask them to vertically fold their paper in half and label the left-hand column with one of the following terms: *Observations*, *Noticings*, or *Initial Ideas*. Students should label the right-hand column with one of the following terms: *Questions*, *Wonderings*, or *Ponderings*. (See Figure 4.4 for an example of an Inquiry Chart.)

2. Provide students with a source of information or an object related to the science content at hand. Use pictures, text, a video, or artifacts to stimulate students' thinking. These different sources of information help students get their minds around the topic and begin to question what they know and what they want to learn. The item or source of information to be explored can be placed at individual student tables for more careful exploration at longer time intervals. Or, it can be placed around the room. If the source of information is placed at individual student desks, provide each student with an Inquiry Chart to complete. If the items are placed around the room for students to rotate through and explore, place one Inquiry Chart at each station.

3. Ask students to explore the information and document their thinking on the left side of their Inquiry Chart. Ask probing questions such as *What do you see? What do you notice? Describe what you observe. What do you know about the object?* Provide students ample time to document their initial ideas.

4. Direct students to think about any questions they may have about the source or sources of information. Students are to document their questions, wonderings, or curiosities on the right side of their Inquiry Chart.

Figure 4.4 Inquiry Chart

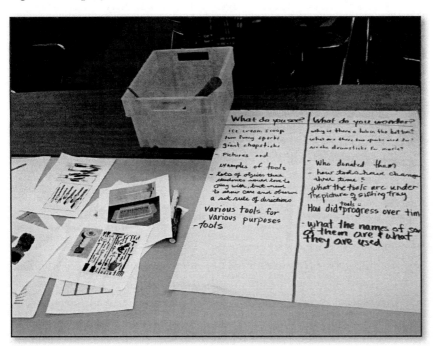

Whip-Around

Whip-Around is a strategy that allows each student to quickly share his or her thinking. After exploring a concept or topic, students have an opportunity to verbally share out one thing that is on their mind. This allows students to hear what their peers know and understand about the content and add to their own thinking.

For English language learners, it is important to establish expectations for a Whip-Around when used as an *Engage* strategy. In this initial stage of the 5E model, ELLs are asked to orally share known information about the content. Students need to feel safe trying out the language of the science content and understand that this is an initial idea that will be built upon through the 5E process. It is important for all students to take some time to think about what they will share out during the Whip-Around. This wait time helps students feel prepared in the content and the language they will have to share orally. In addition, Whip-Around can be used as an informal assessment as the teacher takes note of what the students are sharing about the content and the language they use to participate in the activity.

Though Whip-Around is presented here as a stand-alone strategy, it is commonly used in conjunction with other strategies. As part of *Engage*, students participate in an activity that generates prior knowledge. This can be done through another Engage strategy such as those presented in the scenarios (Natural Language, Inquiry Charts, or K-W-L Charts). At the end of the experience, teachers can then use a Whip-Around as a way for students to share something they knew or learned as a result of the experience or activity.

How Do You Do It?

1. Provide students with an opportunity to generate prior knowledge by presenting an activity, an artifact, an experience, or other source of information.

2. Ask students to think about what they have experienced, observed, or reviewed and have them decide on one thing they want to share about it. Provide at least two minutes for students to think about the content and prepare to orally share their thinking.

3. One at a time, ask students to call out their idea. This is just a share-out; there are no questions asked or elaborations made. Students simply share their thinking aloud.

K-W-L Charts

K-W-L is a strategy that provides students with a graphic organizer that guides them through the learning process. Students document their thinking from initial thoughts and ideas to new learning. The organizer is set up in three columns labeled *K* (What do you know?), *W* (What do you want to know?) and *L* (What did you learn?) The K-W-L Chart was initially developed by Donna Ogle (1986) to support students' reading of expository text.

Like the Inquiry Chart, the K-W-L Chart is a graphic organizer that supports students' learning. For English language learners, a K-W-L Chart provides a safe place to document their thinking. They can bullet their initial ideas about what they already know about the topic at hand and refer back to their initial ideas and questions as they return to the K-W-L Chart throughout the lesson.

In the *Engage* stage of the 5Es, a K-W-L Chart serves as a tool for recording students' prior knowledge and initial questions, curiosities, or wonderings about the topic. As students progress through the 5E process, they will build their knowledge and can revisit the K-W-L Chart to add to the final column. A K-W-L Chart can be revisited throughout the 5E process as students generate more questions and continue to learn. It provides an ongoing record of learning.

How Do You Do It?

1. Provide students with a sheet of paper and ask them to fold it into three columns. Have them label the columns from left to right, as follows: *K* (What do you know?), *W* (What do you want to know?), and *L* (What did you learn?).

2. Present students with a prompt, an artifact, a topic, or other source of information around the content objective.

3. Using the first column, *K* (What do you know?), ask students to document their prior knowledge around the content provided in Step 2. This can be done individually, with a partner, in small groups, or as a class. The key is to document students' prior knowledge about the topic.

4. Ask students to generate questions or wonderings about the topic. They are to record their questions in the middle column, *W* (What do you want to know?).

5. Explain to students that they will revisit their K-W-L Chart to complete the last column to document what they learn as they continue their learning around the topic.

Assessing ELLs in *Engage*

As described in Chapter 3, the expectations for ELL language performance are derived from the English-language proficiency standards for a region. An in-depth analysis of the grade-level science curriculum and standards to identify the vocabulary, functions, and forms that can be acquired through science content is an important additional process for establishing the academic language goals of instruction. To achieve the instructional language objectives, attention must be given to modifying the instruction to the proficiency levels of English language learners during each stage of the 5E model. This process begins with determining the academic language students begin with in order to design instruction that will help them attain the academic language targets for the unit of study.

The *Engage* stage provides ample opportunity for informally assessing ELLs at the beginning of a unit of study. The preassessment of English language proficiency can be captured through careful observation and documented in anecdotal records. Analyzing the language use of English language learners at the onset of instruction will provide insight into what students understand, the level of vocabulary they already know and use, and their ability to communicate their understanding in the appropriate grammatical forms that match their thinking. This initial data will aid teachers in determining the language support ELLs will need in order to maximize the acquisition of academic language through science content.

The classroom scenarios shared in this chapter represent a range of approaches that teachers can use to informally evaluate the language comprehension and use of English language learners. The teachers in these scenarios use various techniques to gather information: observing and listening, circulating among the students to check understanding expressed in language and gestures, and using probing questions or prompts to provoke language use or demonstrate comprehension. The teachers make anecdotal records of the language students are using for future reference. The second-grade students in Ms. Cortez's classroom have created Inquiry Charts that now can serve as student assessment artifacts, documenting the language of their wonderings and observations.

Science Notebooks as ELL Assessment in *Engage*

Science notebooks are powerful tools for evaluating the multidimensional aspects of ELL learning: language use and academic-content understanding. Utilizing science notebooks as formative assessment can help teachers make ongoing decisions about English-language-development instruction—in addition to content instruction—as ELLs move through the 5E process.

In *Engage*, the science notebook can be used as an additional tool to diagnose students' language level at the beginning of instruction so that changes in their language use can be monitored throughout the learning activities. English language learners should be encouraged to communicate what they know about the phenomenon under study, formulate initial questions, or make connections to their real lives in the language they bring, whether in their primary language or in English. In addition to words and drawings, other visual representations should be encouraged in science-notebook entries.

An example of a science notebook entry produced during *Engage* can be found in Figure 4.5. This example comes from one of the English language learners in Mr. Asaad's middle school science class (described earlier in one of the chapter scenarios). The notebook entry of this Intermediate-level student provides Mr. Asaad with concrete written examples that indicate the student's level of academic language and understanding of language structure. Mr. Asaad can use this language data to guide his future instruction in order to support the English language development of his students and to ensure that they have the academic language they need to express their understanding of science content.

Figure 4.5 Sample K-W-L Chart

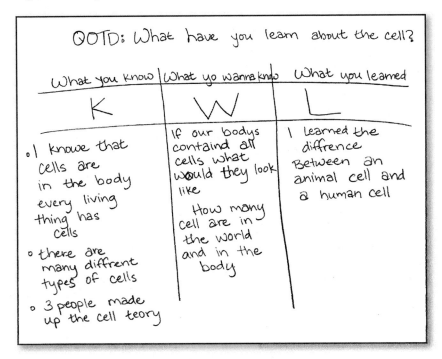

Tips for Planning *Engage* for ELLs

When planning *Engage* for English language learners, consider the following:

- Be sure that you know the English-proficiency level designations of your English language learners and each level's expectations.

- Make sure that students are grouped—either heterogeneously or homogeneously, depending on the situation—in small enough numbers to ensure comfort and the opportunity to be heard and to listen to one another's ideas.

- Carefully study the science curriculum and standards for the grade level.

- Thoughtfully consider how to capture the scientific concepts for the unit through the actual phenomena that surround students in the school environment or the broader community (accessed by field trips).

- Identify the English-language demands and opportunities for your students. Think about the academic language you want your students to practice and acquire by the end of the 5E inquiry cycle. Identify and plan how you will model the targeted language in your interactions with students. Select supplementary materials and strategies that will be appropriate for their level of proficiency.

- Create a learning environment that grabs your students' attention and invites conversation. Gather real photos that depict the concept. Rummage through your science kits, old textbooks, and the Internet. Set up your materials around tables, in corners, or on the rug so that they are accessible to clusters of students.

- Develop a system for gathering information while students are thinking and talking to guide your ongoing instruction. Along with clipboards, notepads, or sticky notes for jotting down observations, make sure that you have the opportunity to circulate among students working in groups to record the language they are using. Prepare a set of target questions, with an emphasis on *why* and *how* questions, that uncover what students understand and can express. Decide upon the types of science-notebook entries and other artifacts that will provide you and the students with a record of progress in language and concept attainment.

Reflect on Wonderings

1. What preparation will you need to ensure that your English language learners have abundant opportunities for exploration and access to the language and knowledge they possess?

2. How can you design tasks that compel your English language learners to interact with one another and use the language they possess?

3. How will you ensure that the students consistently have access to quality language models?

4. What techniques will allow you to frequently monitor the language practice and use of English language learners in your teaching?

CHAPTER 5

Mediating Language Through *Explore*

You May Wonder:

- What do I need to think about when designing scientific exploration tasks for English language learners?

- In what ways can I support the development and understanding of language and science in *Explore*?

- How do I approach the assessment of students' language performance in the *Explore* stage?

This chapter focuses on the essential instructional components that maximize academic language opportunities for English language learners through the 5E model stage of *Explore*. We revisit Ms. Cortez's second-grade classroom to begin.

Ms. Cortez's Class—Grade 2 Scenario
ELD Levels: Early Intermediate and Intermediate
Part A: A First Glimpse at English Language Learner Instruction During Explore

Clear plastic bins half filled with dirt are placed in the middle of two tables. Some children jump up and down as they realize that they are now going to observe real earthworms and not just look at photographs of them. In groups of four, students are instructed to use their senses of sight, hearing, and touch to learn more about earthworms. Ms. Cortez reminds her students that earthworms are living organisms that need to be treated with care. She demonstrates this by delicately placing an earthworm in her hands and leaning down to take a closer look at it. The students pick up a magnifying lens to more closely observe what is moving in and out of the dirt.

As the students' talk fills the room, Ms. Cortez walks from group to group holding a clipboard and listening to conversations focused on these wiggly organisms. She takes note of some of the language that the students are using. She not only records information about their knowledge of the content, but also listens carefully to their language use and linguistic structures.

She approaches a group of seemingly shy, reluctant students peering through magnifying lenses with their noses very close to the dirt.

Ms. Cortez: *What are some things that you observe?*

She bends down and brings her ear closer to one of the boys, who whispers his response without raising his head.

Nathan: *Earthworms are long.*

Lin: *Earthworms shiny. Has curly body.*

Ms. Cortez: *Keep looking closely and see what else you notice about the worms.*

Ms. Cortez records what these students say and then moves to another table. As she approaches a different group, she notices that these students are holding the earthworms in their hands and watching how they slide from one hand to the other. One student giggles as the earthworm wiggles and slithers across his hand. Then, they place the earthworms back into the bin. Within seconds, the earthworms burrow into the soil.

Ms. Cortez: *What are you noticing about the earthworms?*

Jose: *I noticed that the earthworms are long. Why is he so long?*

Ms. Cortez: *Are they all long?*

Jose: *No, they are different.*

Ms. Cortez: *How else are they different?*

Lily: *One is moving and the other isn't.*

Ms. Cortez: *Watch its body and how it moves as the earthworm slithers out of your hands. Is there some way that you notice in which they are the same?*

Jose: *They both are slimy when you feel them. They are both earthworms.*

Lily: *They both like soil. Do they smell?*

Ms. Cortez: *That's a good question. Write it down so you don't forget it.*

Again, she writes down their responses and notices that the members of this group are more confident in speaking English than the previous group.

Then, Ms. Cortez raises both arms into the air and shakes her body to represent a slithering worm as she calls out "Earthworms!" The students respond to this signal by stopping and raising their arms in the air and wiggling their bodies while repeating the word *earthworms*. This is their transition signal as they move on to the next task.

Ms. Cortez asks the students to record any questions they have based on their observations. With partners, students write their questions on sentence strips. Afterward, each pair of students stands in the front of the room and reads their questions. After reading, they place their sentence strips in a pocket chart. Their questions include *Do earthworms have a life cycle? How do earthworms see? How do earthworms eat? Do earthworms poop? What is that little red thing on their body?*

Figure 5.1 Working with Partners

When students help one another to complete a task, it leads to a higher level of language use and accomplishment.

Figure 5.2 Shared Writing

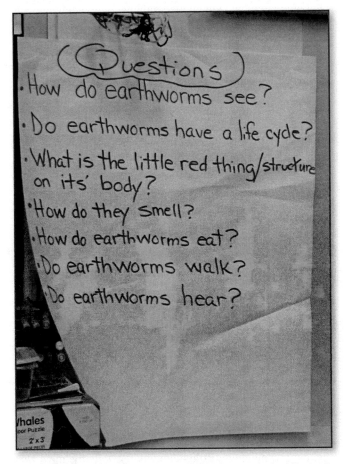

Using shared writing to record students' responses allows the teacher to model how to structure questions.

As a homework assignment, the students are told to ask their parents what they know about earthworms and to write down any additional questions their parents may have in their science notebooks. On the following day, the students shared their parents' responses in a shared writing activity (see Figure 5.2).

What Is *Explore* for English Language Learners?

Exploration continues the inquiry process through hands-on learning. At this stage, students are involved in observation, data collection, making predictions, and hypothesizing about what they understand and are seeking to understand. During *Explore*, teachers give students an opportunity to investigate through experiments, observations, and shared inquiry. The teacher serves as a guide for the inquiry process. Through probing, modeling, feedback, and providing suggestions, students are asked to go deeper in their thinking.

English language learners need to understand the language they are receiving in order for language learning to take place. At this stage, comprehensible input remains high as teachers probe students' thinking and language while the students are engaged in hands-on experiences. Through the level of questions the teacher asks, students are asked to use English at higher levels. For example, when looking at the earthworms, Ms. Cortez asks, "Why are they burrowing into the ground?" This question causes students to think deeper about what they are observing. It takes them beyond the concrete descriptions to interpretation of the phenomenon being observed. In turn, they will use language for a different purpose. The deeper they are asked to think, the higher the level of language they will use naturally in their minds, on paper, or orally to express their thinking. Once again, as students use language to engage in the thinking and doing of science, teachers can informally assess students' language and content knowledge.

Building upon a common base of learning from their discovery and interaction, English language learners can be provided with the opportunity to acquire some specific types of language in *Explore* as they engage in natural conversation. Questioning, naming, describing, predicting, and relating ideas about what is observed can be promoted in carefully designed instruction. Focusing on Ms. Cortez's teaching, we see how she has intentionally promoted and supported language through the careful selection of materials, interactive structures, and procedures. Thus, she purposefully creates compelling tasks that nudge students toward specific concept and language goals.

Mediating Language in *Explore*

A key goal for the *Explore* stage is to maximize the opportunities English language learners have to develop understanding of academic English and use it in meaningful ways. This is accomplished through instruction that appropriately facilitates the use of English as students explore scientific phenomena. A critical factor for the development of a second language is ensuring the dynamic relationship of comprehensible input and output within instructional practices (see Chapter 2). English language learners comprehend new, unfamiliar language through meaningful and engaging input. Simultaneously, English language learners must make repeated and ongoing attempts to practice and use the language they are coming to understand as they express their thinking.

Figure 5.3 Essential Features of Developing Academic Language in *Explore*

- Providing hands-on experiences for thinking and talking
- Utilizing and reinforcing one-to-one correspondence for language development
- Facilitating language use through teacher questioning
- Monitoring the language use of English language learners

In some cases, a teacher may decide to provide students with two opportunities for exploration. Such is the experience Ms. Cortez has set up for her students in this next scenario.

Ms. Cortez's Class—Grade 2 Scenario
ELD Levels: Early Intermediate and Intermediate
Part B: English Language Learner Instruction
During Explore

On the following day, to remind the students of the work from the previous day, the class choral-reads the questions that the groups had generated. Then, Ms. Cortez gives directions for the exploration activity of the day.

Ms. Cortez: *Yesterday, we observed earthworms in the classroom. Just like scientists, you observed and generated questions. Today, we will go outside and observe earthworms in their natural habitat. This time, you will write down your observations in your science notebooks. I want you to use the strategy* Look *and* Draw *as you sketch what you see. Then, label what you know about the earthworm you are observing. On the bottom of the page, write what you observe. Now, turn and tell your partner what you are going to do.*

After clarifying the task, the students pick up tin pans that each contain an earthworm and walk to the grassy area outside their classroom. They place the tin pans on the ground and release the earthworms onto the grass. They open their notebooks. One set of partners hunches over to more closely examine their earthworm as they draw it on their page.

Figure 5.4 Earthworm Observations

Observing animals in their natural environment optimizes the opportunity to observe details.

Holding her clipboard, Ms. Cortez squats down next to a set of boys who are intently observing their earthworm.

Ms. Cortez: *What are you observing?*

Carlos: *He is going under.*

Ms. Cortez: *Ah yes, he is digging under. You're right. He is burrowing. How does he burrow?*

Samuel: *I think he is chewing.*

Ms. Cortez: *Do you think he is chewing the soil? That is how he is burrowing, digging into the earth. Look, he really has his head under the dirt. Is he moving at all? Do you think that he got stuck?*

Samuel: (Facing the ground he shakes his head) *No.*

Ms. Cortez: *Watch his body as he burrows in. He has slowed down. He is kind of lethargic.*

Carlos: *They don't like the sun?*

Ms. Cortez: *It seems that they don't like the sun.*

Carlos: *That's why they go into the dirt. They don't like the sun.*

Ms. Cortez: *That's a good observation.*

At the other side of the yard, some students stand with their legs spread apart and their arms open wide for fear of stepping on their earthworm that has burrowed into the earth. They bend down and carefully move blades of grass with a pencil to see if they can find it again.

After about 30 minutes, the students return to their classroom, buzzing about what happened outside. Since they are so excited about their observations, Ms. Cortez asks them to share what they saw in a Science Buzz interactive structure. The students stand with their notebooks in hand and find a partner to share their observation notes.

One pair of students shares:

Desiree: *Today, the earthworm was digging a hole, and he was wiggling and he was underground.*

Eva: *Today, my earthworm is going into the dirt. I think my earthworm is lost.*

They thank each other and move to find another partner. Ms. Cortez takes note of the structure of the students' language as she moves to another group.

Providing Hands-on Experiences for Thinking and Talking

The ability to manipulate or observe real objects as evidence of scientific concepts enables students to be active participants in learning. The opportunity to use multiple senses including seeing, hearing, smelling, and touching to make meaning ensures student engagement through multiple modalities in the learning experience. This heightened level of physical involvement will enhance the opportunity for the new language input to be comprehensible as the teacher and more proficient peers model it. It will also set the stage for students to express what is going on in their minds as they are encouraged to interact with their peers and their teacher.

In the second-grade scenarios, the context for *Explore* is a hands-on experience with live earthworms. Ms. Cortez provides her English language learners with both indoor and outdoor experiences with live earthworms. The outdoor experience moves students into the physical habitat of earthworms burrowing into the ground. Tools such as lenses and containers facilitate their ability to observe the earthworm's physical properties and behavior. High cognitive engagement stimulated by the senses serves as the catalyst for student talk.

Utilizing and Reinforcing One-to-One Correspondence

An item or concept that is concrete and visible provides immediate access to scientific concepts, especially for English language learners. Attaching a name or description in words and phrases to what is seen and felt provides students with the language input that directly corresponds to their current experience. Repeated language episodes in which teachers and students focus on naming and describing what is observed and manipulated reinforce language practice and use.

Ms. Cortez utilizes and reinforces one-to-one correspondence through her verbal interactions with students, during which she uses intentionally selected language. For example, in one of the earlier exchanges, she labels the movement of an earthworm across her hand as *slithering*. To further support a purposeful attentiveness to language, she employs the strategy of Look and Draw, with the key feature of drawing what one observes and labeling each detail. As students watch and draw earthworms moving down into the dirt, Ms. Cortez artfully matches words such as *burrow, burrowing,* and *soil* to the event as she explains what she is seeing while also encouraging students to match the new label to what they are drawing. In this way, students are receiving clear and specific vocabulary as comprehensible input. Figure 5.5 below shows a Look and Draw from another classroom activity about building materials.

Figure 5.5 Look and Draw

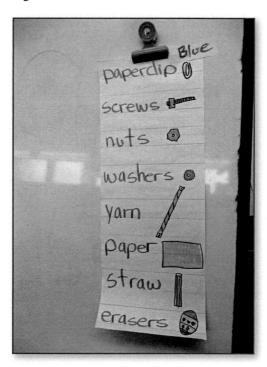

A list of essential words creates a scaffold for language production.

Facilitating Language Use Through Teacher Questioning

In its most literal sense, *mediation* is the use of a tool to accomplish some action. Probing, modeling, giving feedback, and providing suggestions are specific mediating practices, or tools, for language facilitation in *Explore*. As with *Engage*, the teacher is the primary agent for the intentional input of new language. His or her actions serve as the catalyst to activate students' thinking and their talk in social interaction. As with so many practices for ELLs, the goal of questioning is to build on student thinking to stimulate specific comprehensible output in the form of verbal responses, which will lead toward and support scientific-knowledge attainment. The teacher typically asks students questions that are open-ended (e.g., *How do you know that? Why do you think that?*), encouraging expanded stretches of language output appropriate for each proficiency level. For students who are just starting to acquire English, the teacher can utilize types of questions that provide more support, such as either/or questions (e.g., *Is this a _____ or a _____?*) through which students are given the chance to hear the correct label contrasted with a nonexample.

To highlight an example of this type of language facilitation, let us first revisit the mediated discussion led by Ms. Cortez in the second-grade scenario:

Ms. Cortez: *What are you noticing about the earthworms?*

Jose: *I noticed that the earthworms are long. How come he is so long?*

Ms. Cortez: *Are they all long?*

Jose: *No, they are different.*

Ms. Cortez: *How else are they different?*

Lily:	*One is moving and the other isn't.*
Ms. Cortez:	*Watch its body and how it moves as the earthworm slithers out of your hands. Is there a way that you notice in which they are the same?*
Jose:	*They both are slimy when you feel them. They are both earthworms.*
Lily:	*They both like soil. Do they smell?*
Ms. Cortez:	*That's a good question. Write it down so you don't forget it.*

Much is accomplished in this academic language mediation. In this exchange, Ms. Cortez poses a question to the students that not only probes their thinking but also models the use of academic terminology such as *noticing*. The outcome is extended language in a complete statement. The student uses the terminology, not parroting the teacher verbatim but in a manner that is appropriate to the context. The teacher's questioning has provoked thinking and tested the student's acquisition of the academic language. In order to guide the students to draw their own conclusions about the varied characteristics of earthworms, she frames her next question to provoke the students to compare and contrast when she asks whether all the earthworms are long. Students are practicing the language structures of comparison as comprehensible output in a social exchange while also receiving the comprehensible input of specific descriptive vocabulary such as *slithers*. Finally, Ms. Cortez guides students to record their questions as a label for the Look and Draw task.

Monitoring the Language Use of English Language Learners

Effective instruction is reliant upon the teacher's ability to rapidly respond to the needs of the students while the lesson progresses. Often referred to as *making frequent checks for comprehension*, the ELL teacher must assume the additional role of being keenly aware of students' attempts to use English, to evaluate language strengths and needs against the goals of the lesson, and to adapt instruction (e.g., ask a question, restate a point, or make a probing statement). This type of ongoing monitoring embedded within instruction must be utilized at various unanticipated points during a lesson, dependent upon the students' responses and needs. If students are struggling to use proper vocabulary to talk about science concepts, the teacher can provide quick examples of the desired language during interaction with individual students. Or, the teacher can plan explicit vocabulary instruction in the subsequent *Explain* phase. If the teacher observes that the students have a strong grasp of basic vocabulary related to the science concepts, both current and future instruction can be adapted to focus on synonyms at a higher level of academic vocabulary.

Returning to the scenarios once again, there is evidence of language-monitoring techniques employed by Ms. Cortez. She carries a clipboard to record student language data including language use and linguistic structures. She gathers this data throughout the lesson while circulating among the students, listening to conversations and actively mediating their language and thinking. She is aware of both language-proficiency differences and learning characteristics among her students and responds accordingly by approaching a group of shy or seemingly reluctant speakers early in her rounds to monitor their engagement and language use in the task. Because of the proficiency levels of her students, Ms. Cortez wants to ensure that they have enough time to discover and talk and also that she has enough time to circulate, probe, and evaluate their thinking and language. Therefore, she extends the *Explore* time by giving them two types of hands-on experiences.

Examining ELD Practices in *Explore*

In the previous section, we highlighted several ELD practices that are essential to the *Explore* stage, referencing our featured classroom scenario (Ms. Cortez and her second graders learning about earthworms). In this section, we continue the analysis of notable practices for ELLs during *Explore* by focusing on additional scenarios that depict a kindergarten exploration of animal coverings as well as the implementation of exploration stations in a third-grade classroom.

Mrs. Kakuda's Class—Kindergarten Scenario
ELD Level: Beginning

In this study of animal coverings, Mrs. Kakuda sets up a Four Corners activity. She labels the four corners of her classroom as follows: 1) *skin*, 2) *fur*, 3) *feathers*, and 4) *scales*. She places a photograph and/or a real artifact in each corner to help the students identify the word. In addition, she has recruited four parent volunteers to help guide student talk and facilitate at each corner. As the students are sitting on the rug, she explains the task.

Mrs. Kakuda: *I am going to give each one of you a photograph. The photograph will show an animal. I want you to notice the animal's coverings. Does it have fur?* (She holds up a fur pelt.) *Point to the fur.*

Students point to the fur.

Mrs. Kakuda: *Does it have skin?* (She points to her skin.) *Point to your skin.*

Students point to their skin.

Mrs. Kakuda: *Does it have feathers?* (She holds up some feathers.) *Point to the feathers. Does it have scales?* (She holds up simulated scales.) *Point to the scales.*

Students point to the feathers and scales.

Since these students are limited in their use of the English language, the teacher feels that it is important to provide these initial labels prior to the exploratory activity. This will establish a language file in the brain that will help the students classify the photographs.

Mrs. Kakuda passes out the photographs and asks the students to begin to think about the kind of covering their animal has. As she distributes the photographs, she names the covering and asks the students an either/or question (e.g., *Are these feathers or scales?*). She encourages each student to respond and accepts all responses, including gestures.

Then, Mrs. Kakuda moves around the room, pointing out the labels and corresponding visual and/or real artifact at each of the four corners. She instructs the students to go to the corner that corresponds to the covering in their photograph. Students walk around the room, and some are redirected until they reach their correct corner. The adults support students in naming their animal's covering, asking either/or questions and pointing to where they can make their match. Mrs. Kakuda makes a quick note on an index card of students' understanding as well as whether they are able to match the word to the real object.

The children are now divided into four groups, making it more manageable for the young students to explore the new materials. At each corner, they are given other photographs and are asked to sort the cards in a way that makes sense to them. In one group, the students sort the cards by placing the animals that have four feet in one pile and the remaining cards in another pile. Other students match the cards in pairs, such as dog and cat, parrot and dove, or baby and boy. Yet another group classifies the cards by animals that walk, animals that swim, and animals that fly. As they organize these miscellaneous groups of photos, it is evident that the students classify the photographs by their own schema. The concept of an animal covering is still foreign to them. Yet, speaking in their primary language and in English enhances the experience. Adults model targeted language as they facilitate the task and interact with the students.

Notable ELD Practices

The Four Corners task, embedded within the hands-on experience using realia and photos, provokes students' thinking toward classifying objects into groups according to physical features. The thinking inherent in the task serves as a catalyst for language expression as students interact with photos, artifacts, and one another. Through repetition and naming each object and photo, Mrs. Kakuda maximizes the positive effect of one-to-one correspondence for her students' academic language development. The adult volunteers support the language focus through modeling the academic language targets of the lesson: *scales*, *fur*, *skin*, and *feathers*. Either/or questioning enables these beginning-level students to hear a correct response contrasted with a nonexample. Recognizing that her beginning-level kindergartners will benefit from interaction with capable speakers of the new language (English) and an elevated degree of facilitation, Mrs. Kakuda recruited parent volunteers to help her with this stage of the 5E process.

Figure 5.6 Four Corners

Realia and real-life experiences motivate students and enhance language learning in the "scales" corner of Mrs. Kakuda's classroom.

Mrs. Hillman's Class—Grade 3 Scenario
ELD Level: Intermediate

The students in this third-grade classroom have been learning about planets and space. To create an effective *Explore* activity that will build the level of comprehensible language input and expand on the science content, Mrs. Hillman designed Exploratory Stations. Some of the stations she has planned are simulations, while others have been developed to give her students an opportunity to deepen their understanding of some of the concepts. Each station has a literacy element embedded within the task to provide a written record of language use and conceptual understanding. The students in this Spanish-bilingual third-grade classroom know the rituals and routines when exploring science stations. After recess, the 34 students enter the classroom and select a station to explore.

Stations are developed based on students' questions during a unit of study. One of the station options is a taste test of freeze-dried foods such as the packaged meals that astronauts eat on their flights. One student's initial question for the unit had been *What do astronauts eat in space?* In this station (see Figure 5.7), students have the opportunity to taste freeze-dried strawberries, Neapolitan ice cream, and ice cream sandwiches. The station task is to describe the taste and the texture and to vote on whether an astronaut will like it.

Figure 5.7 Astronaut Foods Station

At the second station, students find pairs of snow gloves and mittens and tiny objects such as pencils, paper clips, buttons, coins, and pieces of string (see Figure 5.8). The students had learned that working in astronaut suits is cumbersome. This simulation is set up in order for students to experience some of the difficulty astronauts face by wearing gloves while they are using tools to explore a new planet. Part of the station task is completing a graph that indicates whether items are easy or difficult to pick up.

Figure 5.8 Space Suit Station

The third station includes play dough and photographs of the surface of the moon (see Figure 5.9). Students observe the photographs carefully and then replicate the surface of the moon, using different-color play dough and labeling some of the characteristics that they notice on the surface of the moon. The use of play dough optimizes learning for kinesthetic learners.

Figure 5.9 Surface of the Moon Station

Multiple nonfiction books on outer space fill the table at the fourth station. Students read and look at the space photographs to gain more information. Students make personal connections and practice skills such as skimming, scanning, and asking questions while reading nonfiction books. They add something interesting they have learned to a large chart before leaving the station.

Figure 5.10 Nonfiction Literature Station

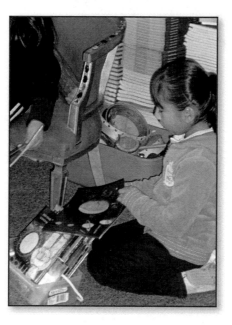

The fifth station is a space-flight simulation computer program that was downloaded for free from the Internet. Students tour the solar system with futuristic spacecraft. Students are asked to jot down a specific skill needed to fly in outer space on a "graffiti wall" in the station.

At the final station, students slip on "moon shoes" (large plastic shoes on coils) to explore how it might feel to walk on the moon (see Figure 5.11). At this station, there is a list of descriptive words (e.g., *heavy, clumsy, awkward, hard, easy*). Students are expected to check off the words that describe how it feels to walk in the shoes. There is additional space for them to enter a word that is not on the list.

Figure 5.11 Moon Shoes Station

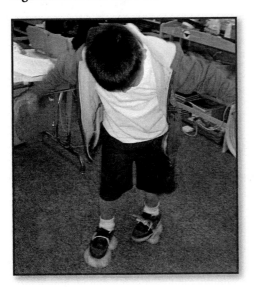

Mrs. Hillman is focused on several activities as she circulates among the students. She has made one round, moving from station to station to clarify instructions and get students started on their tasks. She queries the students with *Do you understand what the task is? Do you have any questions that I can answer? Tell me what you are doing at this station.* Carrying a clipboard with sticky notes, she shifts her focus to listen to student conversations and note the language they are using. She has found that writing initials and quickly noting snippets of language on sticky notes help her to record language use with the large number of students in her class. Later, she will sort the sticky notes onto a class chart she has created and use this information along with the written station logs in her planning for future instruction.

Today, Mrs. Hillman is focusing on evaluating students' independent use of the language developed in previous lessons: *astronaut, surface features, gravity, weightlessness,* and the names of various planets. As students get more involved in the station tasks, she focuses on posing *how* and *why* questions, such as *How does this help you understand weightlessness or gravity in outer space?* and *Why is this important to know if you are an astronaut?* The purpose of these questions is to provoke student thinking and talking related to the unit topic. In her interaction with some students, she probes further, saying, *I heard you say _____. Can you think of another way to say _____?*

Notable ELD Practices

An exploratory station is an effective way to get students to talk, relating inquiry to interaction with scientific phenomena. These sustained periods of *talk, thought,* and *interaction* in hands-on experiences can provide authentic assessment opportunities for the teacher to take anecdotal records, noting students' understanding of the content and the linguistic structures they use to express their understanding. Mrs. Hillman has designed hands-on stations that collectively tap into all learning modalities and include a language and literacy element to probe and stimulate their language practice. The number of stations (six) was given careful consideration because of the size of her class. She wanted to ensure that her students had the opportunity to directly interact with the materials. To facilitate a successful experience with stations, Mrs. Hillman follows a three-step routine as she circulates around the room. In Round 1, she clarifies instructions and solves problems. In Round 2, she observes and listens for language while noting on-task behavior. In Round 3, she interacts with students to mediate their thinking and language with questions or prompts.

Strategies for ELL Instruction During *Explore*

Explore involves strategies that provide hands-on, minds-on experiences for students. Such strategies allow students to *see* the science concept and engage in inquiry-based discussions with peers. Strategies that teachers can use during *Explore* include the following:

- Look and Draw
- Science Buzz
- Four Corners
- Concept Sort
- Exploratory Stations

Look and Draw

Look and Draw guides students through the practice of observation. Students are guided to look closely at an artifact, an object, or a live subject and draw what they see. It begins with a distant view of the object. Then, as the teacher prompts students to look closer, students learn to see the fine details of the object. Through this experience, students learn more about the content because they take time to look at the finest details of the object or artifact to better understand it.

As teachers draw students closer to the object, they begin to ask questions. These questions cause students to want to learn more about the object and lead to an interest in the language of science. The closer they look, the more questions they have. For example, when looking closely at and drawing worms students may ask *What are those things called? They look like little, straight lines all over its body.* This observation can lead to learning new content vocabulary such as *segments*. Allowing students the opportunity to view the content more closely enhances content comprehension. With a solid understanding of the concept students will be able to connect academic vocabulary terms to the concept. Look and Draw provides an authentic opportunity for students to experience the words and concepts. Attaching a label to a known concept is easier than learning a new word and its meaning at once.

Using the Look and Draw strategy in the *Explore* stage of the 5E process supports students in taking a closer look at the topic or concept at hand. They are probed to use their prior knowledge at a deeper and more focused level of observation. This builds content knowledge and supports academic language development.

How Do You Do It?

1. Present an artifact or live object, large enough for all students to see. Ask students to observe the object carefully. A very large artifact can be placed in the front of the room, but all students should be positioned to be able to carefully examine the object. Multiple objects representing the concept or topic can also be used and placed at small group tables for closer observation. All students must be able to see the object closely. When available, each student can be provided an object to observe closely.

2. Provide students with a blank sheet of paper and pencil and ask them to begin by drawing what they observe.

3. Ask students to take a closer look at the object and add to their drawing. Teachers can probe students to look more closely by modeling their own observations and asking students to share their observations.

4. Continue to probe students to observe more closely and note finer details on their drawings. Walk around the room and monitor students' drawings to determine how much more questioning and observations are needed for students to create detailed drawings.

Science Buzz (Science Conference)

When scientists engage in the practice of observation and experimentation, they share their preliminary findings and questions with one another. Science Buzz is a strategy that gives students a chance to share their thinking with their peers just like real scientists. During or after an observation or experiment, students are encouraged to talk with one another about their experience.

For English language learners, a Science Buzz is a great way to hear the language of science being used by their peers. They not only hear models, they also serve as models for one another in both language and content knowledge.

The key to a successful Science Buzz is presenting students with rich content to talk about. In the *Explore* stage of the 5Es, this strategy takes students deeper in their thinking as they learn from one another and explore more content. Their prior knowledge is enhanced as they hear new ideas and questions from their peers.

How Do You Do It?

1. Provide students with content. This can come in the form of an object, an artifact, an image, text, a video, and more.

2. Based on an observation of the content provided in Step 1, students must prepare notes, questions, or observations to share with their peers.

3. After students have documented their thinking, ask them to stand behind their seats with their notes in hand. They will be asked to walk around the room, finding a partner with whom to share their ideas. What did they see? What did they experience? What did they do? What questions do they have? Students casually walk around, sharing their thoughts with one another. There is no order to the Science Buzz; they continue to walk around finding a new partner to talk to. Ensure that all students have a partner and encourage students to move on to another partner when they are spending too much time with one peer. Informally listen to students' language and content knowledge as the Science Buzz is going on.

4. After students have had time to share with multiple partners, ask them to return to their seats to bring closure to the Science Buzz. Once all students have settled back into their seats or a common meeting space, review the science content that the students have demonstrated understanding of so far, as well as the language that they were using. This can be done as a shared writing experience, where students share out what they heard during the Science Buzz while the teacher records their thinking on a large sheet of chart paper. Seeing the learning in writing also captures the academic language of the strategy. This chart then serves as a resource for both science content knowledge and language.

Four Corners

Four Corners is a strategy that allows students to think about a concept from four different perspectives or points of view. The students get an opportunity to physically move to the four corners of the room and eventually settle at the corner that best represents their perspective. In some cases, the corners will represent a correct answer to an individual question or item the student was given. Four Corners can be adapted for all grade levels and content areas.

Four Corners challenges students to think deeply about the content that is presented. When they look at what is presented in each corner they will need to show a level of depth in their content knowledge to select the appropriate corner to settle at. This is a great strategy at the *Explore* stage because it causes students to think about the content they were introduced to in *Engage* from different perspectives. In addition, it builds on students' prior knowledge as they think about the content as it is presented in each of the four corners.

To support English language learners, it is also helpful to allow students to discuss what they are thinking and seeing at each corner with their peers. In addition, as students talk with one another and eventually make a final decision, the teacher can use their actions as an informal assessment. Depending on which corner the students select, the teacher can get a sense of their content understanding.

How Do You Do It?

1. Clear walkways in the classroom to the four corners of the room. In each corner, place a question, topic, label, artifact, picture, or concept.

2. Provide each student with a source of information. This can be a picture, a word, a statement, or another form of input.

3. Ask students to walk around and visit each corner of the room. As they walk around, they are to decide which corner best fits or represents the picture, word, or statement they have been individually provided. As students walk around the room, encourage them to share their thinking with their peers. Also, take note of the students' use of language and demonstration of content knowledge.

4. Once all students have settled on a corner ask them to stay standing at their corner. Have students share with a classmate at their corner why they selected that corner for about two minutes. This provides you with another opportunity to observe students' language use and content knowledge.

5. Invite all students to return to their seats and ask several students from each corner to share why they picked that corner.

Open Sort

Sorting is a practice that helps students learn to classify information in logical ways. Open Sorts are as the name implies, an opportunity to sort the content as the student sees fit. There are no pre-set categories or labels as would be the case for a closed sort. In an Open Sort students demonstrate how they make sense of information.

There are no right or wrong answers in an Open Sort. The items or information the students are provided can lead students to sort the items in a particular way; however, regardless of what the teacher may have had in mind, the students may demonstrate different categories. In the end the teacher will get a good sense of where students are in their thinking around the content and how they are thinking about it at the *Explore* stage of the 5E process.

How Do You Do It?

1. Provide students with a variety of content to sort. This can be in the form of words, picture cards, or objects. The number of items to sort will vary based on the topic or content to be sorted. The key is to have enough information to sort into different categories.

2. Ask students to look carefully at all of the objects, pictures, or words to sort. They can work individually, with a partner, or with a small group to separate the items into groups. For English language learners, it is helpful to allow them to work with a peer or small group to enhance the language learning experience. The groupings they create should show a connection between the items.

3. Students must label/categorize the grouped items to represent why the items have been put together.

4. Ask students to share the Open Sort with a classmate, partner, or group. This helps students see how their peers are thinking about the content and organizing it.

Exploratory Stations

Exploratory Stations bring the experiences of the real world into the classroom. The purpose of Exploratory Stations is to provide students with authentic learning experiences in which they get to use language for real-life purposes.

Figure 5.12 An Exploratory Station

When students have fun exploring, it lowers the affective filter, opening opportunities for talk.

To prepare for Exploratory Stations, decide on a general unit theme. For example, if the unit theme is *Habitats*, re-create those habitats in the classroom. If the unit theme is *My Community*, create stations that give students the chance to experience different parts of the community. As students travel around the stations they will engage in an authentic exchange of language around a given topic. This builds communicative competence as students practice using language for a variety of purposes.

How Do You Do It?

1. Based on the unit of study, re-create real-world experiences in the classroom that students can engage in. Set up the various stations for students in a manner that allows them to move easily from one station to another when asked. Based on class size, create enough stations for approximately four students to participate in each station at one time. The goal is to provide students with an authentic opportunity to use language. And though it takes a significant amount of time and preparation, the experience provides many rich opportunities to use and develop English. If desired, provide students with a language script to follow so they learn the proper way to "talk" in the simulated context when appropriate.

2. Demonstrate each station to the class, one at a time. Elicit questions from the students to ensure clarity of what is expected at each station.

3. Divide the students into small groups (maximum of four). Assign each group to a station and ask them to take their place at the station.

4. Invite students to begin their exploration at the station. Take note of the language the students are using as they interact with the content and with each other at the station. This is a great opportunity for informal assessment of language and content. When the class comes back together as a whole group, share out the language that was used.

5. The time spent at each station can vary depending on the station's content. About five to seven minutes at each station is standard. Determine how much time students should spend at each station. After that time has elapsed, have groups take one minute to straighten

up the station for the next group. Ask each group to walk carefully clockwise around the room to the next station.

6. Once all groups have reached the next station, they can begin exploring. Continue to rotate students to the various stations in an orderly fashion by repeating Steps 4 and 5.

7. After all groups have explored all stations, invite students to return to their seats. Then, ask students to share out one thing they learned. This provides a great opportunity to share the academic language documented during the station rotations.

Assessing ELLs in *Explore*

When developing English through the 5E model, each stage has particular implications for assessing language performance. In the *Explore* stage, formative assessment is used to help teachers understand the progress students are making in comprehending concepts as well as practicing and using new language. Finding out what students are struggling to express orally and in writing helps guide the design of future instructional interventions in the remaining phases. In addition to science notebooks, the main assessment techniques delineated in our scenarios are ongoing monitoring throughout the lesson, use of anecdotal records, and questioning to check for understanding.

In each scenario, examples were given of teachers actively and frequently circulating among the students as they explored the content. Adopting rituals or procedures for monitoring can ensure the success of a task as well as the gathering of meaningful data. To facilitate a successful experience with stations, Mrs. Hillman follows a three-step routine as she circulates around the room. In Round 1, she clarifies instructions and solves problems. In Round 2, she observes and listens for language while noting on-task behavior. In Round 3, she interacts with students to mediate their thinking and language with questions or prompts. This routine serves multiple purposes. In addition to ensuring that students are on task by refocusing their attention, the teacher can shift her purpose to capturing performance data in varied ways. First, she listens in on the thinking and language that is independently generated at a surface level. Then, she provokes responses to get at students' deeper thinking and ways of communicating, using open-ended questioning or prompts such as *How do you know that?* or *Tell me more about...*

There are multiple formats that teachers can use to record anecdotal notes of student's language use. In several scenarios, you have read about teachers carrying clipboards and recording notes on sticky notes or on a sheet of paper. Mrs. Hillman demonstrates what is done with this type of record. Because of the size of her class, she realizes that she will not be able to observe each student at every lesson. So, she has devised a system in which she posts her sticky notes onto a chart in a corner of the room. The chart is large enough to create a box with each student's name. At the close of instruction on a given day, or when she has information posted for all her students, she can use the information to guide her planning for the next sequence of instruction. She can also capture at a glance students whom she has not assessed on an ongoing basis. An additional benefit is that this archive of anecdotal notes will serve as a handy reference of student performance for conversations with parents.

Ms. Cortez provides strong examples of questioning to check for understanding. The questioning that she engages in with her students serves the dual purposes of provoking student thinking and action and providing her with insight into student language performance. The questions represent a range of levels such as surface-level questions (e.g., *What are some things that you observe?*) and deeper-level, analytical questions (e.g., *How else are they different?* or *Do you think that he got stuck?*).

Science Notebooks as ELL Assessment in *Explore*

As has been stated before, the science notebook has many uses for capturing the developing understanding of students learning scientific content (see Chapter 3). English language learners in our scenarios use the notebooks to make scientific records of their learning in varied ways. The notebooks are used as a tool for students to share their findings and thinking—using oral and written language—with their peers and their teacher.

It is important to note that all of the notebook work presented in this chapter was preceded by lengthy periods of talking and thinking. Often the notebooks are scaffolded for second language learners at each round of academic talk about science. The Look and Draw strategy employed by students in Ms. Cortez's classroom emerged from hands-on exploration, which in turn emerged out of the questions students entered as they were observing and touching live earthworms. Moving from the concrete and the visual supported by ample language interaction, these entries served as the platform for additional language practice and use related to what students were discovering and asking themselves.

Figure 5.13 is an example of a science notebook entry from a fourth-grade, Intermediate-level ELL that captures a rich range of language data. As she moved through Exploration Stations related to a unit on rocks, she recorded information for each station. The graphic organization of the entries provided the student with a repetitive and predictable structure.

Figure 5.13 Sample Exploration Station Notebook Entry

Name of Center	What I did	Questions	Observations
Books + photos	I read and looked at rock pictures	Where on earth are IGNEOUS Rocks? What are some kinds of IGNEOUS Rocks?	almost all of the rocks had crystals in the pictures that I looked at
Rock mass	I weighed some rocks and then was...		The rock that I weighed weighed 300 grams
Sand Lab	I dropped drops of water in some sand	Why does the sand have holes when we drop water at it?	When we drop water on something it makes holes. When we wet the sand the sand gets wet and sometimes makes holes.
Observing Rocks	I observed different kinds of rocks	Why do some rocks have holes?	In every rock I observed I saw crystals in them.
Types of Soil	I observed soil.		They all had crystals.
Computers	I saw Images of rocks and minerals in google		The rocks were different Aon other rocks.

Her writing provides a record of various forms of language (action statements, questions, and descriptions) that reflect facets of her language proficiency associated with her thinking (reporting, describing, analyzing, questioning) about rocks. Through this type of evidence, the teacher can gain valuable insight into the strengths and needs of her students for the conceptual and linguistic focus of the remainder of the unit.

Tips for Planning *Explore* for ELLs

When planning *Explore* for English language learners, consider the following:

- Be sure that you know the English proficiency level designations of your English language learners and each level's expectations.

- Make sure that your students are grouped, either heterogeneously or homogeneously depending on the situation, in small enough numbers to ensure comfort and the opportunity to be heard and to listen to others' ideas and talk.

- Consider how you can capture the scientific concepts for your unit through multisensory, multiliteracy, and multimedia experiences: concrete objects, outdoor exploration, nonfiction trade books, videos, photos, and technology. Taking the time to gather these resources will come in handy when planning exploration station tasks.

- Identify the English language demands and opportunities for the students you have in your classroom. Think about the academic language you want your students to practice and acquire by the end of the 5E inquiry cycle. Identify and plan how you will model the targeted academic language in your interactions with students. Prepare varied types of questions that support and provoke students at different proficiency levels to talk.

  - Either/or questions provide language support for limited English proficiency students. Example: *Are these feathers or fur?*

  - Focused questions challenge students to dig into their language pools. Example: *I heard you say _____. Can you think of another way to say _____?*

- Probing questions nudge students to think and talk. Example: *What are you observing? How else are they different? Is there something that you notice in which they are the same?*

- Open-ended questions encourage students to use language in extended discourse. Example: *How does this help you understand _____? Why is this important to know?*

- Design exploratory tasks that grab your students' interest and invite conversation. Thoughtfully designed tasks ensure that students have ample time to interact with each other and the instructional materials. The tasks must also allow the teacher to circulate and interact with the students.

- Think through how you will manage instruction to maximize opportunities for students to practice and use the language. Make sure that the environment is set up in such a manner that students have room to explore and that all materials are available and accessible. Provide students with clear directions and expectations. As you circulate among the students, plan how you will establish purpose, clarify the task, and motivate students.

- Develop a system for gathering valuable information while students are thinking and talking, to help you plan for ongoing instruction. Beyond clipboards, notepads, or stickies for jotting down notes, make sure that you have the opportunity to circulate amongst students working in groups to record the language they are using. Prepare a set of target questions, with emphasis on *why* and *how* questions, which probe into what students understand and can express.

- Decide upon the types of science notebook entries and other artifacts that will provide you and the students with a record of progress in language and concept attainment.

Reflect on Wonderings

1. How can you design hands-on experiences for exploration that promote thinking and encourage English language learners to practice and use English?

2. What can you do to maximize English development as you guide students to match language to what they see, touch, and smell (one-to-one correspondence)?

3. How can you prepare the type of questioning that will provoke student thinking and language use?

4. What techniques will allow you to consistently and frequently monitor the language use of ELLs in your teaching?

CHAPTER 6

Explicit Language Instruction Through *Explain*

You May Wonder:

- What do I need to think about when designing explicit academic language development instruction for English language learners in *Explain*?

- In what ways can I support the understanding of language and science in *Explain*?

- How do I approach the assessment of students' language performance in the *Explain* stage?

This chapter focuses on the 5E stage of *Explain* and outlines the various essential components. These components are intended to maximize the English-language-development opportunities for English language learners.

Ms. Cortez—Grade 2 Scenario
ELD Levels: Early Intermediate and Intermediate
A First Glimpse at English Language Learner Instruction During Explain

After observing earthworms, Ms. Cortez clarified some of the language she heard outside.

Ms. Cortez: *What did you notice when you placed your earthworm on the grass?*

Michael:	*He was digging under.*
Ms. Cortez:	*Yes, it was digging into the soil. Scientists use the word* burrow. *Say* burrow *with me.*
Students:	*Burrow.*
Ms. Cortez:	*Earthworms burrow into the soil. Burrow means to dig or to make a hole. I am going to write the word* burrow *on this chart. I would like Isabel to come up and draw a picture of an earthworm burrowing into the soil next to the word. Meanwhile, I want you to think: What does* burrow *mean?*

Ms. Cortez pauses.

Ms. Cortez:	*Now turn to a partner and explain what the word burrow means.*

Ms. Cortez circulates among the students as they speak to one another, actively listening to the thinking and language use of as many students as she can. As students complete their sharing, Ms. Cortez calls out examples of what she heard.

Ms. Cortez:	*It is clear that you noticed the earthworm burrowing. Some of you commented that it appeared that the earthworm didn't like the sunlight. Something else I noticed was that some of you observed another way the earthworm moved. You talked about how the earthworm's body seemed longer and at other times looked shorter.*
Natalie:	*The earthworm moved like this.* (She stretches her arms out and then she brings them close to her body.)

Ms. Cortez: *You are correct. Take a look at this Slinky. Notice what happens when I stretch out this Slinky. It* extends. *When I let go of it, it* contracts *to become shorter. Similarly, this is how an earthworm moves. It extends, or stretches its body, and contracts and becomes shorter. Practice this with me.*

Ms. Cortez models by stretching out her arms in front of her and then bringing them close to her body and moving her feet. The students join in. She writes the words *extend* and *contract* on the chart and has another student draw a visual for those words.

With notebooks in hand, the students form groups of three and find a space to sit around the room. They share the drawings that they drew outside and describe what they saw. It was Ms. Cortez's intent that they use some of the vocabulary she inputted because she understands that language practice and use are essential elements of *Explain*. Ms. Cortez circulates among the student triads, commenting positively when students use the new vocabulary. She employs a particular technique of giving them a brightly colored strip of paper with an illustration of a worm saying, "Congratulations! You're really speaking like a scientist now." At other times, when students are challenged to use the new words, she informally restates what she heard to model how the new vocabulary can be used.

During the observation of earthworms in their natural habitat, various initial questions were answered, yet this group of budding scientists was still perplexed as to how the worm moved. Their query still remained: *How do earthworms walk?*

Ms. Cortez shifts her lesson and decides to focus on identifying some of the earthworm's structures and explaining their functions. This will lead to answering some of their questions and will provide additional opportunities for explicit language development. She continues the lesson with a Pictorial Input chart, which she begins by drawing a simple line drawing of an earthworm. As she draws the earthworm from top to bottom, she discusses and labels each part (see Figure 6.1).

Ms. Cortez: *Watch and listen as I draw an earthworm. I want you to focus on the different parts of the earthworm. Notice how it is pointed a little at the top. Near the top is its mouth. Each part is not straight; it is uneven. The body has these dividing lines. Each part is called a* segment. *All of these parts are called segments. Repeat the word with me. Say* segments. *(The students repeat the word. Ms. Cortez continues to draw.) This middle part of the earthworm is wider and longer; it is called a* saddle.

Kimi: *What's a saddle? Do you mean like a horse?*

Ms. Cortez: *Yes, you are right. Some horses do have a saddle. A saddle is placed on a horse for a rider. This is different. This saddle is part of an earthworm's body. We are going to have to look at one of our science resources later to find out the function of an earthworm's saddle. Now look at this final part. As we get to the other end of the earthworm, notice that it is called the* back.

Figure 6.1 Pictorial Input Chart

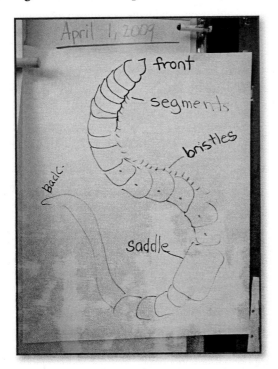

After she finishes the Pictorial Input Chart, she asks students to draw an earthworm and label its parts in their science notebooks. Upon finishing, the students turn to a partner and identify the parts of the earthworm, using specific sentence forms that Ms. Cortez has written on a chart. She reviews the language forms as possibilities for students to talk like scientists: *An _____'s body is divided into segments. An _____ has several parts. It has a _____, a _____ and a _____.*

Ms. Cortez understands that as a science teacher, she does not have to know the answers to all of the students' questions. Often, there is no correct answer; in fact, there can be several responses to one question. At other times, the answer is left to speculation. She feels that it is essential for an effective science teacher to have a bank of resources. Consequently, Ms. Cortez engages in a Shared Reading using the book *Earthworms* by Claire Llewellyn to further research the students' queries.

She places the book under the document camera, which enables all of the students to see the text. She begins by asking the students to choral-read the title and the author's name. Then she turns to the Table of Contents and scans the titles of the chapters.

Ms. Cortez: *We are going to read this book. Let's see if it has the answer to the question of how earthworms walk. Let's read some of the titles of these chapters to see where we might find the answer to this question. Let me read some of the titles.* (She places her finger along the side and begins to read.) *"All Sorts of Worms," "Finding Earthworms," "A Worm's Body," "Feeding," "Moving"… I think that there are two chapters where we might find our information. Let's begin with "A Worm's Body."* (She turns to page 10.) *Let's scan the information found on this page. Turn to a partner and share what you notice on this page.* (She pauses to allow students to quickly talk about what they see.) *The first thing that I notice is that this page has an illustration that is similar to the picture I drew on this chart. It also has labeled parts of an earthworm. Take a closer look under the word* saddle. *Earlier, you wanted to know about the use, or function, of a saddle. It says, "where a worm's eggs are made." I see—the worm uses its saddle to make eggs. That is the function of the saddle. How interesting! I'm going to write that information on our chart. Turn to a partner and explain the function of a saddle.*

Ms. Cortez quickly reviews a particular sentence form displayed on a chart that students can use to speak like scientists about what they observe.

While the teacher writes the information about the saddle on the chart, the students discuss the function of the saddle in partners.

Carlos: *It looks like a bag. A worm's eggs are there.*

Other students glance at the charted sentence form repeatedly to support their explanation.

Next, the teacher shifts the students' attention to the actual text. She uses Shared Reading to model behaviors of fluent readers and thinks aloud to model how to clarify unfamiliar terms. Some examples are charted as follows:

Vocabulary	Facts
skeleton	Worms don't have skeletons. This allows worms to twist and turn.
tube or cylinder	A worm's body is a tube made of tiny segments.
bristles	Bristles help a worm move.

Ms. Cortez scaffolds instruction in this new vocabulary by providing photographs of other skeletons, using a sheet of rolled-up paper to show an example of a tube and comparing the bristles on an earthworm to the bristles on a toothbrush.

Ms. Cortez: *I'm going to read this first page. Listen for the answer to our question, How do earthworms move? "A worm is a very simple animal. It has no skeleton, no lungs, no eyes, and no ears." That is interesting information about an earthworm. A worm doesn't have a skeleton.* (She places some photographs of other skeletons under the document camera.) *Here are skeletons of other animals. Worms don't have skeletons.*

Arelia: *That's why a worm can go back.* (She tries to lean back like a worm.)

Ms. Cortez: *Yes, we have skeletons. We can't twist and lean all the way back like a worm. It also doesn't have lungs. Lungs are those sacks we have inside that help us breathe. Let me keep reading. "Its body is a tube made of many tiny segments." Here is a tube I made by rolling up a sheet of paper. It is the shape of a cylinder. Look at this straw. This is also a tube or a cylinder. The worm's body is a tube like these examples I just showed you. Listen to this last sentence. "Each segment is filled with liquid and has bristles that help the worm move." Here is part of our answer. Bristles help a worm move. Take a look at this toothbrush; it has bristles. The bristles are rough. An earthworm has tiny bristles. Those bristles help it move. The bristles are used as anchors to help the earthworms move forward and backward. Some of you may have seen these bristles, but they are really tiny. That means that these bristles help the earthworm to grab onto a surface as it extends, or stretches, and contracts using its muscles. I want you to turn to a partner and explain what you have learned about earthworms.*

As the students talk to their partners, Ms. Cortez circulates among the students to listen to their understanding and the way they are using language. Once again, she acknowledges the use of the new vocabulary with praise or restates what a student says, modeling the use of the target vocabulary. After several minutes, she has two to three students share out to the whole class.

Ms. Cortez: *Next, on our chart, I'm going to label the bristles and write the function of the bristles and how they help the earthworm to move.*

Ms. Cortez draws tiny bristles under the earthworm and labels them. Then, she writes: *Bristles grip the ground to help the earthworm push itself forward or backward.* The students write this information in their science notebooks. Then, they are asked once again to identify the parts of an earthworm and explain to a partner the function of the parts they have learned so far. Ms. Cortez reminds them of the charted language forms that can help them speak like scientists.

What Is *Explain* for English Language Learners?

By this point in the 5E inquiry model, students have had opportunities to think deeply and develop questions for key science content and concepts as they explored scientific phenomena and made connections to what they know. Students are guided to articulate their scientific understanding in their own words. And, subsequently, they will be guided further to represent what they have come to understand, using the formal academic thinking and language of science. At this stage, misconceptions are clarified and new questions are generated. Key academic terms are analyzed, and information is shared. Teachers can offer alternative points of view and explanations to enhance student understanding.

It is in the *Explain* stage that teachers must focus support for English language learners on understanding, practicing, and utilizing content-specific language. Of all the stages within the 5E model, the *Explain* stage may require the most dedicated time to develop the academic language of science. Teachers focus on making English language learners' previous experiences and understanding easier to describe and explain in order to set the stage for further development in the remaining stages of their inquiry. As ELLs are asked to explain their learning orally or in written form (e.g., diagrams, charts, drawings, or text), they will benefit from explicit instruction and focused support in the vocabulary, functions, and forms of science needed to communicate their thinking. The active role of the teacher—as facilitator and assessor—in this focused language instruction is critical.

Teacher decision making about language goals build on the earlier stages of the 5E learning cycle for ELLs. The selection of the language forms, along with the determination of specific academic vocabulary instruction, must depend upon the level of English language development the students exhibited during the *Engage* and *Explore* portions of the lesson. This careful attention to the varying levels of second-language acquisition in order to target the appropriate language is an important consideration for ongoing language development.

The integration of literacy gains greater prominence in *Explain*. As students interact with multimedia resources through the use of demonstrations, direct teaching, modeling, read-alouds, and guided or shared reading of content texts, teachers can guide ELLs to find the answers to their questions. The language of the print resources provides additional models of academic language vocabulary and structure.

Developing Language Explicitly in *Explain*

Because the *Explain* stage marks the shift into expanding and confirming scientific knowledge, there are expectations for students to be able to use language to question, predict, analyze, interpret, justify, and report. The scientific functions of providing precise evidence, contrasting data, and drawing conclusions pose particular demands on English language learners to use content-specific language effectively. It is at this stage that language must be used in tandem with high levels of cognitive processing to achieve greater concept understanding. Therefore, instructional practices that embed focused explicit language instruction within the scientific processes are a critical component of the *Explain* stage. The essential features of these practices are discussed in this section.

Figure 6.2 Essential Features for Developing Academic Language in *Explain*

- Providing explicit language instruction
- Appropriately selecting language for instruction
- Differentiating instruction for language
- Utilizing graphic organizers to connect thinking and language
- Integrating literacy to support language development

Providing Explicit Language Instruction

The importance of explicit, or direct, instruction for English language development has been discussed earlier (see Chapter 2). Three fundamental components exemplify an effective cycle of explicit language instruction: 1) language input, 2) teacher-facilitated language output, and 3) independent language output. Although presented separately, they often overlap. Depending on the language needs of the students, emphasis in the form of time and/or resources may be placed on some components over others. Nevertheless, they are each a critical factor in the sequence of explicit language instruction.

1. **Language input:** A key construct for acquiring a new language is comprehensible input (see Chapter 2). In order for language to be acquired, it must be understood. With explicit instruction, the teacher builds the meaning of select content-related language by tapping into the contexts of previous experience and familiar language, by matching language (oral or written) directly to visuals or printed materials, or by using physical movement and concrete objects to expand and elaborate on meaning. The language input is often a set of extended intervals of modeling or demonstrating content-related language.

2. **Teacher-facilitated language output:** The intervals of language input are followed by opportunities for students to process the new content-related language, often in interactive structures that support thinking and talking—comprehensible output—in exchanges between the teacher and students as well as students with their peers. In the early stages of the lesson, the language output of the students is highly facilitated by the teacher. Depending on the language needs of the students, there may be significant repetition in this step. The teacher focuses the students' language use by providing particular prompts or interactive structures that will compel students to use explicit language targeted for the lesson. The use of visuals or printed materials, concrete objects, and physical movement may continue to be implemented in this step as needed. The teacher constantly monitors the understanding

and use of the new language by students as he or she facilitates their language output.

3. **Independent language output:** As the teacher becomes confident that the students have had enough focused, facilitated practice, the teacher decreases the level of direct guidance and prompting. Students move into tasks designed to encourage their independent output of the new language, for example, creating and sharing a science notebook entry, creating and sharing a diagram or visual, or giving an oral report. Many of the same practices utilized in the second step can be used here without the explicit guidance and support of the teacher. The teacher now becomes an active listener and observer, assuming the important role of assessor. The information gathered as the teacher observes the students use the target language independently will aid him or her in making decisions for future instruction: whether to reteach, to extend and expand the lesson, or to move on to the next level of inquiry.

Thus far, the teacher's role in 5E ELD science has been characterized as highly conscious of the language needs of students as well as the language purposes of the instruction. An additional element of explicit language instruction that must not be overlooked is establishing clear purposes for student involvement from a language perspective. As learners of a second language, English language learners benefit from practices that develop their language consciousness. Teachers do this by establishing clear purposes for developing academic language as well as developing awareness of language features and language-learning strategies as they encourage their students to speak like scientists.

The opening scenario in Ms. Cortez's classroom provides an example of explicit attention given to language practice and usage. Within the context of sharing their outdoor exploration, Ms. Cortez explicitly inputs new language to her students (*burrow, extend, contract*), using the context of their shared experience as well as concrete objects (the Slinky), and gestures (stretching her arms in and out) to elaborate. Students process the meaning in brief partner sharing. This is followed by an extended interval of guided language practice as her students use the scaffold of their drawings to talk in small groups. As her students talk, Ms. Cortez is actively monitoring and facilitating the use of the select vocabulary she inputted. In addition to restating student language, she uses a particular technique of passing out colored strips as recognition of their use of the academic language.

Appropriately Selecting Language for Instruction

When planning instruction for English language learners, teachers must ask themselves a critical question: What is the language that science instruction demands of and provides to English learners? Because language is so vast and complex, the selection of the language to target for instruction can seem to be an overwhelming task for the teacher of English language learners. As has been discussed previously (see Chapter 2), we support a functionalist communicative perspective for second-language development. This theoretical perspective gives us the tools to talk about language development as the acquisition of academic vocabulary, functions, and forms. The functions of language refer to the thinking processes of language or the purpose of language—to analyze, to compare and contrast, to express relationships of cause and effect. When we refer to the language forms, we are referring to the syntax of language—how language is organized into the grammatical structures of phrases, clauses, and sentences. There are characteristic forms of language that correspond to the way one thinks about the world. For example, expressing a relationship of cause and effect would require using the language form, or structure, *If they _____, then _____.*

Tiered Vocabulary Approach

Academic vocabulary refers to content-related vocabulary. We prefer to think about this vocabulary through the lens of Tiered Vocabulary.

Figure 6.3 Tiered Vocabulary

Tier	What It Is	Examples
Tier 1	**Basic Words.** These words often represent familiar, simple, or concrete concepts.	*run, ball, is, thing, fish, sky, home, work, boy, girl, dog, air, bug*
Tier 2	**Academic Words.** These words represent concepts already known by students but expand and specify knowledge of the concepts; they are found in a variety of reading contexts and across curricular areas.	*vocabulary, example, varied, structure, adapt, predict, slightly, accurate, patterns, current, pump, surface, probe*
Tier 3	**Content Words.** These are low frequency and are limited to specific domains. They do not necessarily need explicit instruction but require clarification for understanding a concept or text.	*salinity, submersible, intertidal, reef, plankton, stratosphere, ultraviolet, trough, chlorofluorocarbons*

Figure 6.4 Science Notebook Entry

The teacher might encourage this student to use more precise language, such as *uneven, coarse, jagged, sleek,* or *opaque.*

The Tiered Vocabulary approach helps teachers identify, categorize, and prioritize the vocabulary that can be optimally developed in the 5E ELD model. Because they build on previous conceptual understanding that will be reinforced across the curriculum, Tier 2 words are ideal targets for ELL student mastery. Tier 3 words can be targeted for additional elaboration and clarification as science conceptual understanding is developed.

Teachers can use the elements of vocabulary, functions, and forms to identify specific language objectives for their ELD instruction. These language elements assist the teacher in designing focused, purposeful tasks as they move their students through each stage of the 5E model. In the previous stages, *Engage* and *Explore*, we highlighted instructional features that enhance opportunities for students to utilize the language they bring to the instructional setting. Emphasis was placed on designing instruction that exposed students to content-related language. The teacher's role was to model the academic vocabulary, language functions, and forms. Modeling the appropriate use of the target language within the meaningful contexts of hands-on science experiences provided students with indirect oral and written language opportunities to communicate their understanding as they thought about scientific phenomena.

Because of the emphasis on explicit language instruction and the practice and use of language by students in the *Explain* stage, thought and purpose must be given to selecting the appropriate language targets. As exemplified in Figure 6.5, the best approach is for teachers to identify the thinking processes their students will be using for science concept development. This can be accomplished through a careful analysis of the curriculum frameworks and standards. Once the thinking processes have been identified, attention can be given to the language forms that communicate that thinking to oneself or to others. Finally, key vocabulary can be identified that relates to the concept, topic, or theme, with particular attention given to Tier 2 words. Consequently, instruction will focus on providing the appropriate scaffolding strategies that will help ELLs acquire the language needed to meet the language demands of academic content.

Figure 6.5 Sample Framework for Identifying Academic Language Targets

Content Knowledge (Standards)	Process Skills/ Cognitive Tasks	Language Skills, Functions, and Forms	Instructional Strategies to Support ELLs
Students know how to compare the physical properties of different kinds of rocks and know that a rock is composed of different combinations of minerals.	**Observation** 1. Observing rocks 2. Gathering information **Communicating** 1. Organizing thinking by completing graph **Inferring** 1. Drawing conclusions	**Vocabulary** *rough, dull, smooth, shiny, polished, minerals* **Functions/ Forms** Describing: *The _____ has _____ and _____.* **Compare/ Contrast** *Both minerals have _____.* *_____ has _____ but _____ doesn't have _____.* **Drawing Conclusions** *The _____ is _____ because _____.*	• Word Bank • Gestures/ Movements • Tree Map • Circle Map • I Notice/I Wonder • Partners • Read Aloud • Pictorial Input • Look and Draw

Referring once again to the featured scenario, it is clear that Ms. Cortez has identified specific language targets in the instructional cycle she designed for her second-grade English language learners. Building on the processes of observing and communicating, she wants her students to develop specific academic language to describe, identify (name), and explain what they are learning about earthworms. She repeatedly models her key vocabulary within the context of discussing what they observed. Orally and in writing, she first uses words that students know (Tier 1 words) such as dig, stretch, part, or job. Then, she inputs more precise academic terms (Tier 2 words) like burrow, extend, segment and function as well as content-specific vocabulary (Tier 3 words) such as bristles and saddle. At the same time, she facilitates her students' use of forms for targeted functions as can be seen in Figure 6.6.

Figure 6.6 Language Functions and Forms

Function	Language Form
Describe	It has a _____, a _____, and a _____.
Identify	This is called a _____.
Explain	The earthworm uses the _____ to _____.

Differentiating Instruction for Language

Because English language learners in today's classrooms are complex socially, linguistically, culturally, and academically, the concept of a differentiated approach is a critical component of ELD instructional decision making (see Chapter 2). In *Engage* and *Explore* scenarios, teachers have accommodated their instruction based on the English language proficiency of their English language learners. For the most part, instructional tasks and purposes were open-ended and allowed for much flexibility for students who had varied language needs.

When considering language development, the *Explain* stage involves heightened emphasis on using specific content-related language to communicate orally or in writing. This necessitates the thoughtful design of direct instructional support to ensure the practice and use of targeted language aided by the careful monitoring of language performance. In order to avoid overwhelming an ELL student with excessive language and content demands, a teacher must make particular considerations when planning and delivering ELD science instruction. When planning instruction the teacher must actively consider cognitive knowledge, culture, relevance, background, and language complexity based on students' ages, learning preferences, and English proficiency levels.

Several key practices, depicted in Figure 6.7, can be utilized to differentiate instruction based on language proficiency:

Figure 6.7 Differentiating Instruction for English Language Learners

Technique for Differentiating Instruction for ELLs	Actions
Adjust teacher talk.	The types of questioning or prompting teachers use should vary for Beginning-level students who have just begun to build language as compared to Intermediate-level students who can draw upon larger reservoirs of language.
Modify expectations for language production.	Expectations for responding orally or in writing should be modified according to students' level of English proficiency. Beginning-level students should be expected to respond in single words and short phrases, while Intermediate-level students can respond in complete sentences with expanded vocabulary.

Technique for Differentiating Instruction for ELLs	Actions
Adapt materials.	Early-Intermediate students may require text with more visual features such as photos, diagrams, and tables, or realia to develop language and concept understanding. In comparison, Early-Advanced students can access information from text with fewer of these visual or concrete supports.
Design adjustable instruction.	Tasks should be designed to allow students to be involved in various ways. Students with fewer language skills may be guided to respond with gestures or drawings and simple labels. Advanced-level students may serve as group reporter or recorder because of their native-like proficiency. Some students may require more time to focus on an objective than other students because they are still developing fluency.
Employ flexible grouping.	Decisions about grouping should take into account how to promote students' acquisition, practice, and use of the target language. At times, speaking to a partner who has greater language skills would be advantageous for exposure to more proficient peer models. Another option would be to group students homogeneously by language level so that the teacher can match instruction directly to student need.

There are several examples of Ms. Cortez employing a differentiated language approach in the featured instructional scenario. Since Ms. Cortez has a classroom that comprises two language proficiency levels—Early Intermediate and Intermediate—she needs to design instruction that accommodates their distinct needs. One example of support occurs when she asks an Early Intermediate student to demonstrate her understanding of the word *burrow* by drawing rather than orally explaining the term. Since Ms. Cortez positions her students in a heterogeneous seating arrangement on the rug (Early Intermediate students sitting next to Intermediate students), Early Intermediate students have the opportunity to listen to a more elaborate response as they are directed to "turn to a partner and explain what the word *burrow* means." As Ms. Cortez circulates among the students, she is purposefully supporting her Early Intermediate students by prompting them or restating their responses to continue modeling the targeted language as needed. This procedure is repeated throughout the lesson. Another grouping pattern is also employed that accommodates the students at both levels when they are grouped in triads and asked to use their notebook drawings and/or notes.

Utilizing Graphic Organizers to Connect Thinking and Language

During the *Engage* and *Explore* stages of the 5Es, students gather a great deal of information. Graphic organizers at the *Explain* stage help students organize the information to support comprehension and the development of academic English.

Graphic organizers are tools for organizing thoughts and ideas in a variety of ways. They are helpful when structuring writing and organizing ideas gained from reading. Graphic organizers vary in design. They can demonstrate cause and effect, document comparisons, show relationships and associations, highlight structural features of written discourse, represent problem-solving approaches, organize research and planning models, and more. Students can get overwhelmed with information. They need to make sense of their learning. Graphic organizers help students wrap their heads around content. A graphic organizer can help create a mind map of students' thinking as they grapple with new content.

As graphic organizers facilitate and reflect student thinking, they are equally compelling vehicles for language development. Students express their thinking with particular vocabulary, phrases, and complete sentences that correspond to specific purposes, or functions, for using language (e.g., identifying relationships of cause and effect, recording similarities and differences). With the focus on developing language, teachers can use a particular type of graphic organizer as a tool to develop or expand language for a particular purpose. With the focus on demonstrating language proficiency, students can use a particular type of graphic organizer as an artifact of how they use language for a particular purpose. With the focus on being a strategic language user, students can use a particular type of graphic organizer as a learning tool to practice and use language for a particular purpose.

Students need guidance to understand the different ways that thinking can be organized and communicated. Teachers can guide students through a preselected organizer that will help students meet the content and language objectives. For many students, it is helpful to clearly model the development of a graphic organizer, using a think aloud/talk aloud strategy. Students may need to see and hear how the ideas are being connected. Thus, students can develop an understanding of the purpose of a graphic organizer as well as its practical application. The goal is for students to learn how to think and talk differently about content.

Figure 6.8 Process Grid

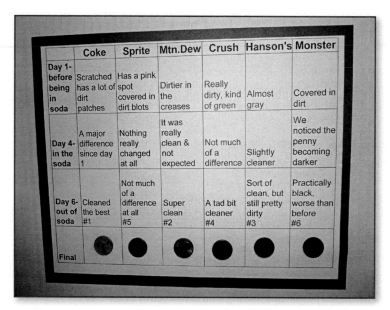

	Coke	Sprite	Mtn.Dew	Crush	Hanson's	Monster
Day 1- before being in soda	Scratched has a lot of dirt patches	Has a pink spot covered in dirt blots	Dirtier in the creases	Really dirty, kind of green	Almost gray	Covered in dirt
Day 4- in the soda	A major difference since day 1	Nothing really changed at all	It was really clean & not expected	Not much of a difference	Slightly cleaner	We noticed the penny becoming darker
Day 6- out of soda	Cleaned the best #1	Not much of a difference at all #5	Super clean #2	A tad bit cleaner #4	Sort of clean, but still pretty dirty #3	Practically black, worse than before #6
Final						

This process grid depicts the outcome of the use of beverages as a cleansing agent. The chart serves as a resource to more easily explain the results of an experiment.

Integrating Literacy to Support Language Development

Beyond the expected dimensions of listening and speaking, the processes and practices specifically related to reading and writing instruction elsewhere in the daily curriculum help ELLs make meaning of the new language and facilitate its practice and use. Teachers can employ practices introduced and developed in language arts instruction, such as shared reading or think-alouds to help students unlock the meaning of content-area text. As students interact with text resources and read to learn more about science, they also interact with a source of rich academic language. The writing skills students develop in language arts are tapped into and reinforced as students draw, make lists, formulate predictions, and express relationships in their science notebooks. The creation of charts, word banks, and other speech-to-print techniques are typical literacy practices that can be integrated as tools for concept and language development within science content.

While these practices are embedded within all of the 5E stages, their use is emphasized in *Explain* as tools that aid teachers in honing in on explicit language-development instruction. The featured teacher, Ms. Cortez, provides strong examples of the role literacy plays in her instructional delivery. She records key terminology on the board and charts for students to reference, supporting their understanding with drawings. The labeling of new vocabulary in the Pictorial Input chart is yet another example of how literacy practices support both language and content development. Sentence frames are displayed in writing on charts for students to use as a linguistic scaffold. Ms. Cortez guides students through a Shared Reading of a book on earthworms to support language and concept development. She points out text features, models how to read expository text, and defines and explains key academic vocabulary.

Examining ELD Practices in *Explain*

In the previous section, we highlighted several ELD practices that are essential for the *Explain* phase, citing examples from the feature classroom scenario. In this section, we continue the analysis of notable practices for ELLs during *Explain* by focusing on additional scenarios from elementary and middle-school classrooms that depict the development of specific academic language for science.

Miss Gonzalez's Class—Grade 1 Scenario
ELD Levels: Beginning and Early Intermediate

After visiting each of the exploration stations for a unit on plants, Miss Gonzalez gathers her students on the rug to specifically focus on the parts of plants and the function of each part. In her class, she also has an ELL student with a learning disability, so she is sure to seat this student in front.

On chart paper, she has drawn a large red flower with petals. In a previous lesson, she had labeled each part. (See Figure 6.9.) Now she wants the students to explain the function of each part.

Miss Gonzalez: *What words did you say and hear as you visited each station?*

She guides the students to turn to a partner and share. She prompts a pair of students to get them started. As the students share, Miss Gonzalez makes a list of the words she hears. She quickly adds the contributor's initials next to the word. After two minutes, she brings the whole group back. She reviews the words she heard, including *water, leaf, food, roots, stem,* and *dirt.* She draws a quick illustration for each one on the board. Some students begin to read the words aloud.

Figure 6.9 Pictorial Input Chart

This kind of chart is developed in progressively more challenging steps that may include labeling, matching, defining, and elaborating.

Miss Gonzalez holds up a flower with attached roots.

Miss Gonzalez: *Take a look at the roots of this flower. The roots have a function. In other words, the roots have a job to do so that the flower grows. Say the word* function. *(The students repeat the word.) Function means "job." What did you learn about the job of the roots in your exploration stations?*

Serena: *Water.*

Victor: *Get food from dirt.*

Kali: *Roots help the plant get food and water.*

Miss Gonzalez: *I heard you say the roots get food and water from the soil, or dirt. What is the job of the roots? Let's say it together. The roots get food and water.*

Again, the students repeat the sentence. Next, Miss Gonzalez sets up the AB Partner Share strategy.

Miss Gonzalez: *Now, I want you to turn to a partner. Decide who will be partner A and who will be partner B. Partner A will ask the question, "What is the job of the roots?" Partner B will answer, "The roots get food and water." Let's have two students come up to the front of the class and role-play the task.*

Miss Gonzalez guides her students to ask and answer the question with their partners.

Miss Gonzalez uses a particular grouping technique to make sure that the Beginning-level students are interacting with the higher-language-producing Early Intermediate students. This also helps students with different learning abilities. She has preassigned them seats on the rug so that students from different levels are seated next to each other. She reviews her seating chart frequently to make adjustments as needed.

Miss Gonzalez walks over to a set of partners that are sitting quietly and not engaging in conversation. She sits next to them to get them started.

Miss Gonzalez:	*Liana, I see you have a flower in your hand. Point to the roots.*

Liana lowers her head to look at her plant and points to the roots.

Miss Gonzalez:	*Yes, now tell me, what part of the plant is this?*

Liana, a Beginning-level student with a learning disability, hesitates for a few seconds before answering.

Liana:	*Root.*

Miss Gonzalez then turns to Liana's partner.

Miss Gonzalez:	*What part gets food and water for the plant?*
Ryan:	*The root.*
Miss Gonzalez:	*Yes, you are correct. The job of the roots is to get food and water. Say that with me. Roots get food and water.*

It was difficult for these particular students to engage in the AB Partner Share. In this instance, it was critical for Miss Gonzalez to mediate the language in a short guided conversation focused on the lesson objective. After her encounter with the group, Miss Gonzalez goes to a chart by her desk and quickly adds a note in a box with Liana's name.

After several minutes, Miss Gonzalez draws her students' attention to a chart she has prepared and posted at the front of the room. She tells the children that they have been doing a great job of thinking like scientists. She explains that she wants them to learn how to talk like scientists, too.

| Miss Gonzalez: | *We are going to use this graphic organizer to help us think and talk more like scientists.* |

With the help of the students, she adds the parts of the plant vocabulary to the first column, which they focused on earlier in the Pictorial Input Chart.

Science Words	A plant needs its _____ to grow.	The job of the _____ is to _____. The function of the _____ is to _____.
roots		_____ carry food and water to the plant.
stem		
leaves		
flower		

| Miss Gonzalez: | *What did we just finish talking about?* |

| **Students:** | *The roots.* |

Miss Gonzalez then asks for a student volunteer to come to the board and draw a picture of the roots in the second column. (She will guide students to create an illustration in the second column for all the terms.)

| **Miss Gonzalez:** | *We have a sentence here at the top that will guide us to talk like scientists.* (She reads aloud the sentence frame at the top of the second column, pointing to the word and the illustration as she fills in the blank.) *Now, read the sentence with me.* |

The students read the sentence aloud.

Then, Miss Gonzalez points to the top of the third column.

| **Miss Gonzalez:** | *What does it say here?* |

She reads the sentence frame and works with students to record a response in the third column. Miss Gonzalez and her students read aloud the completed sentence frame with the added information.

| **Miss Gonzalez:** | *You sound just like scientists! Now, let's see what else we've learned.* (Miss Gonzalez holds up a stem.) *What is the function of the stem? What is the job of the stem?* (Once again, she is careful to allow students enough time to explain what they observed in their exploration stations. After the students share their understanding, Miss Gonzalez holds up a flower with roots and leaves and points to each part as she restates and elaborates.) *The stem takes the water and the nutrients from the roots to the* |

leaves. This is where the food is stored. Say the word nutrients. *What a great science word!* Nutrients *means food.*

Miss Gonzalez guides the students to ask and answer a question about the stem of the plant with a partner in the same way they shared about the roots.

Miss Gonzalez:	*With a partner, you are to select a plant or a flower with a stem from one of the stations. Partner A will ask the question, "What is the function of the stem?" and partner B will respond, "The stem takes the water and the nutrients from the roots to the leaves."*

Then she asks them to reverse roles.

Miss Gonzalez directs the students' attention back to the graphic organizer they were working with earlier. In a similar fashion as before, she works with students to complete the organizer with additional information about the stem and its function. This time, students practice both sentence frames in the third column. As she calls on different students to orally share, she enters their initials next to the language form they practiced.

Next, Miss Gonzalez directs the students to make an entry in their science notebooks regarding what they learned about the functions of the plant parts they discussed during the lesson.

The first direction is to draw a picture of two plant parts, the stem and the root. She quickly gives an example and reminder of what the students need to do by holding up one of the science notebooks. She calls their attention to the graphic organizer as an additional resource. While students open their notebooks and begin to draw, Miss Gonzalez differentiates the task in the following way:

Levels	Teacher Prompts
Beginning	Label the parts of the plant. What part helps the plant get nutrients (food) and water?
Early Intermediate	What is the job of the roots? What is the function of the stem?
Others	Write what you know about the functions of the parts of plants.

Notable ELD Practices

At various points in this example, the teacher differentiates her instruction to meet the particular language needs and readiness levels of her students. She intentionally arranges the seating of her students so that they can be matched with a more language-proficient partner to practice their academic language usage. She circulates among the students, observing their level of participation and questioning students to elicit language as needed. She is also conscious of the fact that she has to take the time to prompt her student with a learning disability and tailor the tasks to meet her needs. The final activity of completing notebook entries is adapted in various ways according to the language-proficiency levels of her students, giving students with limited language proficiency the benefit of scaffolds such as visual representations and guided oral practice with the teacher.

There is ample evidence of explicit language targets as students are supported to master the language through repeated input of teacher and peer models, oral rehearsal with partners, and the use of a graphic organizer to connect thinking (understanding) to specific academic language. Miss Gonzalez structures the graphic organizer with sentence frames and illustrations to serve as a model of language use to explain the functions of a stem and root for a plant's survival.

It is important to note that the graphic organizer follows students' self-generated explanations. They were encouraged to think and talk about their understanding prior to explicit language instruction.

Mrs. Huang's Class—Grade 4 Scenario
ELD Levels: Intermediate, Early Advanced, and
Advanced

Students in this classroom have been learning about erosion, specifically the effects of flowing water on land. During the *Explore* phase of this lesson, the students create a plateau of sand and clay in a long plastic tray. They pour water into the tray and observe what happens to deposits of sand and clay when water flows through. As students begin to explain what is happening, Mrs. Huang, the classroom teacher, walks around and listens to a small group.

Clarisse: *Look at the water on the plateau!*

Jonathan: *It's spreading. It's cool. It's going fast.*

Clarisse: *The water is going fastest here.*

Silvia: *It's dipping. It's making some holes.*

Figure 6.10 Grand Canyon Simulation

This simulation of the creation of the Grand Canyon serves as a concrete experience that allows students to observe and explain difficult science concepts.

Mrs. Huang notices that most of the students' talk focuses on the water instead of on the effect of the water on the landforms and the flow of the sediments. To aid their thinking, she has each group fill a vial with some sand, clay, and water (see Figure 6.11). The students leave the vials on their desks to allow the sediments to settle. After about two to three minutes, she directs their attention to the vials.

Figure 6.11 Sediment Vial Experiment

The teaching of science requires teachers to anticipate where students may have difficulty understanding concepts and to be prepared with alternatives to clarify misconceptions.

Mrs. Huang: *Look at your vial. It looks like a three-layer cake. What do you notice?*

Ramon: *The sand is on the bottom.*

Mrs. Huang: *Yes, what do you see in the middle?*

Breanna: *Clay.*

Mrs. Huang: *What is left on top?*

Students: *Water.*

Mrs. Huang: *Now, I want you to think. Why is the sand on the bottom? Turn to a partner and share your response.*

Students discuss their ideas with their partners.

Trinh: *The sand is heavier.*

Mrs. Huang: *Knowing that sand is heavier, what do you expect the water flow to carry the farthest, sand or clay?*

The students are given time to share their opinions with the whole group.

Mrs. Huang: *Because we're scientists, we need to be mindful of how we can talk more precisely, like scientists do.*

She projects a language form on the screen that reads: *I expect that _____ flows the farthest because _____.*

Mrs. Huang: *Think about the ideas you just shared with the class and practice expressing them by using this language form with the person next to you.* (Her students share their responses with a partner. Mrs. Huang waits two to three minutes before continuing.)

Mrs. Huang: *In a real canyon, sediments that don't weigh as much travel farther. They get deposited farther away. Your clay got deposited really far away. When sediments get deposited in different places, it's called* deposition. (She writes the word on the board at the front of the classroom.) *Say the word* deposition *with me. Now, whisper the word. Now, sing the word. Yell the word! Deposition is when the earth erodes and the sediments are taken to a different place.*

To better observe the effect of water on the sediments, she has the students pour green-colored water into the trays. The table groups again get an opportunity to explain what occurs.

Ramon: *The clay is lighter. It is white.*

Trinh: *The sand is super-heavy and it stays.*

Breanna: *The clay goes the farthest. The clay flow farther.*

Mrs. Huang: *Breanna observed that the clay flows farther than the sand. The sediments of sand and clay do not move, or flow, the same. Take a look here. What do you notice?*

Trinh: *The water deposited the clay the farthest.*

Mrs. Huang: *When sediments like clay and sand get deposited in different places, what is that called?*

Ramon: (Looks at the board) *Deposition.*

Mrs. Huang: *Yes! This group is really thinking and talking like scientists today! Keep up the good work, scientists. Continue your observations.*

Mrs. Huang continues to circulate from group to group, repeating similar probing and prompting interactions with each group. Then, she asks the students to stop and open their science notebooks to make an entry.

Mrs. Huang: *I want you to explain what you understand about the effects of flowing water on land. You may draw as well as write to communicate what you know. Which scientific terms will be helpful to use in your explanations?*

The students call out the words *deposition, erosion, flow, farthest, expect,* and *sediment.* Mrs. Huang lists these terms on the board as a reference for her students. Ever mindful of the value of encouraging her students to be conscious of their language use, she tells them that she will be evaluating their notebooks today to look for how well they are using scientific language in their notebook entries.

Notable ELD Practices

In this scenario, Mrs. Huang provides a sequence of opportunities for her students to explain their understanding about the effects of water on land as part of their unit on erosion. To aid their thinking and explanations, she incorporates additional hands-on opportunities to explore, such as layering sediments and adding green-colored water to the trays. Mrs. Huang's active interaction with students to probe their thinking and encourage their use of academic language is an exemplary practice. She explicitly calls attention to their use of particular examples of language as a vehicle to create strong scientific explanations. These examples include providing definitions, modeling or restating appropriate language use, employing language forms and partner sharing as scaffolds, and generating student-generated lists of important scientific terms.

> *Mr. Asaad's Class—Grade 7 Scenario*
> *ELD Levels: Early Intermediate, Intermediate, and Early Advanced*
>
> The students in Mr. Asaad's class have just finished comparing and contrasting the depth of detail acquired by observing a photograph with the naked eye, a magnifying lens, and a microscope, the intent being to have students realize that cells were not discovered until the invention of optical tools. In the *Explain* stage of this instructional cycle, the students will learn specific information on cells and the names of the scientists responsible for the discovery of cells. Mr. Asaad also recognizes that his students will need specific language to talk about the academic concepts related to cells. He will guide the students through a chapter in their science textbook as well as a teacher-made Microsoft PowerPoint® presentation.
>
> Prior to reading, Mr. Asaad tells the students that they will learn about the structure and function of cells. He asks the students to listen for certain words as he reads. He begins by reading aloud the first paragraph. Midway through the

paragraph, he stops and says the word *structure* while writing it on a sheet of paper under the document camera.

Mr. Asaad: *This is an important word to understand. Let's read the word aloud.* (Everyone reads.) *What does* structure *mean?* (He pauses and two students call out the words *building* and *playground.* Mr. Asaad shows students a small ball.) *The structure of this ball is a sphere. It is its shape. Grab your pencils. What is the structure of the pencil?* (Students call out words like *long, rectangle, and cylinder.* Mr. Asaad confirms that the structure of a pencil is a cylinder.)

Next, Mr. Asaad writes the word *function* on the board.

Mr. Asaad: *Here is another word that will be important for you to know. What is the word?* (Everyone reads it aloud.) *What is* function? *Have you ever heard the word before?*

Jake: *Fiction is a book that is make-believe.*

Mr. Asaad: *You're thinking and I like that. You said* fiction. *The word is* function. *It means what someone or something is able to do. What is the function of this ball? What is it able to do?* (Students shout out the word *bounce* almost in unison.) *The function of a ball is to bounce. What is the function of your pencil? The function of a pencil is to record words on a paper. Think about what I just read about cells and what I explained about these important words. Then, turn to a partner and share what you understand about the structure and function of a cell.*

Before students get started, Mr. Asaad displays and quickly reviews two different forms of language for students to use as a support: *The structure of a cell is _____. Based on the reading so far, the function of a cell is to _____.*

As the students work in pairs, Mr. Asaad grabs his clipboard and circulates among the students to learn what they understood from the reading and listen to how they are practicing and using the new vocabulary and language forms. He visits the Early Intermediate students who have been partnered with more proficient speakers and takes some notes that he will refer to later for planning.

Mr. Asaad continues his read-aloud process, highlighting references to the structure and function of cells within each paragraph. Finally, he sets up the reading for the last paragraph. He tells students that the next section will focus on the size of cells. Instead of reading aloud himself, he directs the students to read with their table partners. They will take turns reading aloud the sentences to each other. He cautions students to use their partner voices, which means reading aloud just loud enough for their partners to hear them. As students read aloud, Mr. Asaad circulates among the students to monitor their completion of the task. He has selected this paragraph intentionally for students to read and process on their own. He is confident that the previous discussion and reading have prepared them all to be successful.

After students have completed the paragraph, he checks for their understanding.

Mr. Asaad: *How are cells measured?*

Penny: *In micrometers.*

Mr. Asaad: *Yes, cells are measured in micrometers. Let's see how big a cell is. Look at this ruler.* (Mr. Asaad places a centimeter ruler under the document camera.) *What is the value of a millimeter? A millimeter would be the space between these lines. Take that tiny space and divide by 1,000. That would be a nanometer. Then take the nanometer and divide it into 1,000 parts. One of those parts is a micrometer! We measure cells by micrometers. Turn to a partner and explain how cells are measured.*

Next, Mr. Asaad further explains how cell theory evolved, using a slide presentation accompanied by brief dialogue with his students. He displays the first slide with the words *Cell Theory.* After asking everyone to choral-read the words, he facilitates the following exchange:

Mr. Asaad: *What is a* theory? *Have you ever heard this word before? Turn to a partner and share what you think* theory *means.*

Marcos: *A theory is sort of a thought and you are trying to look for an explanation.*

Mr. Asaad: *Based on evidence, a theory has to be developed and people have to agree on it.*

He displays the second slide containing a picture of a microscope.

Mr. Asaad: *Here is a drawing of Robert Hooke's first microscope. He designed his own microscope. He got parts from other people who made lenses and put them in two ends. Then he added an oil lamp and a mirror.*

Trisha: *He needed the oil lamp to reflect it.*

Mr. Asaad: *When he observed the first cells under a microscope, he was looking at a thin slice of cork. In 1663, he found these tiny structures (cells) that made up the piece of cork. Cells are little rooms. Robert Hooke named the tiny structures cells because it reminded him of little rooms.*

Figure 6.12 Robert Hooke Cell Theory Slide

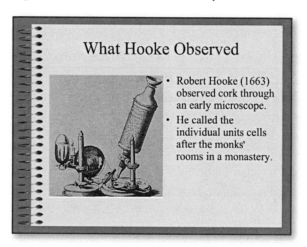

The explanation continues as he moves to the third slide, which shows a picture of a real cork at a normal size side by side with a close-up drawing of a cork.

Mr. Asaad: *Cork is the bark of a tree. It is a dead cell. With the microscope, he saw an enlarged picture of cork cells. This is his drawing. You can tell the difference between our technology today and what he had back in the 1600s.*

Slide 4 contains a picture and description of Anton von Leeuwenhoek.

Mr. Asaad: *This scientist was able to make important discoveries using the microscope. He saw little* *animals. He called them* animalcules. *Back then, people didn't have toothbrushes. From reading his science notebook, we know that he scraped off the stuff that had collected on his teeth, which we now call plaque. He dropped parts of the plaque on a slide. He observed with his microcope that these tiny organisms seemed to move.*

The next slide presents a photo of Matthias Schleiden and a detailed drawing of a plant cell.

Mr. Asaad: *Plants are composed of cells. Schleiden collected plants from all over the world. He looked at them under the microscope. This is what a plant cell looks like. The structure of this cell is a boxlike shape.*

The next slide contains a photo of Theodor Schwann and a drawing of animal tissue.

Mr. Asaad: *Theodor Schwann changed the* theory, *or what people thought, about cells. He believed that animals are composed of cells. Take a look at this slide of animal tissue. How would you describe its structure?*

Odessa: *It's kind of circular.*

Mr. Asaad: *Yes, that is correct. Schwann's scientific investigation helped us understand more about cell theory.*

Mr. Asaad displays the next slide, a photo of Rudolf Virchow and a microscopic image of a cell.

Mr. Asaad: *This scientist discovered that all cells are made of other parts and pieces.*

Mr. Asaad displays the final slide, listing three important points about cell theory. He summarizes these points for the students.

Mr. Asaad: *The scientific investigation of all of these scientists has helped us to understand three important things about cells. One, all living things are composed of cells. Two, cells are the basic units of structure and function in living things, and three, all cells are produced from other cells.*

Once Mr. Asaad finishes the slide show presentation, he tells the students that they will have a chance to see the slide show once again and to talk about what they have learned with their partners. He reviews instructions for the AB Partner Share strategy they have used before in class to share information.

Mr. Asaad: *Partner A explains the information on the first slide; partner B adds any missing facts. Then, you switch roles.*

Before replaying the slide show, he asks students to decide who will be partner A and who will be partner B. He distributes strips of paper to each pair to display on their desks, describing them as "tabletop language strips" to help them speak like scientists. The strips list the focus words' structure and function, along with several language forms that he challenges them to try to practice: *I learned _____. With his microscope, he discovered _____. Based on his investigation, his cell theory was_____.*

Mr. Asaad replays the slide show. He stops after each slide, allowing students to employ the AB Partner Share strategy. As pairs share, he actively circulates around the room. At times, he interacts with the students to guide them to think more deeply and to practice the target language. At other times, he jots down a note about what he hears or observes.

Once the slide show is over, Mr. Asaad asks the students to open their science notebooks to the page where they have completed the first two columns of a K-W-L Chart during earlier stages of the instructional sequence. He asks them to think about what they have learned about cells and add it under the *L* column before the period is over.

Notable ELD Practices

This instructional scenario provides strong examples of several of the essential features discussed in this chapter. Mr. Asaad has designed content instruction that effectively integrates an academic-language focus appropriate for middle school ELLs. He uses varied types of text as resources, including a textbook chapter and PowerPoint slide show for understanding the concept and highlighting key vocabulary. As his students interacted with text resources and read to learn more about science, they also interacted with a source of rich academic language. He positions himself within the interaction as an additional language model while reading and thinking aloud and narrating the slides.

In order to differentiate the content to meet the needs of his English language learners, he chunks the chapter reading for his students. This enables the students to have more support to process the content and new language after each chunk of text with the teacher or a partner. This support is enhanced by the focus on key words, using familiar concrete objects and sentence frames. Moreover, pacing the instruction in segments gives Mr. Asaad multiple opportunities to assess student understanding. The chapter reading sequence culminates with the students reading independently in pairs. Because of the level of explicit language input and teacher-facilitated language output, these seventh-graders successfully comprehend and discuss the academic content on their own.

In this scenario, we have a clear example of adapting materials through the use of a multimedia slide show presentation. By virtue of its structure, slide shows break down information into brief segments of information. Slide shows allow information to be presented through text as well as visuals. These features can support the understanding of complex concepts and language for English language learners. Particular techniques that Mr. Asaad employs are matching concept vocabulary to visuals as well as the repetition of vocabulary and language structures. Language was presented orally and in written captions in the form of accessible phrases and repetitive sentence structures. In the slide show lecture experience, Mr. Asaad once again guides his students through an explicit, deliberate cycle of language input and guided language output in partners. The cycle culminates with students' independent entries in the science notebook.

A final noteworthy point is the utilization of flexible grouping in Mr. Asaad's lesson design. Students receive instruction in whole-group settings, interact with partners to process information, and demonstrate their understanding as individuals. Because he has students who represent a wide range of English proficiency levels, he pairs them at tables in assigned seats to match a student with low English proficiency with a more proficient speaker. The varied grouping configurations and tasks provide students with different opportunities to receive new input and to express their understanding.

Strategies for ELD Instruction During *Explain*

Explain involves strategies that compel students to use specific academic language to express their understanding. Such strategies allow students to delve into their previous experience, to infer meaning and draw conclusions about what they know, and to communicate their concept knowledge to the teacher and peers. Some of the strategies represented in our scenarios and described here rely upon explicit teacher input and modeling balanced by intervals of student processing and language output. Other strategies, such as Think-Pair-Share and AB Partner Share, are characterized as partnership structures that promote student-to-student interaction as students display their concept knowledge and language mastery. The strategies presented include:

- Pictorial Input Chart
- Think-Pair-Share
- 10/2 Lecture
- Shared Reading
- Interactive Read-Alouds/Think-Alouds
- AB Partner Share

Pictorial Input Chart

Pictorial Input Charts are a strategy derived from the work of Project GLAD (Guided Language Acquisition Design) as a way to bring vocabulary words to life (Brechtel 2005). Pictorial Input Charts allow students to see a visual representation of the words they are learning. For English language learners, the visual representation provides an additional language cue to support academic language development.

A Pictorial Input Chart requires teachers to preselect key vocabulary and pre-draw a scene that incorporates all the selected vocabulary. The scene should be pre-drawn using a pencil to lightly outline the image so that it is clear for the teacher, but it must not be easily seen by the students. During a Pictorial Input, the teacher traces the scene clearly for all to see while discussing through a think-aloud the meaning of the key vocabulary. The scene will be further labeled using the vocabulary words.

During the *Explain* stage of the 5Es, students should be given opportunities to confirm their understanding of key vocabulary. In addition, teachers should highlight words or concepts that may have been overlooked during the previous *Engage* and *Explore* stages.

Figure 6.13 Sample Pictorial Input Chart

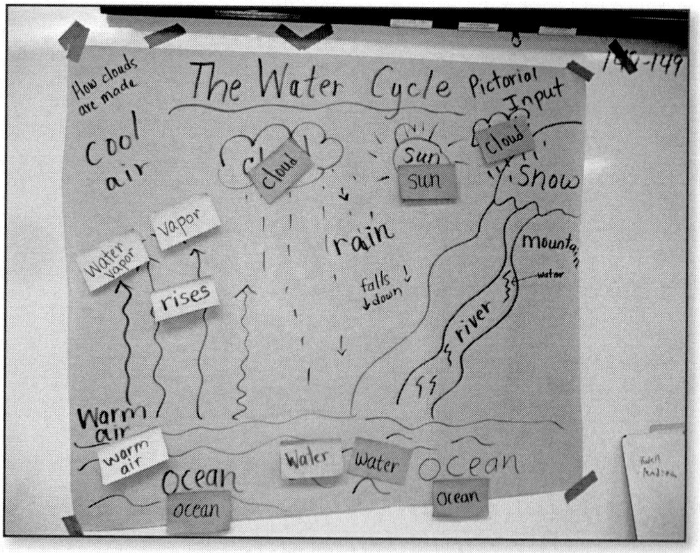

How Do You Do It?

1. Preselect a set of key vocabulary terms based on the learning objectives.

2. With a pencil, draw a scene that incorporates all the selected vocabulary words.

3. Display the pre-drawn Pictorial Input Chart so that all students have visual access to it. Begin to trace the scene with a marker. While tracing, explain what you are drawing in a think-aloud. When a representation of a key vocabulary word is being drawn, label the chart with the vocabulary word and express the meaning orally. For example, say, *Notice that there are different parts to the earthworm. The dividing lines are called* segments.

4. Continue to clearly trace the scene, labeling and discussing the meaning of key vocabulary.

Think-Pair-Share

Think-Pair-Share is a discussion strategy that provides students with time to process their thinking. After students have been presented information, they need time to think about what they have heard or read. They can then share their thinking with a partner to either confirm or extend their ideas. For some students, it serves as an opportunity to clarify misunderstandings and build academic language orally. It is important for students to have frequent opportunities to Think-Pair-Share because this strategy supports comprehension and offers an opportunity for academic dialogue. Students exchange language around academic content in a nonthreatening context. For those students who, for a variety of reasons, may struggle to share in whole group, the partnership context lowers the affective filter (Krashen and Terrell 1983). Students feel safe taking risks with their ideas and language.

To ensure a successful Think-Pair-Share, teachers should be sure to create effective partnerships. Be mindful of who is sitting next to whom. Students need to feel supported by peers but also need to feel like they are part of the conversation. A strong partnership is one in which both students will feel successful in the discussion and learn from each other.

Think-Pair-Share can be used during any phase of the 5Es. During the *Explain* phase it serves as a way to clarify information and offers explicit opportunities for academic language rehearsal.

How Do You Do It?

1. Present content to students.

2. Ask students to pause and think about what they understand about the information just presented. Allow students about two minutes to reflect.

3. Ask students to turn to a partner and share their thinking. Partnership talk can be open-ended or probed. Some examples of prompts that can be used to focus student sharing include:

   • Think about what we have just read. What have you understood so far? Turn and talk to your partner about what you understand about _____.

   • Share with your partner why you think _____ happened as a result of _____.

- Share with your partner two questions you have about _____.

4. As students talk with their partners, walk around and take note of the ideas they are sharing as well as the language they are using.

5. Gather the class together and ask a few students to share their thinking. Share out ideas or language heard while monitoring students during the pair-share.

10/2 Lecture

A 10/2 Lecture, often called "chunk and chew," is a strategy that gives students time to reflect on 10 minutes, worth of information at a time. Art Costa (1991) studied how the mind works and thinks and concluded that people need time to process new information. The brain needs time to assemble, coordinate, integrate, monitor, and evaluate knowledge as it is being presented. When too much information is presented without time for comprehension, students can get lost.

The 10/2 Lecture is a way for students to keep up during a lengthy lecture or long interval of language input. When students are provided opportunities to stop and think about what they have heard, seen, or read, it not only builds comprehension but also helps students make connections.

During the *Explain* stage, the teacher presents key information around the learning objective. This information helps confirm or clarify ideas gathered during the *Engage* and *Explain* phases of the 5Es. The 10/2 Lecture strategy helps students connect to the previous learning as well as extend it in order to build deep comprehension.

How Do You Do It?

1. Present 10 minutes of information or content. This can be done as a traditional oral lecture, a PowerPoint presentation, or by reading a text, as appropriate to the audience and content.

2. After 10 minutes, pause and ask students to process what they have heard for two minutes by thinking about the information. Guide students' thinking using the following prompts:

   - Thinking about what I have just shared, what made sense to you? What are you still wondering about?

   - What have you understood about what I have shared?

   - Let's stop and think about what we have heard. Reflecting on your learning, what have you understood so far?

3. Continue to present information, pausing every 10 minutes to allow students time to think.

An alternative step in the 10/2 Lecture is a pair-share. After students have reflected independently, ask them to share their thinking with a partner before moving on. Whichever process is used, the purpose of the 10/2 Lecture is for students to have time to reflect on their thinking and learning.

Shared Reading

Based on the seminal work of Don Holdaway (1979), Shared Reading builds upon the early lap-reading experiences children share with caregivers in the home. A child sitting on his parent's lap or at his or her side can see how the book is organized and how readers make meaning as they read. Unlike a Read-Aloud, Shared Reading provides students with visible access to the text. Shared Reading gives students the experience of hearing and seeing what it means to read fluently and how print works on a page. Whether through a big book, a chart, a document camera, or individual copies of the text, students get to see the words on the page that the teacher is reading. While the teacher reads, the students are invited into the comprehension of the text. Though all students may not be able to read the text themselves, they can still successfully be part of the experience. They learn reading behaviors and gain new information.

Shared Reading is a great way to introduce students to informational text and provide access to challenging content. As the teacher reads the text, students are able to build their listening comprehension skills. They can focus on the content and not worry about decoding the text. All students will have access to the information.

During the *Explain* stage of the 5Es, students are often presented with text that supports the learning objective. The text may be used to clarify information or extend the learning introduced during *Engage* and *Explore*. A Shared Reading experience helps all students access the information.

How Do You Do It?

1. Select a text that supports your learning objective(s) and/or is necessary to clarify or extend information discovered during *Engage* and *Explore.*

2. Present the text in a format that provides visible access to all students.

3. Read the text, pausing to allow students time to engage in thinking about the content of the text. Ask questions, clarify key ideas, or use a Think-Pair-Share.

4. On occasion, use a think-aloud to model for students how you are making sense of the text.

5. Continue reading and inviting students into the comprehension of the text.

Interactive Read-Alouds/Think-Alouds

A Read-Aloud is an instructional method that provides students with exposure to content, language, and modeled reading. The teacher has the task of reading the text, allowing students to focus on the content of the text. When teachers read to students through a Read-Aloud, it offers an opportunity for students to access texts that may be too difficult for them to read on their own. It further exposes them to new academic language as they hear the flow of language while the teacher reads. Read-Alouds, unlike Shared Reading, utilize a single text that may or may not be clearly visible to students. When there are large pictures available, the teacher often shows the students the pictures to aid in their listening comprehension. Read-Alouds are a great way to share high-quality texts with students and invite them into the content of a story and the joy of reading.

A more structured Read-Aloud, the Interactive Read-Aloud asks teachers to set clear objectives for the reading with predetermined comprehension checkpoints and ongoing Think-Alouds. Prior to reading the text to the class, the teacher decides where to chunk the text and check students' listening comprehension. These checks for understanding can include a quick pair-share or a whole-group check-in. The key is to stop at places where you might want to highlight a key idea or where the content or language may pose a challenge for students. This gives the teacher an opportunity to clarify the information prior to continuing to read. This will guide students' listening comprehension throughout the reading of the text.

In addition to planning for comprehension checkpoints throughout the text, Interactive Read-Alouds provide great opportunities for teachers to model language and reading behaviors through Think-Alouds. Think-Alouds are an instructional approach whereby the teacher makes his or her thinking process transparent to students. While reading, the teacher can pause and share out loud his or her thinking about the text. The use of Think-Alouds not only shows students how to process the information but also models the language a reader should use when drawing meaning from text. Students get an opportunity to hear academic language being used as the teacher thinks about and learns from the text. This is the language we would expect students to use when asked to share their thinking as well. What is essential when using a Think-Aloud is to plan points in the text to pause and share thinking. Places to recount key content, review important language, or model a literacy strategy should all be considered. Interactive Think-Alouds can also be used during Shared and Guided Reading experiences.

Interactive Read-Alouds with Think-Alouds are effective methods to use during the *Explain* stage of the 5Es. At this stage of the process, students are sharing the learning acquired up to this point in the 5E cycle and teachers are providing additional information to clarify misconceptions and preconceptions. Sharing a text can provide clarifying information, while the Think-Aloud further demonstrates the language used to communicate thoughts. For English language learners, Interactive Read-Alouds with Think-Alouds provide support in listening comprehension and academic language development.

How Do You Do It?

1. Select a text that supports the lesson or unit learning objectives and/or is necessary to clarify or extend information provided during *Engage* or *Explore*.

2. Chunk the text into sections, noting strategic points in which language or concepts should be clarified or discussed. Mark your preplanned stopping points with a sticky note, if desired.

3. Read the first text chunk aloud to students, pausing at the predetermined location.

4. *Engage* in a Think-Aloud to model the targeted concepts for students, such as reviewing a key concept, explaining vocabulary, and modeling a comprehension strategy. Call on students to share their thinking as well.

5. Repeat for the remaining sections of the text.

AB Partner Share

....

AB Partner Share is a reading partnership strategy that helps students process information. After reading or listening to information, students have a chance to ask and answer a question with a partner. This helps students rehearse the language of asking questions and giving information. In addition, students take time to process the information with a partner. Similar to the Think-Pair-Share strategy, students get a chance to clarify information or extend their thinking.

During the *Explain* stage of the 5Es, students have already learned a great deal of information. But they have also generated questions to be further explored during *Explain*. This strategy helps students further process new information and continue to question their learning. The teacher guides the questions, often explicitly providing the question to be asked. This helps build students' academic language as teachers carefully craft questions based on the content and based on students' academic language development levels.

How Do You Do It?

1. Read or present content, either in whole or in part.

2. Pause and ask students a question.

3. Pair the class up and direct students to designate an A and a B partner. To ensure that each partnership has an A and a B, ask the pairs to identify who the A partner is and who the B partner is.

4. Partner A should ask partner B the question you presented in Step 2. Partner B should then answer the question.

5. Pairs reverse the roles, with partner B asking the question and partner A responding.

6. Continue to read or present information, pausing to ask questions.

7. Repeat Steps 3–6.

Assessing ELLs in *Explain*

The goal of assessment for ELLs in the *Explain* stage of the 5E model is to determine whether academic language has been acquired to the degree that students can communicate what they know using specific content-related vocabulary and language forms. Finding out how students can express themselves orally and in writing helps the teacher monitor progress along a language-proficiency continuum. Since *Explain* requires greater emphasis on focused, explicit language instruction, teachers place greater emphasis on evaluating language performance. In other words, there is an expectation that students will use the language they have been taught as they articulate the conceptual knowledge they have attained.

The scenarios in this chapter provide examples of how teachers evaluate language performance through oral interactions, charted responses, and other learning archives, specifically science notebooks for science instruction. It is important to note that all of the teacher examplars actively interact with students and circulate among groups or pairs to listen attentively to how they orally express their understanding. These teachers have devised methods in which they efficiently use anecdotal notebooks, data-collection charts, or evaluation rosters to capture how and when students use the target vocabulary and language forms. Miss Gonzalez keeps tabs on language performance by adding students' initials to all recorded responses on charts or the board. Mrs. Huang and Mr. Asaad design their instruction so that they have frequent opportunities to circulate among students to hear and see how they use language.

Although students make entries in their science notebooks throughout the 5E cycle, several teachers emphasize the use of particular language in notebook entries during *Explain*. They specifically call students' attention to available language artifacts and establish a language focus for their entries.

Science Notebooks as ELL Assessment in *Explain*

In *Engage*, the science notebook is used as an additional tool to diagnose the language that students bring to instruction so that changes in their language use can be monitored. Science notebook entries in *Explore* are preceded by expanded periods of talking and thinking. As a tool for language development, they provide ELLs with opportunities to try out language connected to their discoveries in scientific exploration.

In *Explain*, language is developed with considerable specificity and purpose as students are expected to articulate conceptual knowledge. Supported by multiple opportunities for oral rehearsal and clarification, the notebook entries in this chapter expect students to explain what they know about particular concepts by utilizing specific academic content language to express their thinking. At this juncture in the inquiry cycle, teachers are able to use notebook entries to evaluate language as well as learning. The notebook serves as a window into how the student is thinking about a particular concept as well as how he or she can use language to reflect thinking. Figure 6.14 shows a sample notebook entry from an Early-Advanced level fourth-grade student who is learning about magnets. In this entry, she shares what she has come to understand about magnets at the close of the *Explain* stage. She is able to use academic terminology (e.g., *attract, repel,* and *force*) appropriately to communicate some basic understanding.

Figure 6.14 Early Advanced Student's Notebook Entry

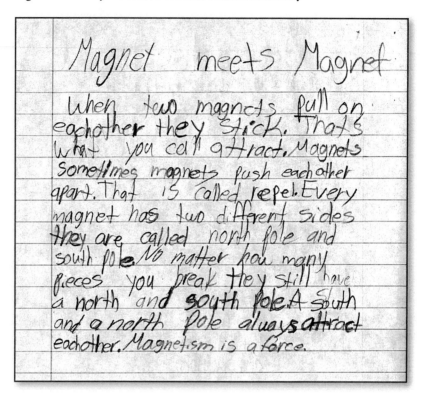

Magnet meets Magnet

When two magnets pull on eachother they stick. That's what you call attract. Magnets Sometimes magnets push eachother apart. That is called repel. Every magnet has two different sides they are called north pole and south pole. No matter how many pieces you break they still have a north and south pole. A south and a north pole always attract eachother. Magnetism is a force.

Notebooks can also be utilized as repositories for words students should know and remember. Writing in notebooks encourages students to think about the structure and meaning of the words. The following entries come from a fourth-grade class in which the majority of the students are English language learners. Since language is essential for her students' understanding of science, she has integrated a language support component into her notebooks that aids the English language development of her English language learners in specific ways: a word study, a glossary, and a list of Spanish and English terms.

Figure 6.15 Sample Word Study

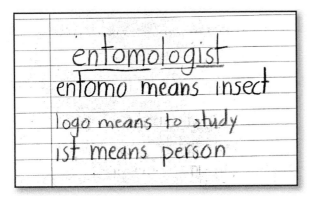

entomologist
entomo means insect
logo means to study
ist means person

Figure 6.16 Sample List of Spanish and English Terms

Spanish Page

atoms - atomos
circuit - circuito
bulb - foco
wire - cable / alambre
D-cell - pila
filamento - filamento
insulator - insulador
conductor - conductor
bright - brillante
din - oscuro
electron - electrones
neutron - neutrones
proton - protón
switch - regulador
motor - motor
rivet - remache
series circuit - circuito en serio
parallel circuit - circuito para leto
electromagnet - electroimán
electricity - electricida

Figure 6.17 Sample Glossary

Word	Definition	Picture
telegraph	A device that uses an elecetromagnet to send coded messages by closing and opening an electric circuit.	rivet, switch, wire, D-cell
code	A set of signals that represents letters or words for sending messages	CLOUD 2 1 4 6 8
gap	A little space beetween something	Gap

Tips for Planning *Explain* for ELLs

When planning *Explain* for English language learners, consider the following:

- Carefully examine available text resources. Search for alternative multimedia formats that will make the content accessible for students through interaction with multisensory or technological features. Select texts that match your language goals and that are aligned to the language strengths and needs of your students. Consider creating your own narration of the content that is better suited to the proficiency level of your students.

- Identify and plan how you will input the targeted academic language in your instruction through strategies, reading, visual representations, or thinking tasks.

- Create optimal opportunity for students to receive comprehensible language input and to practice and use the language meaningfully.

- Thoughtfully designed tasks in this stage ensure that students have ample time to interact with one another and the instructional materials.

- Make sure that your students are grouped either heterogeneously or homogeneously in small enough numbers to ensure comfort and the opportunity to be heard and to listen to others talk and explain their ideas.

- Circulate and interact with students for the ongoing assessment of language strengths and needs.

- Utilize varied grouping patterns in order to maximize opportunities for students to practice and use the language.

- Determine the appropriate format for science notebook entries to best stimulate the use of academic language to express content understanding.

Reflect on Wonderings

1. How can you identify the language targets (vocabulary, functions, forms) for explicit language instruction?

2. What preparation will you need to do to ensure that your students have opportunities to develop and rehearse their explanations?

3. Which tools and resources will assist you in designing instructional tasks for optimal academic language development?

4. What techniques will allow you to consistently and frequently monitor the language performance of ELLs in your teaching?

CHAPTER 7

Academic Language Performance Through *Extend*

You May Wonder:

- What do I need to think about to promote the academic language development, practice, and usage for English language learners in *Extend*?

- In what ways can I support deeper understanding of language through science in *Extend*?

- How do I approach the assessment of students' language performance in the *Extend* phase?

As you have seen in previous chapters, language-development instruction is integrated strategically within all stages of the 5E model, building on the unique features of each stage of scientific inquiry. *Extend*, in this 5E process, offers an opportune time for students to synthesize their science and language learning as they transfer their understanding to new contexts. This chapter will begin with the featured classroom scenario and highlight important instructional elements for the *Extend* stage that promote the academic language proficiency of English language learners.

Ms. Cortez's Class—Grade 2 Scenario
ELD Levels: Early Intermediate and Intermediate
A Glimpse at English Language Learner Instruction
During Extend

In the following scenario, Ms. Cortez facilitates a language opportunity focused on parts of speech. Because precise language is a feature of scientific discourse, she wants to highlight and extend the language that students have been acquiring in their study of earthworms. This language work will be applied in conjunction with their understanding of science concepts as students analyze a video later in the lesson.

In the front of the room, there is a chart written on butcher paper with the following four headings across the top (in this order): *Adjectives, Nouns, Verbs,* and *Prepositional Phrases.*

To provide additional visual support, photographs of earthworms are placed at the students' tables. Ms. Cortez tells her students that everyone has been learning a lot about earthworms. In particular, they have been learning new language that has helped them talk scientifically about earthworms.

Ms. Cortez: *A special feature about the language that scientists use is that it has to be detailed or precise in order to vividly describe what they have learned and create a picture in our minds.* (She holds up a photograph.) *In today's lesson we are going to gather together and practice all the precise language we have learned before we continue learning about earthworms.*

First, Ms. Cortez writes the word *earthworms* in the *Nouns* column. She reinforces the idea that the word *earthworms* is a noun. Then, she asks the students to pair-share words that describe earthworms. After about two minutes, she brings the students to attention and asks for descriptors. As the students share their responses (e.g., *reddish, brownish, wiggly, shiny, sticky*), the teacher writes the words in the *Adjectives* column. She explains that words that describe nouns are called *adjectives*. She asks the students to choral-read their responses, guiding them to the words listed in each column.

Next, Ms. Cortez asks the students for action words for the movement that earthworms make. The students share their responses with a partner. Afterward, the students call out their responses (e.g., *wiggle, slide, slither, dig, stretch*) as the teacher writes the words in the third column. She explains that all of these words describe the earthworms' behavior, or what the earthworms can do. These words are *verbs*.

Ms. Cortez notices that the students have not called out a new word that was introduced earlier in their inquiry. She knows that some students have been using it instead of the word *dig*.

Ms. Cortez: *Like scientists, we closely observed behaviors of earthworms. Here you have given me the word* dig. *Can someone tell me more about this behavior? What was the earthworm doing precisely?*

Isabel: *He was digging. He was digging underground.*

Ms. Cortez: *I heard you say that you observed that he was digging underground. Let's think. When you use a shovel, you dig. The earthworm did not have a shovel. Is there another word we can use to describe what the earthworm was doing in the ground?* (She makes digging gestures with her hands.)

Brian: (Gesturing with hands.) *Burrowing.*

Ms. Cortez: *Another way we can describe this digging behavior is with the word* burrow. *We can say that earthworms burrow. Say that with me. I am going to write the word* burrow. *That is a precise word that scientists would use.*

For the last column, Ms. Cortez asks the students to first think about places where earthworms could live. Then, after they have had some "think time" the students share their ideas with a partner. As previously demonstrated, the teacher writes the students' responses on the chart under *Prepositional Phrases.* The students share phrases such as *beneath the grass, in moist places, underground,* and *in the garden.* She explains that words such as *beneath, in,* and *on* are prepositions. When those prepositions are combined with a noun, they are called *prepositional phrases.* At this point, the students have been exposed to these terms and are not at the usage stage, but with time and lots of repetition, the students will master these grammatical terms. Below is the chart that was created:

Adjectives	Nouns	Verbs	Prepositional Phrases
shiny	earthworms	wiggle	in moist places
wiggly		slide	in the garden
sticky		slither	beneath the grass
slippery		dig	
reddish		stretch	
brownish		burrow	

The final task for this activity is to compose a grammatically correct sentence using the familiar tune of "The Farmer in the Dell." First, students select three adjectives. Then, they vote on a verb, and finally, they choose a prepositional phrase. Ms. Cortez underlines the words the students select and points to each of the words as she sings the first example.

Ms. Cortez: (Singing) *Reddish, sticky earthworms; Reddish, sticky earthworms; Reddish, sticky, wiggly earthworms burrow beneath the grass.*

The students then join in as the sentence is repeated. As a group, another sentence is composed. Then in partners, students create their own sentences and write them down in their science notebooks. Noise fills the room as the students sing their descriptive sentences with prepositional phrases.

Now that the students have more precise language that they can use to talk about earthworms, Ms. Cortez prepares them for their next task. She tells them that they are going to study, or analyze, a video for the information it shows about earthworms.

She shows brief clips of the short video, pausing once to allow the students to briefly talk about what they have seen. When the students have seen the complete video, Ms. Cortez asks the students to open their science notebooks to the descriptive sentences they have just created.

Ms. Cortez: *Did you see any of the behaviors that you have on your list?*

Two students read aloud an item from their notebook.

Next, Ms. Cortez provides all the students with an extended opportunity to share information about what they saw through the use of the Think-Pair-Share strategy (see Chapter 6). She asks them to take their science notebooks with them for the pair-share in order to review language forms they can use to share their information. Such language forms include *I saw _____. But, I didn't see _____.*, and *An important fact I learned about earthworms is _____.*

She models the task with a student, showing how they can use the language forms and their science notebooks as resources to think and talk scientifically about the video. Students face their partners and take turns sharing out what they saw and did not see in the video. This lasts about five minutes as Ms. Cortez moves through the room listening, taking notes on her clipboard, and prompting students to share out as needed.

Finally, Ms. Cortez brings the group together on the rug where they talk about what was not included in the video. She asks whether the video left out important information about earthworms and prompts the students to explain their thinking. She encourages them to reference the information they have in their science notebooks by asking them to put a check mark next to what is shared in the whole group discussion. Ms. Cortez explains that their next step is to create a script with pictures, called a storyboard, for their own class video on earthworms and tells them to be extra careful to think about and include all the important facts they have been learning. Once the storyboards are done, they will present their video scripts to the class.

She displays a storyboard with space for captions beneath each box. She tells students that they will work in teams to think about the important information that must be included and complete the storyboard. Ms. Cortez asks the class to give her an important fact they think must be in the class video. She models how to create a quick sketch and caption using the information displayed around the classroom in charts, books, photos, and the students' science notebooks. She is careful to model using precise scientific language, reminding students once again about the language resources they have just entered in their science notebooks. Students are sent to assigned tables with their notebooks to begin the task. Ms. Cortez actively circulates among the groups to support them in elaborating on their conceptual understanding and language application. They have a few minutes to start on their plan and will continue their collaboration the following day.

What Is *Extend* for English Language Learners?

The words *extend* and *elaborate* are often used interchangeably to describe this stage of the inquiry cycle. Regardless of which term is used to label it, the focus of this stage is on providing students with the opportunity to put their learning into practice, extending their exploration of scientific concepts in such a way that allows them to use what they have learned in a new context. Students get the opportunity to carry out a new project that involves the thinking and language processes they have developed to this point. Too often, students are heavily guided in their learning but not provided enough opportunities to apply their learning. Without the opportunity to transfer their knowledge into new contexts, students may not reach the deep level of understanding that leads to long-term retention.

Figure 7.1 Student Generated Poster

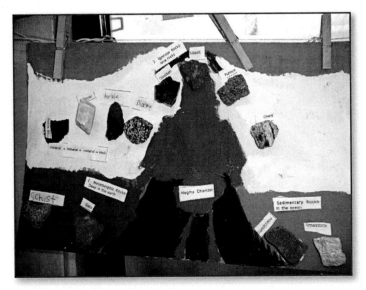

Creating a poster to exemplify learning provides another context for applying new knowledge.

Within the 5E ELD framework, *Extend* must also provide the opportunity to deepen the understanding and usage of academic language for English language learners. The instruction thus far has been aimed at moving ELLs successfully toward using the language of the curriculum as they progress through the 5Es. Students in earlier scenarios have had numerous and varied comprehensible experiences doing, thinking about, and talking about science.

At this stage, the instructional opportunities build on newly acquired academic language by applying the language in new situations. Language that is normally beyond student comprehension is much more likely to be understood and used effectively when students bring previous experience and understanding as a basis for interpretation. Teachers will give students the opportunity to elaborate on and extend their understanding of language in order to increase their academic language proficiency. Students are encouraged and enabled to clearly describe events, to account for outcomes, and to summarize in words what they have learned. Literature is viewed as a source of academic expression as well as scientific understanding. The goal for language is to gain access to the discourse of science. This stage also provides an opportunity for teachers to evaluate how English language learners use newly-developed language in new contexts.

Figure 7.2 Dissection Activity

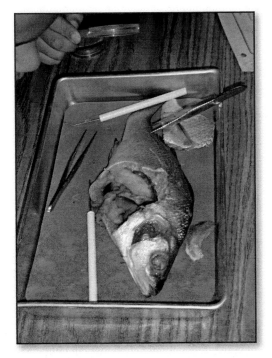

Applying book knowledge to a real context extends students' learning. This experience may develop a future biologist!

Promoting Academic Language Performance Through *Extend*

In the scenarios presented in this chapter, greater emphasis has been placed on describing the language component of instruction to highlight support for English language development. The importance of the extended content experience as the catalyst for using and reusing the language meaningfully should not be discounted. A thinking-and-doing curriculum is imperative for the language development of ELLs. The essential practices and language strategies we depict in the scenarios serve as valuable tools that promote the application and internalization of language.

Figure 7.3 Essential Features for Developing Academic Language in *Extend*

- Ensuring a gradual release of responsibility for language production

- Employing teacher-student exchanges that compel students to use appropriate scientific discourse

- Extending students' linguistic resources through planned cognitively engaging social interaction

- Deepening academic language competence through novel applications of language and science understanding

Ensuring a Gradual Release of Responsibility for Language Production

A long-established goal of second language instruction is that as students acquire more language, the teacher's dominance in language production will diminish (see Chapter 2). This gradual release of responsibility for talk manifests itself strongly in the *Extend* stage. Instruction in this stage is designed to allow students to use the language they have been developing, with a reduction in explicit language instruction or heavily guided facilitation. Regardless of their English language proficiency level, ELLs must be given ample and appropriate opportunities to think about and use the language they have been acquiring in order to independently communicate their scientific knowledge.

In our featured second-grade scenario, Ms. Cortez guides her students through a progression of steps that gradually shifts the responsibility or control of language use from the teacher to the students. The beginning segment involves students in language tasks that are heavily facilitated by Ms. Cortez and the graphic-organizer structure. As the students watch the video and discuss its content with a partner, the level of facilitation diminishes. The teacher's role is to listen in and provide limited support. Ms. Cortez is able to naturally monitor students for their use of the syntactic structure created in "The Farmer in the Dell" as they share their learning. She will continue to release responsibility as students have the opportunity to independently collaborate on a group project, thus taking on complete autonomy for language production.

Employing Teacher-Student Exchanges Using Scientific Discourse

A language behavior that is important to note is that when eliciting language from English language learners, they will often provide simpler language. Along with the goal of gradually releasing responsibility for language performance, a critical role for the teacher of ELLs will always be to mediate, or push, students beyond their comfort zones toward using higher academic language, appropriate for the students' level. While recognizing that language mediation is employed in the other 5E stages, note that there is a particular emphasis in *Extend* on the teachers' role to provide linguistic scaffolds through questioning, prompting, and even the design of tasks that support the communication flow of their students. The mediating practices in *Extend* focus on giving students access to elaborate ways of expressing the meaning they wish to create. Thereby, students continue to rehearse language structures that are closer to formal academic discourse. The teacher's questions allow for students to extend their responses as they probe deeper into thinking about what they have learned. The teacher leads from behind, recasting or reformulating what the student says to model options for language that are more appropriate in the context of talking about science. Recasting and support is precisely timed so that learning is confirmed and the student is supported in using appropriate language for talking about science.

In Chapter 6, as Ms. Cortez develops academic language in *Explain*, she also skillfully leads her students to be mindful of and use scientific language to express their understanding of earthworm behavior.

Ms. Cortez notices that her students have not called out a new word that was introduced earlier in their inquiry. She knows that some students have been using it instead of the word *dig*.

Ms. Cortez: *Like scientists, we closely observed behaviors of earthworms. Here you have given me the word* dig. *Can someone tell me more about this behavior? What was the earthworm doing precisely?*

Isabel: *He was digging. He was digging underground.*

Ms. Cortez: *I heard you say that you observed the he was digging underground. Let's think. When you use a shovel, you dig. The earthworm did not have a shovel. Is there another word we can use to describe what the earthworm was doing in the ground?* (She makes digging gestures with her hands.)

Brian: (Gesturing with hands.) *Burrowing.*

Ms. Cortez: *Another way we can describe this digging behavior is with the word* burrow. *We can say that earthworms burrow. Say that with me. I am going to write the word burrow. That is a precise word that scientists would use.*

Ms. Cortez leads students to remember and use the term *burrowing* by building on what they have observed and understood. She uses gestures and restates the known term, *dig*, to connect to what the students are familiar with. When Brian provides the more academic term, she recasts his statement using the academic term. She also reaffirms a relevant purpose for using the academic term, which is to speak "like a scientist."

Extending Students' Linguistic Resources Through Social Interaction

In this stage, the planning and design of particular types of interactive tasks assumes prominence. The *Extend* focus challenges students with tasks that demand that they apply their critical thinking and problem-solving skills through periods of extended language usage, not simply a language rehearsal. For ELLs, a well-designed *Extend* task should compel them to talk, think, and interact with peers within the broader context of their science-content knowledge.

Coming together through cognitively engaging social interaction around shared experiences can ensure that partners or group members will share similar ideas about their thinking in a variety of different ways. New vocabulary verbalized within collaborative structures is articulated by the students. The need to get information or clarify meaning increases the opportunities for learners to ask questions that genuinely seek new information. Thus, there is further input and practice in authentic communication. As they move through the task, students enter scientific discourse with the resources they have acquired, taking on the role of experts. Asking questions, exchanging information, and solving problems in interactive tasks provide a context in which words are repeated, ideas are rephrased, problems are restated, and meanings are refined.

The best-designed tasks have clear procedures and expectations. They are open-ended, allowing students to have partial or complete control over how the task will be completed. The teacher takes on a secondary role of monitoring on-task behavior and adherence to procedural steps. Because of the release of responsibility for direct teaching, the teacher has additional opportunities to monitor and assist language usage as needed on an individual basis. Moreover, less-proficient learners who are not confident in English often feel more comfortable working with more proficient peers than performing in a whole-class situation. Individuals are scaffolded by the language and learning of the group as a whole.

Deepening Academic Language Competence Through Novel Applications

Taking up, or *appropriating*, new language is clearly an aim of second-language development. This refers to the ability of English language learners to use the new language competently to communicate what they know across varied contexts. Novel applications of language in an atypical genre or through a different modality challenge students to think deeply about what they know as well as the forms of oral and written expression they have at their command to express their understanding. As the language they have acquired through science inquiry is used for different purposes and/or audiences, students will naturally be involved in exploring distinctions between forms of language and discourse. For example, a nondisciplinary science task such as dramatization requires students to manipulate the information, ideas, and language they have previously developed in order to synthesize, generalize, explain, and interpret. Through novel applications of scientific conceptual knowledge and academic language (e.g., writing a haiku about rocks), students have the opportunity to transform what they have learned into different forms, representing their knowledge in a new medium or artifact.

By this stage, the language ability and content knowledge students have acquired should empower them to approach any kind of related task or problem creatively and they should be able to see it from multiple perspectives. Because of the learning and experiences that have occurred, students should have the ability to read any new context in a fresh way. Some novel applications, such as creating a brochure or a family conservation plan, not only compel students to think and talk critically and creatively about what they have learned but also serve as valuable and authentic purposes.

Figure 7.4 Sample Novel Application in *Extend*

Integrating art into science opens vup opportunities for application, creativity, and more talk.

Figure 7.5 Sample Novel Application in *Extend*

This model allows the student to demonstrate his learning and critical thinking about the life cycle of the sea turtle, regardless of English proficiency level.

The second-grade scenario provides two examples of this type of application. The first example occurs as the students sing using the concept-related language with the familiar tune "The Farmer in the Dell." The integration of music engages these students in a new way of thinking and talking about what they know about earthworms. A second example of an atypical multimodal application is creating the storyboard for an earthworm video in collaborative groups. This task moves beyond a mere written report of information to involve the use of visuals and scripts. The goal of Ms. Cortez's lesson is to help her English language learners manipulate language in a novel way, thereby strengthening their language competence as they move toward appropriating stronger scientific discourse.

An additional application of this practice for students with a more advanced level of English proficiency would be to include an additional column in the parts of speech chart, labeled *Adverbs*, which would follow the *Verbs* column. This would challenge students to create a more complex sentence (e.g., *Reddish, sticky, wiggly earthworms burrow slowly beneath the grass.*).

Examining ELD Practices in *Extend*

In the previous section, several ELL practices that are essential instructional features of the *Extend* stage were described. These examples referred specifically to the second-grade classroom inquiry of earthworms. This section continues the analysis of notable ELD practices during *Extend* by focusing on additional scenarios from kindergarten, second-grade, and fourth-grade classrooms. Within these scenarios are examples of the essential features for developing academic language that have been adapted for varied language-proficiency levels as well as for grade-level maturation expectations. Additionally, strategies that were introduced in earlier chapters have been repurposed for this stage of the 5E learning cycle to provide students with more opportunities to speak like scientists.

Mrs. Kakuda's Class—Kindergarten Scenario
ELD Level: Beginning

Since the students have been learning about the similarities and differences of animal coverings, Mrs. Kakuda repurposes the Four Corners strategy in combination with the Shared Reading approach so that her students can apply their basic understanding of animal coverings. She is confident that the students will be even more successful in the second execution of these activities since these are familiar instructional procedures.

Using Shared Reading, Mrs. Kakuda repeatedly reads *Sheep in a Jeep* by Nancy Shaw (1997), a rollicking tale about sheep who get stuck in their jeep. During the first read, she asks the students to make predictions. Making explicit predictions encourages active learning and keeps students interested. In subsequent readings, she uses the illustrations along with physical movement and the text to make meaning of verbs such as *shove, grunt, leap* and *shrug*. She also explains the development of the story as these sheep attempt to get the jeep out of the mud.

After a few readings, she shows the students a ball of raw wool.

Mrs. Kakuda:	*What animal is covered in wool?* (Several students call out that sheep are covered in wool or point to the illustration of sheep in a jeep on the book cover.)
Samara:	*My uncle has a ranch. He has sheep. He cuts the wool.*

Mrs. Kakuda confirms the connections her students make:

Mrs. Kakuda:	*Yes, the bodies of the sheep in the story are also covered in wool.*

Then, Mrs. Kakuda walks to each of the four corners of the classroom and places a different picture book at each corner.

Mrs. Kakuda: *Let's see how these books can help us use what we have been learning in science. (As she places a book at each corner, she reads each title:* I Like Myself *by Karen Beaumont,* Bear Shadow *by Frank Asch,* Little Green *by Keith Baker, and* Fish is Fish *by Leo Lionni. At each corner, she prompts the students.)* What animal covering does this animal have? What other animals have the same covering?

She provokes student responses carefully and patiently as they identify various types of body coverings.

Afterward, the students are directed to select a picture card of an animal from the table and walk to the corner that corresponds to the type of covering that that animal has. For example, one student chooses a flamingo. First, he has to remember that feathers cover the body of a flamingo. Then, the student has to make the association that the hummingbird in *Little Green* also has feathers and walk to that corner. Once in their corners, the students are prompted to share their cards by talking like scientists about what they know about body coverings.

Notable ELD Practices

Inherent challenges for students in accomplishing this task are the multiple levels of cognition and language required of the ELLs in this kindergarten classroom. By this stage in the 5E process, students have had significant amounts of comprehensible input and guided opportunities to practice the new language as they develop an understanding of varied animal body coverings. Mrs. Kakuda has designed a task that releases the responsibility to her students for thinking and talking about what they have learned. Through the use of familiar picture books and photographs, students are supported in making important applications and connections and in more closely mirroring scientific discourse.

Figure 7.6 Song Activity

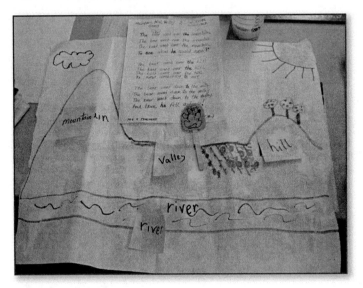

With simple props and a familiar tune, students can practice language structures to build fluency.

Additionally, it is important to reiterate that students at this age require various opportunities for language development in multiple contexts. The most appropriate setting is play-based learning that comes from scientific exploration and discovery. For example, after a trip to the park to identify animals and name their coverings, students might continue to practice their knowledge with puppets. At the beginning, the teacher will take part in their play as is evidenced in the following example:

Mrs. Kakuda:	(Pulling a squirrel puppet over her hand.) *Hi, I'm a squirrel. I live at the park. My fur keeps me warm.*
Rachel:	*Woof! Woof! I am going to chase you.*
Mrs. Kakuda:	*I am going to climb a tree. You can't catch me! I see that you have fur, too! Dogs have fur, too. Donaldo, you have a scaly fish.*
Donaldo:	*I gonna to get you.*
Mrs. Kakuda:	*Look! You aren't covered with fur. Fish do not have fur. What covers a fish?*
Donaldo:	*Scale.*
Mrs. Kakuda:	*I wonder why a fish is covered with scales and not fur.*

The opportunity to apply what Donaldo understands and can articulate is realized in this brief exchange. The teacher exploits the playful novelty of a hand puppet to prompt Donaldo's language use through artful questioning and recasting.

Mr. Rutherford's Class—Grade 2 Scenario
ELD Level: Intermediate

In this classroom, Mr. Rutherford has developed a series of lessons around the concept that different materials make different sounds. Prior to today's instruction, he has guided his students in exploring the sounds of objects made of metal, wood, and plastic. Students have explored and understood the different sounds made by different materials. The evidence of their previous exploration is displayed throughout the classroom.

Based on past explorations, Mr. Rutherford developed a chart of sound words with his students and has posted it on a classroom wall.

Wood		Metal		Plastic	
Object	**Sound**	**Object**	**Sound**	**Object**	**Sound**
rhythm sticks	clickity-click	pie tins	bang	yogurt cups	clip-clop
maracas	chaca-chaca	bells	ding, tinkle	pvc tubing	click
blocks	sh-sh-sh	keys	jangle	bottle tops	tic-tic

The class has also previously explored and discovered other dimensions of sound related to amplitude, such as *loud* and *soft*. A second two-column chart was co-created and posted on the wall. It lists instruments that have loud sounds and instruments that have soft sounds.

To further explore sound, the students constructed simple sound boxes out of cardboard boxes, metal fasteners, and rubber bands (see Figure 7.7). They discovered that different actions also produce different sounds. Thus, the class developed an action-word bank that was posted on the wall. It included words such as *scratch, flick, bang, knock, rub, pluck,* and *tap*. The class also created a chart showing the relationship between vibration and the quality of the sound. This chart recorded the following information:

Action (or movement)	Pitch (high or low)	Vibration Features
flick	high	tighter, stiffer = tension

Figure 7.7 Sound Box

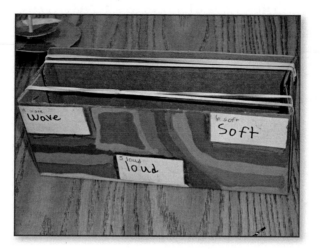

Today, Mr. Rutherford tells the students that they will make an adaptation to their sound-box instruments so that they make a new and different sound. He tells them that he wants them to learn more about what causes different sounds. He holds up an example of a sound-box instrument and plucks the rubber band wrapped around its middle.

Mr. Rutherford: *Who can describe the sound that it makes? What is the volume, or* amplitude, *of the sound it makes? What action did I use to make the sound? Who can explain what causes the sound we hear?*

The students respond to Mr. Rutherford's questions using some of the vocabulary inputted in previous learning activities.

Mr. Rutherford: *You're really sounding like scientists! I want to challenge you now to think harder about what you have learned about sound and vibration. What can I do to change the sound this instrument makes?*

The students' hands shoot up.

Mr. Rutherford: *Before you tell the whole class, rehearse your idea with a partner.*

The students share using a Think-Pair-Share structure.

Mr. Rutherford: *Who is ready to share an idea?*

Paola: *Hit the box with a stick.*

Jun: *I think use a different box.*

Eden: *Move the rubber band so it's tighter.*

After each response, the teacher probes further:

Mr. Rutherford: *Why does that change the sound?*

This allows the students to review some of the concepts and language they have been developing as they offer answers.

Ernesto: *The volume is louder.*

Eileen: *The vibration wave is stronger.*

Mr. Rutherford: *Now it's your turn, scientists, to think of a way to change the sound of your instrument by changing one thing, or what scientists call one variable. Repeat the word after me,* variable. (Students repeat the word in unison.) *You have to be able to report three things to your fellow scientists in the room: One, what you changed; two, the new sound it makes; and three, what you believe happened to the vibration or sound waves to make it change.*

Mr. Rutherford shows the students sample frames he has written on the board at the front of the room. He tells the students that they can use the frames to report their findings to their partner, if needed: *I changed _____. Now my instrument sounds like _____. It makes this sound because _____.*

At their tables, students work with an assortment of materials, including plastic bottles, cans, jars, and wooden boxes along with rubber bands in a variety of thicknesses, craft sticks, tape, and brads. They record the changes in their science notebooks. Mr. Rutherford circulates among the students to focus them on getting started and to help them complete the steps of the task on their own as much as possible. Meanwhile, students are making changes that create fast and slow sound waves. They are alternating plucking with strumming. They are changing some of the materials. They call out excitedly to one another and the teacher, reporting on the changes in their instruments and the effect on the sound. Mr. Rutherford encourages them to express their thinking and reasoning:

Mr. Rutherford: *I like the adaptation you made. Remember, you're going to report your findings to a fellow scientist. How would a scientist explain what he or she is doing? Where can you find the words that you can use to talk like a scientist?*

After a period of 20 minutes, Mr. Rutherford asks the students to take their sound boxes and their science notebooks to a large space located on one side of the room. He explains that the strategy they will be using to report their adaptations will be Inside/Outside Circles, which the students have used before. He helps the students split into two equal groups and then stand in two concentric circles facing a partner. Before starting, Mr. Rutherford asks for two students to volunteer how they will share with a partner. He brings the two students to the middle of the circles, where he guides them to model how to share their report with a partner.

Mr. Rutherford asks the students who are in the inner circle to raise their hands to signal where they are.

> **Mr. Rutherford:** *You will report first. When you are finished, raise your hands to let me know.*

The room fills with noise as the students in the inner circle begin to share. Mr. Rutherford walks around to listen. He quickly adds notes to a roster on his clipboard. When all of the students have signaled that they are finished, he shares aloud what he heard students say and do.

> **Mr. Rutherford:** *I saw students listening closely and carefully. I saw students demonstrating the sound their instruments make. I heard students reporting their findings using their science notebooks. That was a great time of sharing! Now, the students in the outer circle will report.*

Once again, Mr. Rutherford walks around to listen. He quickly adds notes to the roster on his clipboard. After a few minutes, the teacher raises his hand and asks the students to stop. Once everyone has stopped, Mr. Rutherford comments on what he heard and saw:

> **Mr. Rutherford:** *I heard a student explain that the vibration was caused by moving his hand back and forth. That made him think of the tension he created. What an interesting finding! Did anyone else hear something interesting from a fellow scientist?*

| Eileen: | *Strumming vibrates soft.* |

| Mr. Rutherford: | *It is interesting to know that strumming can make an instrument vibrate softly.* |

The teacher then asks that the students who are standing in the outer circle move two students to the right. Now they are facing a new partner.

| Mr. Rutherford: | *Now, you get to learn something from a new scientist. The inner circle will report first, and then the outer circle will share. Raise your hands when both partners are finished.* |

Mr. Rutherford moves around the room, adding information to his clipboard. After approximately six to eight minutes, the majority of students have finished and have their hands raised. Mr. Rutherford asks some students to share their findings out loud.

| Enrique: | *I changed how tight my rubber band is. I hear pitch. High. I see the rubber band move fast like waves.* |

| Daniel: | *I used to have a box. Now it's a jar. When I pluck it, I hear a hm-hm-hm when it vibrates.* |

| Leslie: | *When I do this,* (shakes the box with two brads inside) *it makes rat-a-tat sound when it shakes. It makes the sound because it vibrates hard.* |

After a third round of sharing, Mr. Rutherford directs the students to set their sound boxes on their desks before sitting on the rug in front of the following chart:

Focus Question: What happens when I change a variable in my instrument?			
Variable	How did you change the pitch or the volume of your sound?	How did the sound change?	Why did the sound change?
Action			
Material			
Position			
Other			

He tells the students that he likes the way they are thinking and talking about science.

Mr. Rutherford: *There is so much that you discovered. We're going to use the chart to display your findings and your understanding of the features of sound and vibration.*

He asks for the students who changed an action to raise their hands. After he lists their names, he quickly notes the actions they changed, the sound that was created, and the reasons students think the sound changed. He repeats this procedure for students who changed the material they used as their variable and for the group of students who changed the position/location of materials. He creates a category for students who changed a variable other than *action, material,* or *position.*

He will use the information on the chart along with his anecdotal notes and individual student science notebooks to determine how he will approach the next stage in the 5E cycle.

Figure 7.8 Stepbooks

Stepbooks can serve as a tool for students to retrieve academic language.

Notable ELD Practices

Mr. Rutherford provides his Intermediate-level students with multiple opportunities for language practice through a purposeful sequence of instruction. Prior to this lesson the students engaged in extensive exploration of sound and were guided through a process of developing charts to depict sounds that were heard, actions that create sounds in instruments, and dimensions of volume and pitch. As he developed the charts with students, Mr. Rutherford was able to expand their language and develop precise vocabulary that would be exploited in this scenario's instruction.

Changing a sound variable allowed students to apply their understanding at a deeper level. Mr. Rutherford designs his instruction to heighten the level of discovery for his students because he has learned that the level of their language increases when they are thinking hard to try out new ideas. Strong language reinforcement occurs through the strategy of Inside/Outside Circles. It provides Mr. Rutherford and the students with a participatory structure that promotes scientific thinking and academic discourse at each interval. The teacher has ample opportunity to check on students' understanding and language use.

Reading processes support the students in their language practice as they access the vocabulary from the co-created charts, utilize the sentence frame text, and interact with Mr. Rutherford to develop the summary chart for their work.

Mrs. Huang's Class—Grade 4 Scenario Part 1
ELD Levels: Intermediate, Early Advanced, and Advanced

Mrs. Huang has previously engaged her students in scientific reasoning as they created a simulation of the Grand Canyon and observed the effects of erosion as water flowed into their model. Students were challenged to make logical arguments as to why certain landforms were created by the flow of water. They came to know that water reshapes the land. Now, the teacher wants to extend and apply their new scientific knowledge and vocabulary and to look for evidence of these phenomena on their schoolyard. At this point in their inquiry, the students design a slide show presentation that illustrates a specific term.

Each group of four students selects a term (e.g., *plateau*, *delta*, *basin*, *erosion*, *canyon*, *chemical weathering*, and *mechanical weathering*). They take a photograph of their simulation tray that illustrates an example of their term (see Figure 7.9). Then, the class walks outside and looks for evidence on the grassy area of the schoolyard (see Figure 7.10).

Figure 7.9 Simulation Tray Photograph

This photograph serves as documentation of student work.

Immediately, evidence of weathering and erosion is identified as a group of students huddle around a cluster of rocks and examine how plants affect changes in rocks. The students label the area and snap a photograph.

Then, another group spots evidence of erosion around the dirt of a sapling. The dirt had recently been watered, causing it to be moist. Soil particles had shifted as water pushed the dirt, causing it to erode. The students place a label in the eroded area and take a photograph of their example of erosion.

Figure 7.10 Schoolyard Photograph

Applying classroom knowledge to real-life environments extends students' learning.

After about 20 minutes, the students gather back in the classroom to begin work on their slide shows. Each slide includes a photograph of their selected word as seen in their simulation activity, a definition of the word, and a photograph of what they found in the schoolyard (see Figure 7.11).

Figure 7.11 Student-Generated Slide

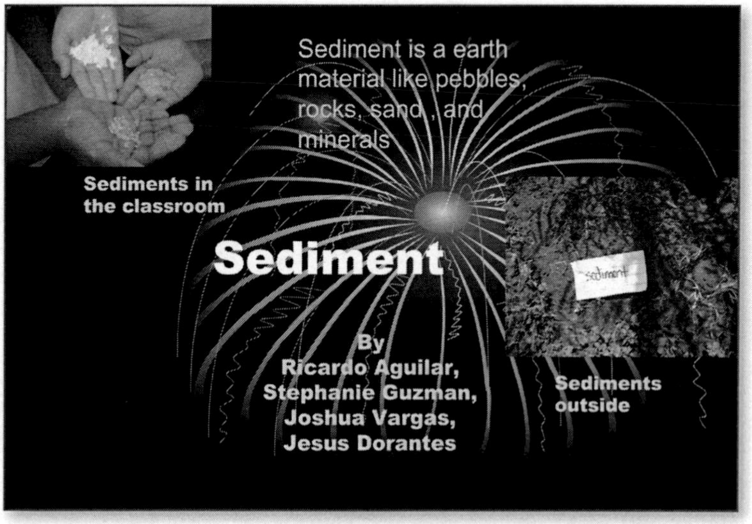

Technology can serve as an effective tool for demonstrating the depth of group knowledge. It is important to provide a structure for language learners.

The students decide how they are going to divide up responsibility for the tasks in order to orally present their slides. Some of the students decide to take turns sharing, while other groups plan to choral-read their slides. What naturally emerges is a period of preparation and oral rehearsal peppered with academic vocabulary couched within declarative statements that define, elaborate, and describe.

Mrs. Huang's Class—Grade 4 Scenario Part 2 ELD Levels: Intermediate, Early Advanced, and Advanced

Mrs. Huang decides to continue maximizing opportunities for academic talk related to what the class has been studying. In her next round of instruction, she structures a content reading experience using the Travelers and Talkers structure in which students read and select important scientific concepts to share with peers. Mrs. Huang encourages students' use of scientific discourse:

Mrs. Huang: *It is time for you to think more deeply about what you have been learning in this unit. Sometimes, scientists confirm, or extend, what they know by reading information written by other scientists.*

She tells them that their challenge will be to scientifically examine information from various texts to find important knowledge about weathering and erosion. They will share what they discover with their classmates, or fellow scientists.

Mrs. Huang divides the class into heterogeneous groups of four students. She explains the task to the students, which requires them to read their assigned page, identify the scientific information that is important to know and share, draw a visual that captures the important information on an 8.5"-by-11" sheet of paper, and finally replicate the visual on a large sheet of chart paper (see Figure 7.12).

Figure 7.12 Visual Representations of Learning

Visually representing information from a textbook taps into learning modalities that support conceptual understanding and language learning.

Mrs. Huang circulates among the student groups, carrying her clipboard to take notes. Her primary focus is on helping students follow the procedures for the task. She guides students to make connections to earlier investigations and to justify their decisions. After 25 minutes of reading, discussing, negotiating, and drawing, the students are ready to share. Mrs. Huang directs them to tape their large visuals around the room and to stand by their drawing. The teacher asks the students to orally rehearse as a group how they will share their information with others. Specific language forms are projected onto the interactive whiteboard as an option for those students who need the additional support. The language forms include *The important information we selected from the text is* _____., *It is important to know this because* _____., and *This information helps scientists understand that* _____.

Then Mrs. Huang asks the groups to divide themselves in half. Two students stay by their drawing; they are called *talkers*. The other two students move from chart to chart sharing their information based on their small drawing clipped onto a clipboard. They are called *travelers*. At a signal, the travelers move to the right to the next group. The travelers are the first to share their findings, using their visual as support. After several minutes, the talkers have a chance to share their important points displayed on the chart.

At a signal, everyone stops talking and the travelers move to the next chart. The sharing continues in this same manner until the travelers have rotated to each chart. Mrs. Huang meanwhile moves from group to group, listening to the conversation and taking notes.

Notable ELD Practices

This scenario is actually two separate instructional events (Part 1 and Part 2). In both events, Mrs. Huang creates a context for small groups of students to independently transfer their knowledge and talk about academic concepts in extended intervals. Making oral presentations is especially important for English language learners. It provides an opportunity for students to describe an experience, to clarify terms and thinking, and to rehearse language, which are important components for promoting language fluency.

The teacher also uses additional strategies (aside from hands-on experiences), to help the students expand their knowledge of the scientific concepts. The use of the science textbook provides opportunities for further inquiry and clarification during this stage of the 5E process. It is important to note that the hands-on experiences enable students, especially ELLs, to observe phenomena, formulate concepts, and arrive at generalizations. This type of background knowledge broadens their understanding of complex concepts necessary for understanding their textbooks.

Interaction with text can benefit ELLs with appropriate scaffolding. Text provides rich examples of certain types of academic discourse. It is a resource that can be accessed repeatedly by a student at an individual pace of learning to deepen understanding. Mrs. Huang uses the Travelers and Talkers structure to enable her students to collaborate together to make meaning of the text. Visualizing the content provides the students with an alternative form of their conceptual understanding and is another form of scaffold. Finally, the oral rehearsal and repetition of the task provides students with many meaningful opportunities to hear and use their own as well as their peers' scientific academic language.

Strategies for ELD Instruction During *Extend*

Instruction during *Extend* involves utilizing strategies that ensure extended intervals of thought, talk, and interaction, such as the following:

- Farmer in the Dell

- Four Corners

- Inside/Outside Circles

- Storyboards

- Travelers and Talkers

While utilized in the *Explore* stage, Four Corners can also be used as a strategy during *Extend*, as it offers students an opportunity to apply their thinking in new contexts. Four Corners is explained again here, with a slight modification to demonstrate its role in *Extend*.

Farmer in the Dell

Farmer in the Dell is a language-acquisition strategy that was initially developed and presented by the Guided Language Acquisition Design Project (Project GLAD™) (Brechtel 2005). This strategy helps guide students through the building blocks of crafting complete sentences and using music to build oral-language fluency. The name of the strategy comes from the tune that is sung as students connect the parts of speech to create sentences. It is a great strategy for supporting English language learners' oral language fluency through a nonthreatening approach. Students enjoy putting the sentence to music, and it helps them see how parts of speech come together to create complete sentences. Students have progressed through the inquiry model having learned a great deal of content. Farmer in the Dell offers students an opportunity to share what they have learned through a structured language model. At the *Extend* stage of the 5E process, students are ready to share orally and in writing the academic language and vocabulary they have learned through the exploration of core science content and concepts. As students share what they have learned, the teacher can place their ideas in a parts of speech chart. The students can then read across the chart to create a complete idea/sentence. The chart should include the following column headers: *Adjectives, Nouns, Verbs, Adverbs,* and *Prepositional Phrases*.

In the opening scenario, Ms. Cortez uses Farmer in the Dell to record her students' learning about earthworms. Students are not only demonstrating their content knowledge but also are sharing vocabulary they have acquired to add to the chart. The students will then have an opportunity to share their learning orally.

How Do You Do It?

1. Prepare a chart that includes five columns with the following headings: *Adjectives, Nouns, Verbs, Adverbs,* and *Prepositional Phrases* (in this order). Invite students to share what they have learned about the subject. Begin by writing the main subject in the *Nouns* column. Then, encourage students to share adjectives that describe those nouns. Guide students to share what the subject is able to do, how it moves or acts, and where it does these things. Put these words in the *Verbs, Adverbs,* and *Prepositional Phrases* columns, respectively.

2. Add another noun to the chart, if applicable, and repeat the procedure.

3. Model for the students how to read across the chart to create a complete sentence.

4. Invite students to create complete sentences using additional information on the chart.

5. Using one of the sentences created, model for students how to read the sentence to the tune of "Farmer in the Dell."

6. Ask students to repeat the sentence to the tune of the song.

7. Continue to sing different sentences created by reading across the chart to the tune of "The Farmer in the Dell."

Four Corners

....

Four Corners can be used as a review strategy in which students apply their content and language learning thus far. It provides an opportunity for students to revisit four main topics, concepts, or ideas that they have previously learned. The information presented is placed in four corners of the room, giving students options as to which corner they will visit. The element of choice is helpful for all students. It can serve as a form of motivation and comfort. Students who may not have a full understanding of the content can select a corner with familiar content. Students who are very confident with the material may feel empowered to have a choice in what they want to review. In either case, Four Corners serves as an informational assessment as the teacher monitors the corners students visit and the discussion they have with their peers.

The content placed in the four corners of the room can differ based on content and grade level. For younger students, place broad categories around the room and ask them to match items or images to the correct corner. For older students, place a variety of materials at each corner related to a particular topic or concept they have studied. Each material should present the information in different ways. The students can then gravitate to the corner that is of interest to them and explore the materials in the corner. In both cases, when the students visit a corner, they engage in academic conversations with their peers. They discuss what they understand about the content at the corner they have visited. This is a great opportunity for students to practice the language they have explicitly learned during *Explain*.

Four Corners is a great strategy at the *Extend* phase of the 5Es because it allows students to demonstrate their understanding of the content they have learned thus far. In addition, it helps students revisit the big ideas by exploring the concept in a new context or form.

How Do You Do It?

1. Select four big ideas, concepts, or topics that are part of what the students have learned through the first three stages of the 5Es cycle (*Engage, Explore,* and *Explain*).

2. Place a large sheet of chart paper, books, manipulatives, pictures, or any representation of the four big ideas in the four corners of the classroom. Each corner should have one of the four big ideas.

3. Ask students to go to the corner they would like to explore further. Provide students with a picture or word and ask them to go to the corner where their word or picture fits best.

4. Have students explore the materials at their corner.

5. Invite students at each corner to share with one another why they selected the corner and what they have learned about the content presented.

Inside/Outside Circles

Inside/Outside Circles is a strategy in which students share their thinking and learning. It gives students an opportunity to talk with different partners and exchange academic language. Based on the work of Spencer Kagan (1994), Inside/Outside Circles can serve as a summarization activity. For English language learners studying science, the strategy is extended to further include an opportunity to explicitly rehearse oral academic language. As students summarize, they exchange language. They are asked to talk with multiple partners, repeating their ideas with each new partner. This repetition of academic language helps build fluency. In addition, students hear what their peers are learning and can confirm or extend their knowledge base.

Inside/Outside Circles gets students up and moving. Though it is similar in nature to a pair-share, students get to stand up and talk to peers. They form a circle and, in a structured manner, engage in a brief discussion with a peer. This strategy can help students who have been struggling to make meaning of the content by giving them a chance to talk with a peer and clarify misunderstandings. As students are talking, teachers have an opportunity to listen in and gather information about the students' content knowledge and use of academic language.

The use of Inside/Outside Circles during *Extend* provides an opportunity for the students to share what they have understood from the *Engage*, *Explore*, and *Extend* stages. The teacher can focus the discussion on the learning objective to assess students' comprehension of the previous explorations. This information can help the teacher select appropriate text or plan instruction to clarify information or extend learning.

How Do You Do It?

1. Have students stand up and form two concentric circles. The students in the inside circle should face the students in the outside circle. If there is an odd number of students, a triad can be formed. Ideally, there is an even number of students in the inside and outside circles. Direct the students in the inside circle to share something they have learned with the person standing in front of them. This can be focused on your learning objective or it can be an open-ended question. On average, two minutes is a good amount of time for students to share their ideas. Provide sentence frames to guide students as they share, if desired.

2. Call time and ask the outside circle to share their ideas around the same prompt or question.

3. Call time again after approximately two minutes. Direct the outside circle to stay in place. Ask only the inside circle to move. They will rotate clockwise to the next partner.

4. Once again, ask students to share with their new partner the same information they just shared with their previous partner. Use the same prompt or question. This helps students rehearse the academic language and continue to clarify their ideas.

5. Continue the process, allowing students to share their ideas with multiple partners. It is easiest to always keep the outside circle in place and only ask the inside circle to rotate.

Storyboards

Storyboards are graphic organizers in the form of visual representations. Students are able to lay out their thinking through the use of drawings or pictures. A storyboard was originally introduced in the field of animation in the 1930s as a way to organize a story that was to be developed into a film. Though storyboards have historically been used to tell stories in film and in printed comics, they can be used in the classroom as a form of presenting one's thinking and learning of both fiction and nonfiction.

For English learners, storyboards are a nonthreatening way of showing complex learning. Where students may struggle with the academic language to produce text around their thinking, a storyboard can be used as an alternative to represent the same complex ideas. In addition, storyboards can be used as springboards for spoken and written language. Students use them as a form of rehearsal or prewriting before having to share their ideas in more traditional text and oral formats.

During the *Extend* phase of the 5E process, a storyboard provides students vehicle for sharing what they have learned in a novel way. This application of their learning helps teachers see where students are in their thinking. Encourage students to share their storyboards orally with a partner or group to further apply the academic language learned at this point in the 5E process.

How Do You Do It?

1. Provide students with a storyboard. The boxes on the storyboard should be large enough for students to draw their ideas. Be mindful of students' grade level

when providing the storyboard. Younger students will need more space to draw their pictures as they are still developing their fine-motor skills.

2. Ask students to use the boxes provided on the storyboard template to show their thinking in a linear fashion. When using the practice for fictional text, students can sequence the main events of the story. For nonfiction text, students can show a process, a sequence, a series of key ideas, or a chronology of events. Optionally, when students complete their illustrations, they can add captions to each of the picture boxes. Younger students still working on early writing skills may only be able to create the images.

3. Ask students to orally share their storyboard with a peer or small group.

Travelers and Talkers

Travelers and Talkers is a strategy in which students can visually and orally share their interpretation of key vocabulary or content. It allows students to work as a team to think through their assigned concept or term and engage in negotiation and creative thinking with one another. Through Travelers and Talkers, all students will get to learn from one another and explain what they have learned.

The group collaboration in the preparation and execution of the strategy provides high levels of support for ELLs. During the preparation, teams of students are asked to create a visual representation of the meaning of a given word or concept. At this step, the students negotiate meaning and try to come up with a creative way to represent their thinking. Students who enjoy drawing and creating visuals feel empowered to represent their ideas in this way. Students who excel in leadership positions enjoy facilitating the group's collaboration. For all group members, there is support around the thinking and the language needed to share their ideas. When groups prepare to share their posters, they get a chance to rehearse what they will say, and they always travel in partners. This peer support helps all students feel successful as they take turns using the group's ideas and language. Partners are asked to share their visuals repeatedly, which helps ELLs build oral fluency of the academic language.

Using Travelers and Talkers during the *Extend* stage provides an opportunity for students to share their thinking in a new context. They demonstrate what they have learned by creating a visual. Additionally, they have to talk about the visual in a way that shares their learning of the content and emulates scientific discourse.

Figure 7.13 Collaboration During Travelers and Talkers

How Do You Do It?

1. Divide the class into groups of four.

2. Provide each group with a large sheet of chart paper, a regular 8.5"by 11" sheet of blank paper, and drawing materials such as markers, crayons, or colored pencils.

3. Assign each group a concept or vocabulary term. Ask the team to discuss the meaning of the word or concept and agree on a shared understanding.

4. Have each group create a visual representation of the meaning of the concept or term on the large chart paper as well as a replica of the visual on the small sheet of paper. The visuals should be identical on the large and small papers. To save time, instruct the groups to have two members working on the visuals. Often, students like to have the "artist" of the group do both, but it will take longer. Ask the "artist" to create the large visual while someone copies it onto the small paper at the same time. On average, groups may take about 10 minutes to complete Steps 3 and 4.

5. Have the groups post their large visuals around the room. Be sure there is enough room between visuals for students to move from one group to another and hear the presentations clearly. Ask all group members to stand in front of their large poster.

6. Ask each group to divide themselves up into two travelers and two talkers. Explain to the class that everyone will be presenting, the only difference being who moves and who stays at their large poster.

7. Explain that the travelers that they will hold on to the smaller replica of their visual as they travel. Talkers will not leave their large visual posted on the wall.

8. Ask the groups to rehearse what they will be sharing about their visual.

9. Instruct the travelers to rotate one poster to the right. Talkers do not move.

10. Once the travelers have arrived at the next poster, ask the talkers to share their visual with the travelers. Once the talkers have finished sharing, ask the travelers to show their small replica of the visual and share it with the talkers. This should take about three minutes. If needed, structure this piece by calling time after about one and a half minutes. Ask the talkers to stop talking, and allow the travelers to share for about one and a half minutes. Asking the talkers to always share first allows the teacher to visually know how far along the students are in their sharing. If you see talkers still talking, you know the travelers have not yet shared. If you see travelers sharing, you know they are almost done and ready to move on to the next poster. Have students wait until time is called before rotating.

11. After calling time, ask the travelers to rotate once again to the next poster to the right.

12. Repeat Steps 10 and 11 until the travelers arrive back at their original group visual.

13. An adaptation to Travelers and Talkers is to have students use their notebooks to take notes as they move around the room.

Assessing ELLs in *Extend*

The role of assessment in *Extend* is to gauge how well English language learners demonstrate their ability to apply and transfer their understanding to new contexts as well as how students use formal representations of scientific knowledge such as terms, formulas, and diagrams. The outcomes can help teachers determine what will be important to assess in the next stage.

When developing English for language learners through the 5E model, each stage has particular implications for assessing language performance. The goal of assessing ELLs' language performance in *Extend* is to determine how English language learners demonstrate their language ability as they transfer acquired academic language to new contexts and approximate scientific discourse (oral, written, and visual) in the expression of their scientific understanding. For teachers of ELLs, forming opinions about student progress in English will be important in determining the final summative assessment steps of inquiry.

The classroom scenarios shared in this chapter represent a range of approaches that teachers can use to assess content understanding in their English language learners as well as their use of the language of science.

Science Notebooks as ELL Assessment in *Extend*

Utilizing science notebooks is a powerful tool for evaluating the multidimensional aspects of ELL learning—language use and academic content comprehension. Using science notebooks as formative assessment can help teachers make ongoing decisions about instruction for English language development as well as content as ELLs move through the 5E process.

As has been stated before, the science notebook has many uses for capturing the developing understanding of students learning scientific content (see Chapter 3). English language learners in our scenarios are using the notebooks to make scientific records of their learning in varied ways. The notebooks are used as a tool for students to share their findings and thinking—using oral and written language—with their peers and their teacher.

Supported by multiple opportunities for oral rehearsal and clarification, the notebook entries in *Extend* expect students to apply what they know about particular concepts by utilizing specific academic content language to express their thinking. At this juncture in the inquiry cycle, the notebook serves as a window into how the student's thinking about a particular concept is deepening as well as how they can use targeted scientific discourse to reflect their thinking. Teachers of English language learners must analyze student performance for more than what students understand about the scientific concept; they must employ the additional lens of academic language when examining notebooks.

Figures 7.14 and 7.15 provide examples of the extended thinking and academic language use of two fourth-grade English language learners. Figure 7.14 comes from a unit on electricity in which students are asked to apply what they know about electromagnets by examining what happens when one of the variables is changed. The notebook entry reflects varied levels of thinking and language in the form of questioning, predicting, graphic recording of data, and drawing conclusions. In contrast, Figure 7.15 shows an example of academic language use in an alternative genre, in this case, poetry. This notebook entry reflects the applied use of specific academic language related to the concept of metamorphosis in brief statements or stanzas that rhyme.

Based on student language-proficiency levels and teacher expectations, a notebook entry becomes data that will guide the teacher's instructional decision making as to the language objectives for future lessons.

Figure 7.14 Sample *Extend* Notebook Entry

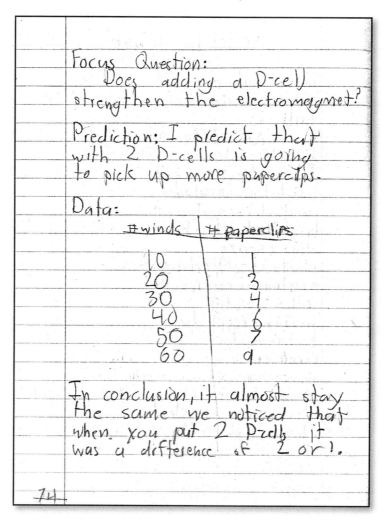

Focus Question:
  Does adding a D-cell
strengthen the electromagnet?

Prediction: I predict that
with 2 D-cells is going
to pick up more paperclips.

Data:

#winds	# paperclips
10	
20	3
30	4
40	6
50	7
60	9

In conclusion, it almost stay
the same we noticed that
when you put 2 D-cells it
was a difference of 2 or 1.

74

Figure 7.15 Sample *Extend* Notebook Entry

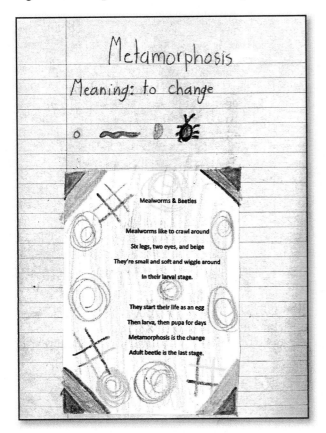

Tips for Planning *Extend* for ELLs

When planning *Extend* for English language learners, consider the following:

- Review the academic language you want your students to practice and acquire by the end of your 5E inquiry cycle.

- Reacquaint yourself with the scientific discourse appropriate for the content you are teaching and adapt it to the English proficiency levels of your students.

- Analyze the assessment data you have gathered thus far to determine the language your students still need to strengthen.

- Create optimal opportunity for students to practice and use the scientific academic language meaningfully in varied novel contexts. Thoughtfully designed tasks in this stage ensure that students will deepen what they understand and can articulate this deeper understanding more concisely and capably. Plan to use thinking and talking strategies in which students interact in pairs or small groups within cognitively engaging experiences. The more novel the task, the more deeply students will have to understand the content in order to communicate about it.

- Design notebook entries at this stage to provoke the use of academic language to express deeper content understanding.

- Think through how you will manage instruction to maximize opportunities for students to practice and use the language with the least amount of teacher or adult facilitation so that you can circulate and assess students. Students should access and use the academic language that has meaning for them.

Reflect on Wonderings

1. How can you create opportunities for students to independently use the language they are acquiring while decreasing explicit teacher facilitation?

2. What are the kinds of tasks that will encourage students to use the appropriate scientific language to express scientific thinking?

3. What are the types of tasks that will help you know that students have acquired a deeper understanding of academic language?

CHAPTER 8

Communicating Content Knowledge Through Evaluate

You May Wonder:

- What do I need to think about in *Evaluate* when teaching English language learners?

- In what ways can I support English language learners in *Evaluate*?

- How do I approach the assessment of ELL language performance in the *Evaluate* phase?

L anguage is an essential interwoven element within inquiry-based science instruction when working with English language learners. There is great potential to enhance academic language development in science content instruction. In the final phase of the 5E process, *Evaluate*, the focus of instruction shifts to illuminate what has been learned and how it was learned through demonstration and reflection. The discussion of *Evaluate* begins with our featured classroom scenario.

Ms. Cortez's Class—Grade 2 Scenario
ELD Levels: Early Intermediate and Intermediate
A Glimpse at English Language Learner Instruction
During Evaluate

At the end of a series of lessons focused on earthworm characteristics, Ms. Cortez holds up a large index card. She tells the students that they are going to write a postcard to their parents telling them everything that they learned about earthworms. On the front of the postcard, they are to draw a picture of the most interesting fact they learned about earthworms. On the back, they are to synthesize what they have learned into a simple culminating statement explaining why that fact is important to know.

Before the students begin to write on their own, Ms. Cortez demonstrates the task through Modeled Writing. She thinks aloud what she is considering in her mind as she writes. The students are able to see her writing projected on the screen.

Ms. Cortez: *Boys and girls, I am going to show you how I would begin my postcard. It will be addressed to my mom. I would begin "Dear Mom." I would add a comma after Mom because it is a part of my heading. Below that, I will begin with a general sentence that would sound something like this: "I learned a lot about earthworms in school this week." Then I will tell them about the most interesting fact I learned. I can use our word chart if I get stuck on a word. At the end of my message, I will write my name.*

After modeling the format, Ms. Cortez wants the students to research and rehearse their ideas. She begins the process by asking students to leaf through their notebooks to review everything they have learned about earthworms. Following an interval of five minutes, she explains, "It's important that we use the best language we have learned to show our parents and families that we can communicate like scientists. Where can I find the best scientific language to use?" The students call out instructional charts that are displayed around the room, such as the word wall and question charts. They skim through their science notebooks and identify sources such as a definition page or a technical drawing. Ms. Cortez solicits the students' responses based on the sources they have discovered.

Ms. Cortez: *What are your ideas for the best language we can use?*

She listens to their responses, which include words like *burrow, segments, bristles, contract, moist,* and *saddle.* As the students call out, she asks them to tell her how they learned these scientific words. Ms. Cortez jots down notes onto her clipboard.

Then, she asks them to stand in two parallel lines, facing a partner and holding their science notebooks. She models thinking and looking through a science notebook with another student. To provide language support and focus, Ms. Cortez calls the students' attention to a sentence frame displayed on the whiteboard. It reads: *The most interesting fact I learned is* _____. She begins the Lines of Communication activity by identifying the east-facing line of students. They will be the first to share one fact about earthworms. After the first student shares, the other partner shares an interesting fact. After this first exchange, Ms. Cortez directs the students from the east-facing line to slide to the right so that they face a new partner. The students share another interesting fact. The process is repeated once more. For the final sharing, she asks the partners to share one question that they still have about earthworms using the sentence frame: *A question I still have about earthworms is* _____. The teacher moves between the partners, recording their responses and their questions. Satisfied that her students have had enough opportunity to rehearse the language that they need to express their understanding, Ms. Cortez asks the students to go to their desks to begin their postcards.

As the students compose their postcards, the teacher circulates among them.

Ms. Cortez: *Why is this interesting fact important to know?*

As she interacts with the students, she elicits from them the statement: *It's important to know that earthworms _____ because _____.* She does this by modeling and restating student responses. On a prepared evaluation sheet attached to a clipboard, Ms. Cortez places a check mark next to the student's name if they can relate a physical characteristic or behavior to its function (e.g., *It's important to know that earthworms can burrow because they need soil to keep moist*). She checks off students who can articulate the importance of knowing a particular earthworm characteristic and also notes examples of academic language used by the students.

What Is *Evaluate* for English Language Learners?

For ELLs, moments of demonstration and reflection represent opportunities for teachers and students to gauge language performance in addition to conceptual understanding. With any lesson, students need an opportunity to reflect on their learning. Thinking about the content and language developed as part of the 5E learning cycle helps students internalize their learning and work toward developing metacognition.

In *Evaluate*, students are encouraged to assess their understanding as they access what they know. *Evaluate* as a culminating phase in the 5E model can include formal assignments such as final presentations, creative projects, written reflections, or formal assessments such as exams. However, *Evaluate* can also involve a quick end-of-lesson opportunity embedded within ongoing instruction in which students are asked to simply stop and think about their learning and share it. These brief oral discussions can be carried out through strategies like Think-Pair-Share, a whole-class Whip-Around, or Stand Up and Share, which will all be discussed later in the chapter. What makes the *Evaluate* stage of the 5E model powerful is the time students are given to think about their learning. Often, through content-area instruction, students can feel overwhelmed by the amount of information learned. This gives them an opportunity to stop and process their learning before starting the inquiry cycle again and adding on to their content knowledge and language development.

Teachers rely on evaluative practices to determine the direction of future instruction. When addressing English language development through content, teachers of ELLs must keep focused on dual aspects of learning: language and content. The challenge is to engage in practices that capture the language dimensions of content learning.

Capturing Academic Language Performance Through *Evaluate*

This section focuses on features that teachers of ELLs must include in their instructional planning in order to maximize the potential for acquiring academic language through science.

Figure 8.1 Essential Features of *Evaluate*

- Designing assessment to capture both targeted concept and language goals
- Allowing students to communicate their understanding in varied modalities and formats
- Providing appropriate language scaffolds
- Prompting students to reflect on the language they learned and how they learned it

Designing Assessment for Targeted Concept and Language Goals

The arc of good assessment practice is to correlate, or align, instruction to targeted objectives. Assessment should reflect what has been previously taught. For English language learners, instruction in *Evaluate* must be connected to both the intended science concepts and the desired academic discourse appropriate for students' language-proficiency levels.

Authentic language assessment is designed to capture how students use language to express their thinking. With respect to science, ELL teachers must design assessment that compels students to use scientific discourse to express their scientific thinking, utilizing sentence forms such as *Our evidence showed us that* _____, *This is important because* _____, or *We can find out more by* _____. One way to stimulate optimum levels of scientific talk is to ask students to communicate their learning to various audiences, including peers, teachers, parents, younger children, experts, and school and community members.

The integration of authentic language assessment with the evaluation of attainment of the science objectives is demonstrated in Ms. Cortez's second-grade scenario. She has designed a series of tasks that will allow her and her students to grasp what has been learned and to share it with multiple audiences. The assessment is scaffolded by a strategy that engages students in an oral language rehearsal of what they learned in Lines of Communication. Thus, the teacher encourages her students to use the content language they have acquired prior to the formal task of writing a postcard. Although parents and families are established as the formal audience of the postcard and its report of learning, students are compelled to share what they have learned with peers during Lines of Communication and with the teacher during the questioning exchange. Ms. Cortez communicates clearly that students are expected to demonstrate the best thinking and language possible from the study of earthworm characteristics. These practices enable her to effectively capture evidence of spoken and written language.

Allowing Students to Communicate Understanding in Varied Modalities and Formats

Currently, there is strong support for the use of multiple measures to assess performance, preventing an overreliance on any single measure to determine what students have mastered. This approach to assessment is particularly important because the opportunity to capture multiple aspects of language proficiency is important when analyzing ELL learning outcomes.

To gain as complete a picture as possible of what has been learned about science and about language, assessment must be diversified. Students must have multiple, varied ways to communicate what they understand that correlates to their language proficiency level, favored learning modality, and critical-thinking capability. The use of formal and informal assessment types in oral (e.g., presentation), visual (e.g., poster or diagram), written (e.g., written reflection or report), and even kinesthetic (e.g., simulations) formats can ensure that students, especially ELLs, have adequate opportunity to demonstrate their achievement in language and in content. Moreover, analysis of what students receive from their instruction is enhanced by consideration of both individual assessment results as well as those outcomes derived through group work.

Figure 8.2 Student Work Sample

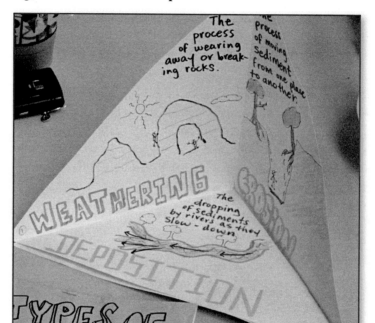

Student content knowledge and language can be assessed in a variety of ways, including three-dimensional displays. Providing choice promotes agency.

The assessment sequence in the opening second-grade scenario guides students through a varied series of tasks in which students use oral language, visuals, writing, and even kinesthetic movement standing and moving in lines to communicate their understanding. At times, Ms. Cortez asks her students to work with a partner. At other times, they work alone. Although the main task is completing the postcard for their parents, all tasks capture the performance of students at varied proficiency levels through diverse modalities of learning. Thus, Ms. Cortez has multiple sources of data to determine academic language progress and science knowledge.

Providing Appropriate Language Scaffolds

Throughout our discussion of the other phases of the 5E cycle, we have emphasized the use of appropriate instructional scaffolds for ELLs. In *Evaluate*, the support of language scaffolds can optimize the assessment experience for English language learners. A language scaffold, such as adding a drawing that expresses understanding, can minimize the effect of limited language proficiency. Engaging in oral rehearsal with a partner prior to producing an assessment artifact can stimulate scientific understanding and the language needed to express it. These types of language scaffolds presume students can benefit from an alternative mode to communicate their understanding that is less reliant on language mastery and more reliant on socially mediated conversation with a peer.

In Ms. Cortez's second-grade scenario, we can identify specific examples of providing language support for the range of students in her classroom, starting with the Modeled Writing of the postcard. Although all the students benefited, ELLs in her classroom with less proficiency were supported by the opportunity to draw what they knew and to orally rehearse and listen to the varied responses of more proficient peers. In the final step of this *Evaluate* sequence, as students were completing their postcards, the teacher orally assessed the students one-on-one. This enabled Ms. Cortez to directly modify her interaction to meet the individual needs of her students.

Figure 8.3 Student Reflection

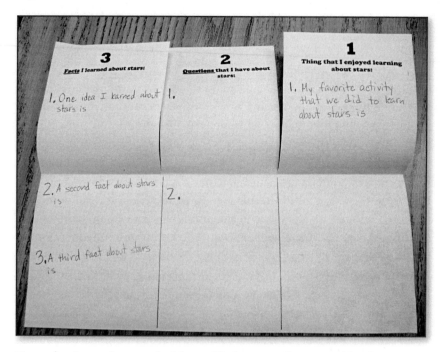

For evaluation, using a tool with specific language forms provides the necessary structure for students to feel successful when sharing.

Prompting Students to Reflect on Language Learning

To be effective, learning must encompass more than just acquiring facts. Learning involves focusing on what has been assimilated, understanding the relationship between the new information and what is already known, understanding the processes that facilitate learning, and being aware when something new has actually been learned.

Metacognitive thinking is a key element in the transfer of learning. It means that through reflecting on what and how one learns, a student can gain control of the strategies and skills they can use for subsequent learning. The teacher can ask students about the successes and difficulties they have had with problems. Students can be encouraged to reflect on the kinds of thinking they have been engaged in and to be conscious of those processes that have been helpful or have hindered their progress.

For ELLs in the *Evaluate* phase, metacognitive thinking should be applied to what has been learned both about science and language. This is an important component of the inquiry cycle.

Ms. Cortez builds in the opportunity for her English language learners to reflect on the significance of their concept learning as a final step in her *Evaluate* sequence. She decides to apply metacognitive thinking about the concepts learned into the postcard task by interacting with her students orally on an individual basis. She has prepared a particular type of question intended to provoke reflective thinking. Convinced that it's important to her work as a teacher, she is careful to capture this element of evaluation on her clipboard notes. Metacognitive thinking about the language the students have learned occurs earlier in the sequence when Ms. Cortez guides the class to think about the best scientific language they can use for the discussion activity and asks them to reflect on and call out how they learned the language.

Examining ELD Practices in *Evaluate*

The analysis of notable ELD practices during *Evaluate* continues by focusing on additional scenarios from first-grade through fourth-grade classrooms. Because of the importance of language in all instructional considerations when teaching ELLs, we place greater emphasis on the language dimension of instruction over concept understanding in these descriptions. Nevertheless, we hope that scientific understanding is clearly apparent in each scenario. Both elements are vital in the 5E inquiry process. Scientific thinking is a critical catalyst for academic language.

Miss Gonzalez's Class—Grade 1 Scenario
ELD Level: Beginning and Early Intermediate

After reviewing plant parts and the function of roots for plant growth, Miss Gonzalez moves to the *Evaluate* stage of her 5E model for instruction. She chooses to evaluate the students' learning through a strategy called Draw and Remember. She feels that this multilevel strategy will best accommodate the Beginning and Early Intermediate proficiency levels of her students. She has paired Early-Intermediate students with Beginning-level students at their tables as support for completing the evaluation task.

Miss Gonzalez:	*Today I'm going to ask you to think about everything you've learned in science about what plants need to grow and survive. You've done such a great job thinking and talking like scientists. I want to ask you now to demonstrate, or show, your table partner and me what you can do.*

She gives her students a blank half-sheet of paper and asks them to fold it into four equal parts. Then she has them number each square on the top-left-hand corner. She proceeds to demonstrate the task step by step. The students listen carefully to each prompt and use crayons to draw their responses. The teacher repeats each prompt twice and provides one minute for the students to complete their responses.

Miss Gonzalez:

1. *Pick up your green crayon. In the first square on the top left, draw a long, green stem.*

2. *Pick up your red crayon. In the second square on the top right, draw a flower with red petals.*

3. *Pick up your black crayon. In the third square on the lower left, draw some black roots.*

4. *Pick up your brown crayon. In the fourth square on the lower right, draw brown soil.*

After completing the drawings, the students pair-share what they drew. Then they turn over their sheets so that they cannot look at their drawings. With a partner, the students respond to the following set of prompts:

1. *What was the first thing that you drew?*

2. *What did you draw next to the long, green stem?*

3. *What did you draw with your red crayon?*

4. *Where did you draw the brown soil?*

Miss Gonzalez has the students pause after each question and asks one student to call out an answer. Because one of her English language learners is a special education student who receives ELD instruction in her classroom, she orally directs the students to point to each thing they drew until she has covered each question. She carefully observes the response of the special education student before moving on.

To make the task a little more linguistically and cognitively challenging, she asks her students to use the back side of their folded sheet and do the following:

1. *In the first square on the left, draw the plant part that gets the plant nutrients and water from the soil.* (roots)

2. *In the second square on the right, draw the plant part that transports nutrients and water from the roots to the leaves.* (stem)

3. *In the third square on the left, draw the plant part that attracts pollinators such as bees and butterflies.* (petals/flowers)

4. *In the last square on the right, draw the plant part that produces food energy from the sun.* (a leaf)

It is important to note that Miss Gonzalez included prompts 3 and 4 to gauge the students' understanding before they move to their new learning cycle that will more intensely focus on the function of the leaves for plant growth.

Miss Gonzalez wants the next level of the task to challenge students' critical thinking about science concepts and the related language. Because she wants to ensure that her students have ample time for evaluation, Miss Gonzalez guides them to share the answers to the following questions one at a time:

1. *What is the first thing that you drew?*

2. *How do the roots help the plant grow?*

3. *What is the function, or job, of the stem?*

4. *Without the roots or the stem, what do you predict would happen to the plant?*

While the partners are sharing, Miss Gonzalez actively circulates to listen and make observations on sticky notes of the students' language use. She will review the drawings later to enhance her understanding of what the students have learned thus far.

Figure 8.4 Teacher Documentation

The teacher scripts students' language for analysis later.

Because Miss Gonzalez wants her students to think about what they learned and how they learned it, they are asked to open their science notebooks and think about what they have learned so far about what plants need to grow. She gives the students time to look through their notebook entries. Then they are asked to write and draw a response to the following: *One interesting activity I did was _____. One important fact I learned is _____. The words I want to remember are _____.*

Once the students have finished, Miss Gonzalez gathers them on the rug to share and talk about their responses. She particularly focuses on the responses related to language. She responds to students sharing their words:

Miss Gonzalez: *Those are all important, scientific terms. Great job! Now, how do you think you will remember those words?*

The students give various responses such as using the vocabulary charts displayed around the room, reading soil poems they have written in their notebooks, looking at the books at the plant center in the corner of the room, and asking experts like Miss Gonzalez.

Notable ELD Practices

Miss Gonzalez designs a multilayered task with the embedded scaffolds of drawing and peer interaction aimed at precisely evaluating concept and language attainment. At the initial level of evaluation, she focuses on plant parts, colors, and functionality. Since the majority of the class is at the beginning level of English proficiency, this task assisted in memory retention and required students to respond in words and/or phrases. (Note that this task can be adapted for students who need additional support by having them cut apart the squares so that they can respond by holding up their drawing or pointing.) The oral response prompts are both cognitively and linguistically demanding. It is important when evaluating student learning that the evaluation task matches the content and is appropriate for the proficiency level of the students.

Figure 8.5 Heritage Language Support

The use of students' heritage language can serve as a bridge for concept and language learning. Using classroom resources can be used as a tool for evaluation.

Miss Gonzalez has anecdotal notes as well as an assessment artifact to refer to for her analysis of student learning. In the final task, she encourages the development of metacognition through a science notebook reflection. She provides a script to guide her students. She has decided not to provide an interval of oral rehearsal for this entry because the students had just finished a period of thinking and talking with their table partners about what was learned. The conversation on the rug about their notebook entries allows her to focus the reflection on the language they learned.

Mrs. Winthrop's Class—Grade 3 Scenario
ELD Level: Early Advanced and Advanced

This instructional cycle represents the launch to a larger unit on the positive and detrimental impact of living organisms on the environment. The students in Mrs. Winthrop's third-grade classroom have just completed an inquiry into their immediate school environment. The instruction centered on an investigation of whether the school was a healthy or unhealthy environment. Student teams were sent out into the school and came back with photographic evidence that resulted in great concern about the state of their schoolyard (see Figure 8.6). The use of photographs and realia to reflect on learning serve as a scaffold, especially for ELLs and students with learning difficulties.

Figure 8.6 Schoolyard Evidence

As a way of closing this cycle of instruction, the teacher asks the students to take some time to reflect on what they gained from this inquiry. She asks the students to pull out their science notebooks and review the contents related to this instructional cycle. They are then asked to complete a self-evaluation with the following information:

Self-Evaluation

Before I started to study the school environment I thought _____. First, I learned that _____. Then I learned more about the school environment by _____. After, I concluded that _____. Now, I understand that _____. I want to know more about _____. My best learning happened when I _____. I learned the most language when we _____. I think I can use this language when I _____. I wish I would have_____.

Before the students begin, Mrs. Winthrop displays the self-evaluation script:

Mrs. Winthrop: *One of the important things you need to do as students is take some time to think about what you learned and how you learned it. We've done this once before in science. Can anyone tell me how this helps you?*

Serena: *It helps me remember what was important.*

Dahlia: *When I think about science, I feel good because I learned something like new words and stuff.*

Mrs. Winthrop: *Thinking about what you learned and how you learned can help you notice what is important about who you are as a student. I hope that this reflection will give you tools, especially new language that you can use in all of your subjects.*

Mrs. Winthrop reviews the script with the students, directing them to use the script prompts as a guide for their self-reflection and giving them the choice to copy and complete the stem as support or respond to these points in another way of their choosing. Mrs. Winthrop adds that their answers will reveal what matters to the students about the science concepts and new language they learned and how well they can express it in writing.

Mrs. Winthrop has decided that she wants to capture more of the students' thinking and language by using a Poetry Frame as a novel alternative, which they have used in language arts instruction. She projects the following frame on the board:

I do not understand

why _____,

why _____,

why _____.

Most of all, I do not understand

why _____

because _____.

What I understand best is _____

because _____.

Before having the students complete this cloze activity, Mrs. Winthrop models how she would begin:

Mrs. Winthrop: *When I was outside, I started coughing. I do not understand why the air isn't fresh outside. There is evidence of air pollution.* (She demonstrated how her first two lines would read by writing this poem:)

I do not understand

why the air outside the classroom is polluted.

Then she asks the students to think about things that they do not understand related to their observations of the schoolyard. After a few minutes, the students have completed their individual poems. Finally, the students turn to a partner and share their poems.

The following is an example of one student's reflection:

I do not understand

why *there was dirty water along the fence,*

why *the grass was dry,*

why *juice boxes were thrown.*

Most of all, I do not understand

why *there were cracks on the floor*

because *I can hurt myself.*

What I understand best is *I can help*

because *I can pick up trash.*

Notable ELD Practices

Mrs. Winthrop begins the *Evaluate* stage of inquiry with a class discussion that queries the students about the value of self-reflection for their learning. This establishes a clear purpose for the tasks that follow.

Because Mrs. Winthrop plans to dedicate a good deal of subsequent instruction to understanding how living things cause changes in the environment in which they live, she feels that devoting the time to creating these evaluation artifacts will be useful in planning her next steps. Her goal for 5E ELD instruction is to refine and deepen her students' language and thinking skills since they already have a strong base of English language proficiency. The challenge for Mrs. Winthrop is to gauge the level of academic language proficiency in this specific content area.

Both tasks will allow her to evaluate how students are expressing their thinking about science, using academic language, and reflecting on their own learning. Both tasks included the scaffold of language frames in a script. However, it is important to note that students at these levels of proficiency should be encouraged to use their own language instead of the frames, if they aren't needed. The prompts are open-ended to invite longer, elaborated responses. The students still receive the support of partner sharing.

Evaluation is not always formal or summative. The following scenario presents an example of an *Evaluate* practice that is embedded within ongoing instruction.

Mrs. Huang's Class—Grade 4 Scenario
ELD Levels: Intermediate, Early Advanced, and Advanced

For the past three days, the students in Mrs. Huang's class have been investigating through a simulation how erosion can alter landforms over time. On this day, the teacher is short on time but recognizes the importance of bringing closure to each of her lessons. She has opted to evaluate what the students have learned so far with a quick evaluation activity called Stand Up and Share.

First, she asks all of her students to think about one important fact that they learned from reading or listening to others during the lesson activities that day. Although the students speak English with some proficiency, she gives them about a minute to stop and reflect on their personal response. Then she asks all of the students to stand up.

Mrs. Huang: *Who would like to share one important point about what they learned today?*

Novak: *I learned that rocks can change through the force of water.*

Mrs. Huang:	*If you learned that rocks can change through the force of water, please sit down.* (Two students with that same response sit down. Then Mrs. Huang asks for another volunteer to share. A student hesitantly raises her hand and is called on.)
Rafael:	*I learned that 18 centimeters are broken off of Big Sur every year.*
Mrs. Huang:	*If your fact to share was that 18 centimeters are broken off, or eroded, from Big Sur every year, please sit down.*

She continues in this same manner until all of the students are sitting down. Very quickly, she is able to hear what students are learning and remembering and can take note of any misunderstandings or struggles with language for future lessons.

Notable ELD Practices

Although this brief scenario presents an example of evaluative practice within ongoing instruction, many of the essential elements of the *Evaluate* stage are evident.

Stand Up and Share represents the type of strategy that can be used over and over throughout instruction as an evaluative tool. It has a flexible structure that allows thinking and language to be demonstrated quickly. The act of standing builds in a kinesthetic aspect to the task of actively listening to responses and making choices. Students are asked to reflect on what they have learned. Students are provided the language scaffolds of a predictable frame—in this case, *I learned ...*—and the opportunity to respond by simply sitting down rather than speaking aloud. The teacher can gain a quick glimpse of students' use of academic language.

Strategies for ELL Instruction During *Evaluate*

Instruction during *Evaluate* involves utilizing strategies that ensure that students have adequate opportunities to demonstrate and think about what they have learned about science. When teaching ELLs, utilizing evaluation strategies that support the use of language to express understanding is integral to the process. The following strategies ensure that social interaction, reflective thought, and intervals of talk have prominence in the evaluative process:

- Lines of Communication

- Stand Up and Share

- Cloze Activities

- Modeled Writing

- Draw and Remember/Draw and Discuss

Lines of Communication

Lines of Communication is a strategy that provides students with an opportunity to demonstrate what they have learned by talking with multiple partners (Christison and Bassano 1995). This strategy affords students the opportunity to talk with their peers while the teacher does a final check for understanding of the objectives at hand. An important feature of Lines of Communication is the opportunity for students to talk to a variety of partners. In a Pair-Share, students talk to only one peer; Lines of Communication, however, exposes students to diverse perspectives and language by talking to multiple partners.

English learners benefit from an opportunity to hear a variety of language models. During Lines of Communication, students will demonstrate the language they have developed as a result of engaging in the first 4 Es (*Engage, Explore, Explain,* and *Extend*). Students will be at diverse levels in their language development; however, the hope is that all students will have reached, at minimum, the language objectives and content-area vocabulary targeted during instruction. In addition to students hearing the language their peers have developed, they also share what they have learned in science content.

Using Lines of Communication at the *Evaluate* stage of the 5E model gives teachers an opportunity to assess students' content knowledge and language development as they share orally. At this phase, the students will have experienced the content and language objectives through a variety of strategies and activities. They are now ready to share what they have learned.

How Do You Do It?

1. Line students up in two equal lines facing each other. Be sure every child has a partner standing in front of him or her. If there is an odd number of students, you can create a triad.

2. Designate an A line and a B line. Explain to line A that they will remain in their place for the duration of the activity. Line B will be moving one partner to the right when time is called. If you have a triad, be sure to place two members of the triad in line A so that they do not move. Allow the single partner of the triad to be in line B so that only one student has to move each time.

3. As the students are standing in line facing a partner, ask line B to share their ideas or learning around the content. After about one minute, ask partner A to share

their thoughts around the same question. If you have a triad, ask the students to share the time, taking turns as to who shares first.

4. After about two minutes, call time and ask line B to move one partner to the right. The student at the end of the line will come to the front of the line to meet up with his or her new partner.

5. Repeat the initial question (Step 3) and ask students to discuss their thoughts with their new partner. After about two minutes, call time and ask line B to move one partner to the right once again.

6. Repeat Steps 3–5 until students have had a chance to talk with about five or six different partners.

7. If students are comfortable taking turns, you do not have to signal when line B talks and when line A talks. You can simply give the students two to three minutes to share with one another, reminding them that they need to take turns and ensuring that each partner has a chance to share in the time allotted.

Stand Up and Share

Stand Up and Share is a quick way to do a final check of student learning. It is a strategy that provides students time to stop, think, and reflect on their learning. After having experienced many engaging activities throughout the previous four Es, students will get a chance to think about what they have learned.

English language learners need opportunities to process language. As part of this process, ELLs make sense of the content they have learned by first accessing ideas through language and then sharing those ideas orally. In Stand Up and Share, ELLs get to think through their ideas first and use the language they have developed to express their ideas. In addition, because the prompt in a Stand Up and Share is open-ended, ELLs do not feel the pressure of using any precise language or sharing specific content.

When using Stand Up and Share at the *Evaluate* stage of the 5Es, students get to share with their teacher and peers what stood out most to them as they experienced the content in the earlier stages of the inquiry cycle. This is a chance for teachers to note key pieces of learning for individuals as well as for groups of students. Because students will be asked to share anything they have learned, this strategy does not check for specific content knowledge. The task is open-ended, and the students choose what to share. Therefore, you may or may not hear whether they met the content and language objective, so there is a potential need for you to couple this strategy with another to get a more comprehensive picture of what the students have learned. This strategy is effective, however, in giving students the confidence to share something they have learned, making all students feel successful. A Stand Up and Share takes about two to three minutes to complete, so it is easy to use multiple *Evaluate* strategies to get a better sense of the complexity of students' learning.

How Do You Do It?

1. Ask all students to stand behind their chairs.

2. Ask students to think about all they have learned throughout the earlier experiences of *Engage*, *Explore*, *Explain*, and *Extend*. Have them consider one thing that stands out to them that they remember about the content or topic. Use prompts such as *Think about one thing you have learned, Take your time and consider this*

item carefully, Who would like to share something they have learned?, or *Who would like to tell the class one important point about what they have learned today?*

3. Call on one student to share. After the student shares his or her learning, ask anyone who was going to share the same thing to sit down with the student who shared.

4. Ask another student who is standing to share what he or she learned. After the student shares, ask everyone who was going to share the same idea to sit down with the student who shared.

5. Continue the same process in Steps 3 and 4 until all students are sitting down.

Many students will sit with their peers. Though teachers may be concerned that not all students have shared out loud, the key is that all students have taken time to stop and think about their learning. They are ready to share one thing they learned, and even though they may have gotten shy and sat down prematurely, they still reflected on their learning.

Cloze Activities

Cloze Activities are fill-in-the-blank activities. Students are provided text with deleted words or phrases to complete. The point of a Cloze procedure is for students to demonstrate their comprehension of the text by properly inserting words or phrases that make sense in the text. Cloze procedures have been used as formal vocabulary assessments in which the deleted word is a vocabulary word. A word bank may or may not be provided, but in either case, the students must show their understanding of the word by providing the correct vocabulary word. Cloze activities have also been used as comprehension assessments. If students are able to complete the blank with a word or phrase that makes sense, it shows that the student is reading for meaning. In the scenario provided in this chapter, the Cloze activity is used in the form of a poem. Students are asked to fill in the blanks in a way that shares what they have learned and any questions they still have. It does not necessarily check for specific vocabulary but is more open-ended so that students may express their own thoughts about their learning. In addition, students are given an opportunity to present content they are still grappling with. Teachers can use this information to make future instructional decisions.

Cloze activities, such as the poem are heavily structured, which helps English language learners jump-start their thinking. The Cloze poem establishes the language to be used. Though it is structured, it is open enough for students to demonstrate their written-language development as well.

How Do You Do It?

1. Provide the students with a Cloze activity frame that will allow them to provide written examples of their mastery of language and content objectives. For example:

I see _____,

I hear _____,

I smell _____,

I feel _____,

I taste _____,

I know _____,

I wonder _____.

2. Individually, ask students to complete the frame in writing.

3. Collect the completed frames for assessment purposes. Students' writing will represent content knowledge as well as written-language development.

Modeled Writing

Modeled Writing is an instructional method that scaffolds writing for students. Through Modeled Writing, the teacher demonstrates the writing process to students as he or she creates a piece of text. The students, meanwhile, watch and learn. The teacher's roles as the thinker and the writer are essential to a successful Modeled Writing. Other writing methods such as shared writing and interactive writing allow students to contribute to the ideas and creation of the text. However, in Modeled Writing, the teacher is responsible for contributing all of the ideas and producing the text. This provides a clear model for students as a scaffold for their own writing. Students will watch as the teacher writes, noting writing strategies as well as listening to the ideas that are being presented. In turn, students will be asked to write their own text that should capture their own ideas and learning in a format that is modeled after the teacher's writing.

For ELLs, Modeled Writing helps them see a strong example of academic writing. They see how to craft their ideas in written form. In addition, Modeled Writing can serve as a form of rehearsal as the English language learners revisit ideas learned throughout the 5E sequence as well as the language that is attached to those key ideas.

As an *Evaluate* strategy, Modeled Writing is a preparation for student writing. The teacher is doing the modeling as a way to prepare students to create a written text that represents their learning. The text that is modeled and in turn is created by students will capture what they have learned in content as well as in language.

How Do You Do It?

1. Identify the piece of writing that you want students to produce in the *Evaluate* activity. This could be a written response to a prompt, a research report, a letter or postcard, or a narrative.

2. Establish the content and language objectives for which mastery should be demonstrated within the piece of writing so that you can communicate your expectations to students. Also, identify activities or artifacts that have been created during instruction that could serve as a resource to students in demonstrating the objectives.

3. Gather students together and model the appropriate steps for completing the writing activity. Give all students visual access to the model as you write. Think aloud as you complete the steps in order to effectively demonstrate the procedure to students.

4. Draw students' attention to any resources that can be leveraged as they complete the writing assignment, including charts, word banks, and science notebook entries.

5. As an option, have students participate in a sharing activity by using one of the strategies for oral discussion introduced in this book. This will activate students' knowledge of science concepts and language, and will also give them time to orally rehearse what they may wish to include in their writing.

6. Instruct students to complete the writing assignment based on the model you have created, with the goal of sharing what they have learned about the given science topic.

Draw and Remember/Draw and Discuss

Draw and Remember is an instructional strategy that helps students review key learning and builds their listening comprehension and working memory (Christison and Bassano 1995). Students are asked to create a four-square organizer that will be used to draw key concepts as reviewed by the teacher. The teacher should guide the students in what to draw by prompting them to demonstrate a key idea in each of the four squares. An essential component of this strategy is the students' listening comprehension. The teacher will prompt students to draw specific items in a particular square. After all the squares have been completed, the students will be asked to recall everything they drew on the paper without looking.

It is important to note that students who have more productive language should be asked more challenging prompts. The evaluation task can also be adapted to become Draw and Discuss. Here is an example of one set of prompts:

1. In the first square, draw a horizontal line. Beneath the line, draw roots.

2. In the second square, draw a flower.

3. In the third square, draw leaves.

4. In the fourth square, draw a plant that is different from the flower you drew in the second square.

The challenge is not in following directions but in the channeling of critical thinking. So, for the prompts given above, the following would be the corresponding oral-response questions:

1. Describe your flower.

2. Which pollinators are attracted to your flower?

3. How long are your roots? What made them grow?

4. Describe the place where your plant is growing.

These final prompts are both cognitively and linguistically more demanding. It is important when evaluating student learning that the evaluation task matches the content and is appropriate for the proficiency level of the students.

How Do You Do It?

1. Provide students with a blank sheet of paper. Ask them to fold their paper into fourths. Walk them through this process by asking them to first fold their paper vertically and then horizontally. Share with the students that you will be asking them to draw something in each of the squares. They must be sure to listen carefully so they know not only what to draw but also where to draw it.

2. Prompt students to draw something in each of the squares. The prompts will connect to what has been learned throughout the 5E process.

3. After all squares have been completed, ask students to share their drawings with a peer or small group.

4. Ask students to turn their paper over and retell what they drew to a partner. You can also have students silently rehearse what they want to share with a partner.

Assessing ELLs in *Evaluate*

The key to ELL assessment in *Evaluate* is to ensure that language learning can be demonstrated along with content understanding. Students and teachers must be able to derive information from the tasks that improves their respective roles in the learning process: to learn effectively and to teach effectively.

We have shared various examples of assessment tasks in the scenario descriptions. They represent the integration of thinking, talking, and reflecting through varied formats. They do not preclude the use of more formal types of science assessment but rather suggest how formal assessment can be enhanced for ELLs through talk, thought, and interaction.

The important point is that *Evaluate* practices enable teachers to assess what students have learned from the 5E instructional cycle in order to make decisions about new 5E learning cycles.

The teachers in our scenarios will rely on data gathered through anecdotal records and assessment artifacts to determine the levels of content understanding and language that have been attained through the instruction they have designed. All of our scenario teachers have designed assessment tasks that will capture multiple examples of concept understanding and language use. They utilize the practice of keeping anecdotal records of oral language expression to augment other assessment artifacts such as written products, visuals, and constructed responses.

Figure 8.7 Matching Activity

Matching activities can provide optimal opportunities for assessment, particularly for kinesthetic learners.

Ms. Cortez, for example, has gathered data from two major sources: the illustrated postcard and her anecdotal records. These sources will enable her to focus on the many dimensions of performance, such as visual expression of concept understanding; written language expression of concepts and language, such as describing and explaining; scientific thinking processes like analysis and synthesis; metacognitive reflection, including what was learned and why it is important; and oral language expression, for example reporting, explaining, and justifying. This data will be correlated appropriately to grade-level expectations and language-proficiency expectations in order to inform the next cycle of science instruction.

Science Notebooks as ELL Assessment in *Evaluate*

As has been stated before, the science notebook has many uses for capturing the developing understanding of students' learning of scientific content (see Chapter 3). English language learners in our chapter scenarios use science notebooks to make scientific records of their learning in varied ways. The notebooks are used as a tool for students to share their findings and thinking—using oral and written language—with their peers and their teacher.

In *Evaluate*, the science notebook can be used as a tool for reflecting on what has been learned and how it was learned, since it is the repository of most of the scientific investigation. At the culminating phase of a particular cycle of inquiry, performance evidence and reflection will be conserved in the science notebook.

The following notebook examples represent a particular approach of a fourth-grade teacher. Because all of her students were ELLs, she recognized that they would require scaffolds for the language they needed to capture their learning at the end of a science unit. Her response was to establish a predictable structure for the end-of-unit notebook reflection. Her belief was that the familiar structure of the reflection would provide her students with a source of support for developing their scientific language and critical thinking. What this teacher discovered was that the reflections evolved from simple statements to more complex examples of scientific discourse across the course of various units of study.

Figure 8.8 Science Notebook Entry after One 5E ELD Cycle

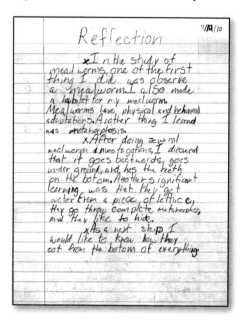

Reflection   4/14/10

    x In the study of
meal worms, one of the first
thing I did was observe
a mealworm. I also made
a habitat for my mealworm.
Mealworms have physical and behavioral
adaptations. Another thing I learned
was metamorphosis.
    x After doing several
mealworm investigations, I discovered
that it goes backwards, goes
under ground, and has the teeth
on the bottom. Another significant
learning was that they get
water from a piece of lettuce,
they go through complete metamorphosis,
and they like to hide.
    x As a next step I
would like to know how they
eat from the bottom of everything.

Figure 8.9 Science Notebook Entry after Four 5E ELD Cycles

Reflection   Room 43
    In the study of electromagnets,
one of the first things I did
was I made an electromagnet.
Furthermore, I made coils around it
and find tested it carefully.
I proved there was magnetism
by using a compass. We tested
it, put it in a table, and
graphed it. Next we used
thicker wire and more D-cells
and it worked better.
    After doing several
electromagnets investigations,
I discovered there is a magnetic
field around an electric circuit.
Another significant learning was
an electro magnet gets stronger
with more coils. Even tho the
electro magnet is stronger it
gets stronger with even
thicker wire. If you use
two D-cells it gets even
stronger and heats up. If
you want it strong you
defenetly need the winds to
be tight.

    As a next step, I
would like to youse it
under water. Also I would
like to ask this question
"What type of matter is
magnetism? Finaly I would
like to know every thing there
is about electromagnets.

With the first early example, we can observe that the language of this Early-Advanced level student was fairly simple, expressed in basic statements with little elaboration or expanded language. He is, however, able to use some key content vocabulary appropriately. We can infer that he relied heavily on the structure provided by the teacher to guide his thinking and prompt the language he used. By the end of the fourth science unit, there is evidence that the student is still following a reflection script provided by the teacher. However, his growth is reflected in his ability to elaborate on his understanding with greater language complexity such as descriptive vocabulary and complex sentence structures as well as his ability to express higher levels of critical thinking about the phenomenon he has studied.

This teacher created an assessment component of her instruction capable of illuminating valuable data for her teaching. Her purposeful planning of science-notebook entries for her English language learners truly reflects the dual aspects of scientific learning—language and content—that all teachers must strive for.

Tips for Planning *Evaluate* for ELLs

When planning *Ecaluate* for English language learners, consider the following:

- Set reasonable expectations for ELL language performance. This will be based on the expectations set by the language proficiency standards for your location. However, another component of reasonable expectations will be based on the evidence you have gathered in previous stages of the 5E cycle. Your students may be reasonably spurred on to a higher level of performance by this practice than by any generalizations derived from English Language Performance standards descriptions.

- If working with an established or published assessment, analyze the assessment for the language demands it would place on the student. Modify or adapt the assessment or the procedure to provide more language support by providing additional time, oral instructions, or visuals. Make sure the assessment measures what was taught. Ideally, your assessment should emerge from the content covered.

- Infuse the essential ELL practices into your assessment design. For example, always consider providing students with the opportunity for oral rehearsal of ideas and language. English language learners benefit from the support of realia, visuals, and interaction with peers.

Reflect on Wonderings

1. What factors should you consider when designing an assessment that will evaluate both concept attainment and acquired language?

2. How will you ensure that your students have adequate opportunity to communicate what they have learned about science and language?

3. How can you appropriately scaffold the evaluation task to accommodate the language needs of English language learners?

4. How do you ensure that your students have the opportunity to metacognitively reflect on their learning?

5. What techniques or tools will allow you to evaluate multiple aspects of ELL performance?

Afterword

Across the country, teachers continue to work diligently and intentionally to meet the needs of English language learners. Understanding that teachers enter and persist in their classrooms with a wide range of knowledge of how to best support their ELLs, we wanted to provide the framework for an instructional approach that has helped us meet the content and language needs of these students. Teachers are in need of a common understanding of English language development and its role in science education. Without this knowledge base, they struggle to provide comprehensible content and language input for students to learn content and develop academic language. An inquiry-based approach to science instruction with a focus on English language development further supports the need for science education at the elementary level. We are passionate about all students receiving a holistic quality education. We believe that children should be in classrooms where they are an integral part of the learning and directly engaged with the content at hand. We want children to enjoy learning and share their learning with one another.

Through our own experiences training teachers and working in real classrooms, we have presented a practical look at how all teachers can find success in their work with English learners. Throughout this book, we have provided a look inside classrooms where teachers are encouraging their ELLs to be successful in language while falling in love with science. These experiences are not only enjoyable and engaging but are also developed with a clear purpose and defined learning objectives. English learners are developing high levels of academic language while meeting grade-level science content standards by utilizing the 5E Inquiry model for science, a framework that effectively marries language and content development. It provides a great opportunity for students to see content in action. It allows students ample opportunities to interact with content and engage in collaborative learning opportunities to both understand the language of science and be able in turn to share their thinking orally and in writing. "The relationship between science learning and language learning is reciprocal and synergistic. Through the contextualized use of language in science inquiry, students develop and practice complex language forms and functions" (Stoddart et al. 2002, 664).

The 5Es—*Engage, Explore, Explain, Extend,* and *Evaluate*—present an inquiry-based approach to the successful integration of language and content. Using science as a vehicle for learning language makes learning relevant, engaging, and comprehensible. In the earliest stage of the 5E model, *Engage,* English learners have an opportunity to build prior knowledge by interacting with science content. They use their natural language to think about the learning at hand and begin to see the key learning objectives that will build throughout the 5Es.

The 5E model then presents English learners with a focused hands-on experience in which the teacher guides the students' attention toward the learning objective by probing students' thinking around the given task. At the *Explore* stage, English learners continue their conceptual development, allowing language to flow in a natural way, while their language is extended through the teacher's level of questioning. These two phases, *Engage* and *Explore,* bring students to a comprehensible level of the learning objectives and lead to an opportunity to use the language they have to share their thinking. In the next phase, *Explain,* teachers clarify misconceptions and explicitly model and support the academic language students will need to share their thinking and learning.

Once students feel confident in new content learning and have had a chance to explicitly learn academic content language, they apply it in order to facilitate deeper levels of comprehension and language development. During *Extend,* English learners once again use their newly acquired language and content knowledge to explore the targeted concepts. Asking students to use what they have learned through new contexts or experiences demonstrates a transfer of knowledge. All the while, the teacher continues to support students' thinking through questioning, modeling language, and providing rich learning experiences.

In the final stage, *Evaluate*, students get a chance to formally share the science concepts they have learned by using the language developed throughout the inquiry cycle. Teachers can take note of both the mastery of academic language as well as progress toward the intended content objectives.

Through an ELD science approach, students are learning content through talk, critical thought, and interaction. They look forward to science and take great risks with language because they are so involved in the learning that they let language flow. Throughout this book, we have attempted to demonstrate how to support students' language attempts and strategically move their language development forward.

Among the three of us, we have so many rich years of learning from our ELLs and from one another. We have come to write this book through a collaborative effort to understand English language development and what it means to provide explicit and authentic opportunities to develop academic language in English. The process was not always clear and simple. We often tried out an idea and fell short, or experimented and felt we could have done better. But in the end, we have learned so much and over the past four years have come to a point in our learning where we not only believe in the work we have done but have also seen its results. We have witnessed students using high-level academic English to enthusiastically share what they have been working on in science. We have heard teachers say, *This is what we have needed for so many years. My students are not only talking, but they are talking science. Thank you for reminding me of the importance of science and how effectively it can help my ELLs learn language.* We are excited about sharing what we have learned and hope this book will serve as a companion for teachers. We can often feel alone in our classrooms and lost when we are not seeing the results we had hoped from our teaching. This book can be a catalyst for conversations with your colleagues to think critically about your work as teachers of ELLs.

The message we wish to convey through our work presented in this book is one of hope. We understand that the work of a teacher is challenging, but it is always rewarding. By implementing inquiry-based approaches such as the 5E model, we believe teachers will be energized about their work as they see a passion for learning and a natural curiosity grow and develop in their students.

—Dolores, Lilia, and Eugenia

References Cited

Abedi, Jamal. 2004. The No Child Left Behind Act and English Language Learners: Assessment and Accountability Issues. *Educational Researcher* 33 (1): 4–14.

———. 2005. Assessment: Issues and Consequences for English Language Learners. In *Uses and Misuses of Data in Accountability Testing*, eds. J. L. Herman and E. H. Haertel, 175–98. Malden, MA: Blackwell Publishing.

———. 2010. Assessing English Language Learners and/or Bilingual Students: Critical Issues. In *Cultural Validity in Assessment: Addressing Linguistic and Cultural Diversity*, ed. M. Basterra, G. Solano-Flores, and E. Trumbull, 49–71. Mahwah, New Jersey: Lawrence Erlbaum Associates, Publishers.

Ada, Alma Flor, and F. Isabel Campoy. 1998. *Effective English Acquisition for Academic Success.* San Francisco, CA: Del Sol Publishing.

Au, Kathryn H. 1980. Participation Structures in a Reading Lesson with Hawaiian Children: Analysis of a Culturally Appropriate and Instructional Event. *Anthropology and Education* 11: 170–180.

August, Diane, and Kenji Hakuta. 1997. *Improving Schooling for Language Minority Children: A Research Agenda.* Washington, DC: National Academy Press.

August, Diane, and Timothy Shanahan, eds. 2006. *Developing Literacy in Second-Language Learners: Report of the National Literacy Panel on Language-Minority Children and Youth.* Mahwah, NJ: Lawrence Erlbaum.

Balderrama, Maria V., and Lynne T. Diaz-Rico. 2006. *Teaching Performance Expectations for Educating English Learners.* Boston, MA: Pearson Education, Inc.

Brechtel, Marcia. 2005. *Bringing It All Together: An Integrated Whole Language Approach for the Multilingual Classroom.* Carlsbad, CA: Dominie Press, Inc.

Brown, H. Douglas. 1994. *Teaching by Principles: An Interactive Approach to Language Pedagogy.* Englewood Cliffs, NJ: Prentice Hall Regents.

———. 2007. *Teaching by Principles: An Interactive Approach to Language Pedagogy.* 3rd ed. Englewood Cliffs, NJ: Prentice Hall Regents.

Bruner, Jerome S. 1986. *Actual Minds, Possible Worlds.* Cambridge, MA: Harvard University Press.

Bybee, Rodger, C. Edward Buchwald, Sally Crissman, David Heil, Paul Kuerbis, Carolee Matsumoto, and Joseph McInerney. 1989. *Science and Technology Education for Elementary Years: Frameworks for Curriculum and Instruction.* Washington, DC: The National Center for Improving Science Education.

California Department of Education. 1999. *English Language Development Standards for California Public Schools, Kindergarten through Grade Twelve.* Sacramento, CA: The California Department of Education.

Center for Applied Linguistics. 1998. *Enriching Content Classes for Secondary ESOL Students: Study Guide.* McHenry, IL: Delta Systems.

Chamot, Anna, and J. Michael O'Malley. 1994. *The CALLA Handbook: Implementing the Cognitive Academic Language Learning Approach.* Reading, MA: Addison-Wesley.

Christison, Mary Ann, and Sharon Bassano. 1995. *Look Who's Talking! Activities for Group Interaction.* Upper Saddle River, NJ: Prentice Hall Publishing.

Collier, Virginia P. 1987. Age and Rate of Acquisition of a Second Language for Academic Purposes. *TESOL Quarterly* 21:6.

Collier, Virginia P., and Wayne P. Thomas. 1999. Developmental Bilingual Education. In *Program Alternatives for Linguistically and Culturally Diverse Students*, ed. Fred Genesee, 19–24. Santa Cruz, CA: Center for Research on Education, Diversity and Excellence. http://www.cal.org/crede/pubs/edpracreports.html#8.

Costa, Arthur L. 1991. *Developing Minds: Programs for Teaching Thinking*. Alexandria, VA: ASCD.

Cummins, Jim. 1981. The Role of Primary Language Development in Promoting Educational Success for Language Minority Students. In *Schooling and Language Minority Students: A Theoretical Framework*. Los Angeles: California State University, National Evaluation, Dissemination and Assessment Center.

———. 1986. *Empowering Minority Students: A Framework for Interaction. Harvard Review* 56:18–36.

———. 1989. *Empowering Minority Students*. Sacramento: California Association for Bilingual Education.

———. 1994a. Knowledge, Power, and Identity in Teaching English as a Second Language. In *Educating Second Language Children*, ed. Fred Genesee, 33–58. New York: Cambridge University Press.

———. 1994b. Primary Language Instruction and the Education of Language Minority Students. In *Schooling and Language Minority Students: A Theoretical Framework*, 2nd ed. Los Angeles: California State University, National Evaluation, Dissemination and Assessment Center.

———. 1996. *Negotiating Identities: Education for Empowerment in a Diverse Society*. Los Angeles: California Association for Bilingual Education.

———. 2000. *Language, Power and Pedagogy: Bilingual Children in the Crossfire.* Tonawanda, NY: Multilingual Matters.

———, ed. 2001. *Negotiating Identities: Education for Empowerment in a Diverse Society.* Ontario, CA: California Association for Bilingual Education.

———. 2003. Reading and the Bilingual Student: Fact and Friction. In *English Learners: Reaching the Highest Level of English Literacy*, ed. G. G. Garcia, 2–33. Newark, DE: International Reading Association.

———. 2005. Teaching the Language of Academic Success: A Framework for School-based Language Policies. In *Schooling and Language Minority Students: A Theoretical Framework*, 3rd ed., 3–32. Los Angeles: LBD Publishers.

Delgado-Gaitan, Concha. 1990. *Literacy for Empowerment: The Role of Parents in Children's Education.* London: Falmer Press.

Dutro, Susana. 2001. Reading Instruction for English Language Learners: Ten Pedagogical Considerations. November 13, 2001, Noyce Foundation ELL Study Meeting [Online]. http://www.noycefdn.org/literacy_programs/ecrwfiles/Ten_Considerations.pdf.

Dutro, Susana, and Lori Helman. 2009. Explicit Language Instruction: A Key to Constructing Meaning. In Literacy Development with English Learners Research-based Instruction in Grades K–6. New York: Guilford Publications, Inc.

Dutro, Susana, and Carrol Moran. 2003. Rethinking English Language Instruction: An Architectural Approach. In *English Learners: Reaching the Highest Level of English Literacy*, ed. G. Garcia. San Francisco, CA: Jossey-Bass.

Echevarria, Jana, Maryellen Vogt, and Deborah J. Short. 2000. *Making Content Comprehensible for English Language Learners: The SIOP Model.* Boston: Allyn & Bacon.

———. 2004. *Making Content Comprehensible for English Language Learners: The SIOP Model.* 2nd ed. Boston: Pearson/Allyn & Bacon.

Elementary and Secondary Education Reauthorization Act of 2011. 2011. Washington, DC: 112th Congress.

Ellis, Rod. 1994. *The Study of Second Language Acquisition.* Oxford, UK: Oxford University Press.

Ellis, Edwin S., and Lou Anne Worthington. 1994. *Research Synthesis on Effective Teaching Principles and the Design of Quality Tools for Educators.* Technical Report No. 5. Eugene: University of Oregon, National Center to Improve the Tools of Educators.

———. 2004. Executive Summary of the Research Synthesis of Effective Teaching Principles and the Design of Quality Tools for Educators. http://idea.uoregon.edu/~ncite/documents/techrep/tech05.pdf.

Enright, D. Scott. 1991. Tapping the Peer Interaction Resource. In *Languages in School Society: Policy and Pedagogy,* ed. M. E. McGroarty and C. J. Faltis, 209–232. Berlin: Mouton de Gruyter.

Ervin-Tripp, Susan. 1991. Play in Language Development. In *Play and the Social Context of Development in Early Care and Education,* ed. B. Scales, M. Almy, A. Nicolopoulou, and S. Ervin-Tripp, 84–97. New York: Teacher College Press.

Escamilla, Kathy. 2006. Monolingual Assessment and Emerging Bilinguals: A Case Study in the US. In *Imagining Multilingual Schools,* ed. O. Garcia, T. Skutnabb-Kangas, and M. Torres-Guzman, 184–199. Clevedon, England: Multilingual Matters, Ltd.

Fassler, Rebekah. 2003. *Room for Talk: Teaching and Learning in a Multilingual Kindergarten.* New York: Teachers College Press.

Federal Interagency Forum on Child and Family Statistics. 2005. *America's Children: Key National Indicators of Well-Being, 2005.* Washington, DC: Federal Interagency Forum on Child and Family Statistics.

Fillmore, Lily Wong, and Catherine Snow. 2000. *What Teachers Need to Know About Language.* Contract No. ED-99-CO-0008. U.S. Department of Education's Office of Educational Research and Improvement, Center for Applied Linguistics.

Fitzgerald, Jill, Georgia E. Garcia, Robert T. Jimenez, and Rosalinda Barrera. 2000. How Will Bilingual/ESL Programs in Literacy Change in the Next Millennium? *Reading Research Quarterly* 35: 520–523.

Freeman, Yvonne, and David Freeman. 1998. *ESL/EFL Teaching: Principles for Success.* Portsmouth, NH: Heinemann.

Freeman, Yvonne, David Freeman, and Sandra Mercuri. 2002. *Closing the Achievement Gap: How to Reach Limited-Formal-Schooling and Long-Term English Learners.* Portsmouth, NH: Heinemann.

Fry, Richard. 2007. *How Far Behind in Math and Reading Are English Language Learners?* Washington, DC: PEW Hispanic Center.

Galguera, Tomás. 1998. Students' Attitudes Towards Teachers' Ethnicity, Bilinguality, and Gender. *Hispanic Journal of Behavioral Sciences* 20 (4): 411–429.

Gándara, Patricia, Julie Maxwell-Jolly, and Anne Driscoll. 2005. *Listening to Teachers of English Language Learners: A Survey of California Teachers' Challenges, Experiences, and Professional Development Needs.* Santa Cruz, CA: The Center for the Future of Teaching and Learning.

García, Eugene, and Julia Curry-Rodriguez. 2000. The Education of Limited English Proficient Students in California Schools: An Assessment of the Influence of Proposition 227 on Selected Districts and Schools. *Bilingual Research Journal* 24 (1 and 2): 15–35.

Gass, Susan M. 1997. *Input, Interaction, and the Second Language Learner*. Mahwah, NJ: Lawrence Erlbaum, Inc.

Gebhard, Meg, Ruth Harman, and Wendy Seger. 2007. Unpacking Academic Literacy for ELLs in the Context of High-Stakes School Reform: The Potential of Systemic Functual Linguistics. *Language Arts* 84 (5): 419–430.

Genesee, Fred, Kathryn Lindholm-Leary, William Saunders, and Donna Christian. 2005. English Learners in U.S. Schools: An Overview of Research Findings. *Journal of Education for Students Placed at Risk* 10 (4): 363–385.

———. 2006. *Educating English Language Learners: A Synthesis of Research Evidence*. New York: Cambridge University Press.

Genesee, Fred, and Caroline Riches. 2006. Literacy: Instructional Issues. In *Educating English Language Learners: A Synthesis of Research Evidence,* ed. F. Genesee, K. Lindholm-Leary, W. Saunders, and D. Christian, 109–175. New York: Cambridge University Press.

George, MariAnne, Taffy E. Raphael, and Susan Florio-Ruane. 2003. Connecting Children, Culture, Curriculum, and Text. In *English Learners: Reaching the Highest Level of English Literacy,* ed. G. Garcia, 308–332. Newark, DE: International Reading Association.

Gersten, Russell, and Scott Baker. 2000. What We Know About Effective Instructional Practices for English Language Learners. *Exceptional Children* 66 (4): 454–470.

Gersten, Russell, and Robert Jiménez. 1997. *Promoting Learning for Culturally and Linguistically Diverse Students.* Albany, NY: Wadsworth Publishing.

Gibbons, Pauline. 1991. *Learning to Learn in a Second Language.* Portsmouth, NH: Heinemann.

———. 2002. *Scaffolding Language, Scaffolding Learning.* Portsmouth, NH: Heinemann.

Gilbert, Joan, and Marleen Kotelman. 2005. Five Good Reasons to Use Science Notebooks. *Science & Children* 43 (3): 28–32.

Goldenberg, Claude. 2008. *Teaching English Language Learners: What the Research Does and Does Not Say.* Washington, DC: *American Educator* (Summer 2008).

Gottlieb, Margo H. 2006. *Assessing English Language Learners: Bridges from Language Proficiency to Academic Achievement.* Thousand Oaks, CA: Corwin Press, Inc.

Guerrero, Michael. 1997. Spanish Academic Language Proficiency: The Case of Bilingual Education Teachers in the U.S. *Bilingual Research Journal* 21 (1): 65–84.

Gutiérrez, Kris D. 2001. What's New in the English Language Arts: Challenging Policies and Practices, ¿y qué? *Language Arts* 78 (6): 564–569.

Hadaway, Nancy, Sylvia Vardell, and Terrell Young. 2002. *Literature-based Instruction with English Language Learners K–12.* Boston: Allyn & Bacon.

Hakuta, Kenji. 2001. *The Education of Language Minority Students.* Testimony to the U.S. Commission on Civil Rights, April 13, 2001 [Online]. *Multilingual News* 24 (6): 10–14.

Halliday, Michael. 1978. *Language as a Social Semiotic.* Baltimore: University Park Press.

Hamayan, Else. 1985. *Assessment of Language Minority Students: A Handbook for Educators.* Arlington Heights, IL: Illinois Resource Center.

———. 2006. Diversity and Differentiated Instruction. *Language Magazine* 5 (6): 26–29.

Hargrove, Tracy, and Catherine Nesbit. 2003. *Science Notebooks: Tools for Increasing Achievement Across the Curriculum.* ERIC Document Reproduction Service No. ED482720. http://www.ericdigests.org/2004-4/notebooks.htm.

Heath, Shirley B. 1983. *Ways with Words.* New York: Cambridge University Press.

Herrell, Adrienne, and Michael Jordan. 2004. *Fifty Strategies for Teaching English Language Learners.* Upper Saddle River, NJ: Pearson Education, Inc.

Hoffman, James. 1992. Critical Reading/Thinking Across the Curriculum: Using I-charts to Support Learning. *Language Arts* 69 (2): 121–127.

Holdaway, Don. 1979. *The Foundations of Literacy.* Portsmouth, New Hampshire: Heinemann.

Housman, Naomi G., and Monica R. Martinez. 2002. *Preventing School Dropout and Ensuring Success for English Language Learners and Native American Students. CSR Connection.* National Clearinghouse for Comprehensive School Reform. http://www.goodschools.gwu.edu/pubs/annual/csrconpsd02.pdf.

Hudelson, Sarah. 1994. Literacy Development of Second Language Children. In *Educating Second Language Children*, ed. Fred Genesee, 129–158. New York: Cambridge University Press.

Irujo, Suzanne. 2007. What Does the Research Tell Us About Teaching Reading to English Language Learners? In *The ELL Outlook: News, Research and Discussion on the Education of English Language Learners.* Course Crafters, Inc.

Johnson, Donna M. 1994. Grouping Strategies for Second Language Learners. In *Educating Second Language Children: The Whole Child, the Whole Curriculum, the Whole Community*, ed. Fred Genesee, 183–211. New York: Cambridge University Press.

Kagan, Spencer. 1994. *Cooperative Learning.* San Clemente, CA: Kagan Publishing.

Klentschy, Michael P. 2008. *Using Science Notebooks in Elementary Classrooms.* Arlington, VA: National Science Teachers Association Press.

Klesmer, H. 1994. Assessment and Teacher Perceptions of ESL Teacher Achievement. *English Quarterly* 26 (3): 8–11.

Koran, Mary Lou, and John Koran. 1980. Interaction of Learner Characteristics with Pictorial Adjuncts in Learning from Science Text. *Journal of Research in Science Teaching* 1:4–483.

Krashen, Stephen D. 1982. *Principles and Practices of Second Language Acquisition.* Oxford, UK: Pergamon Press.

———. 1985. *The Input Hypothesis: Issues and Implications.* New York: Longman.

———. 1994. Bilingual Education and Second Language Acquisition Theory. In *Schooling and Language Minority Students: A Theoretical Framework*, 3rd ed., 33–64. Los Angeles: LBD Publishers.

Krashen, Stephen D., and Tracy D. Terrell. 1983. *The Natural Approach: Language Acquisition in the Classroom.* London: Prentice Hall England.

Kuhlman, Natalie. 2005. The Language Assessment Conundrum: What Tests Claim to Assess and What Teachers Need to Know. *ELL Outlook* (March/April 2005). http://www.coursecrafters.com/ELL-Outlook/2005/mar_apr/ELLOutlookITIArticle1.htm.

Laternau, Joseph. 2003. Standards-based Instruction for English Learners. In *English Learners: Reaching the Highest Level of English Literacy*, ed. Gilbert Garcia, 286–306. Newark, DE: International Reading Association, Inc.

Lightbown, Patsy M., and Nina Spada. 2006. *How Languages are Learned.* Oxford, UK: Oxford University Press.

Long, Michael, and Patricia Porter. 1985. Group Work, Interlanguage Talk, and Second Language Acquisition. *TESOL Quarterly* 19 (1): 207–228.

Marcarelli, Kellie. 2010. *Teaching Science with Interactive Notebooks.* Thousand Oaks, CA: Corwin Press.

McGroarty, Mary. 1993. Cooperative Learning and Second Language Acquisition. In *Cooperative Learning*, ed. Daniel Holt, 19–46. Washington, DC: Center for Applied Linguistics.

Moll, Luis C. 1992. Bilingual Classroom Studies and Community Analysis: Some Recent Trends. *Educational Researcher* 21 (2): 20–24.

———. 2001. The Diversity of Schooling: A Cultural-Historical Perspective. In *The Best for Our Children: Critical Perspectives on Literacy for Latino Students*, eds. M. L. Reyes and J. J. Halcon, 13–28, New York: Teachers College Press.

Moll, Luis C., and Norma González. 1997. Lessons From Research with Language Minority Children. *Journal of Reading Behavior* 26 (4): 439–456.

Moyer, John C., Larry Sowder, Judith Threadgill-Sowder, and Margaret B. Moyer. 1984. Story Problem Formats: Drawn Versus Telegraphic. *Journal for Research in Mathematics Education* 15:342–351.

National Clearinghouse for English Language Acquisition (NCELA). 2011. *The Growing Numbers of English Learner Students 1998/99–2008/09.* http://www.ncela.gwu.edu/files/uploads/9/growingLEP_0809.pdf.

National Science Teachers Association. 2009. *NSTA Position Statement: Science for English Language Learners.* Arlington, VA: NSTA.

Nieto, S. 2003. *Affirming Diversity*, 4th ed. New York: Longman.

Northcutt, Linda, and Daniel Watson. 1986. *Sheltered English Teaching Handbook.* Carlsbad, CA: Northcutt, Watson, Gonzalez.

Ogle, Donna M. 1986. K-W-L: A Teaching Model That Develops Active Reading of Expository Text. *Reading Teacher* 39:564–570.

Olsen, Laurie, and Ann Jaramillo. 1999. *Turning the Tides of Exclusion: A Guide for Educators and Advocates for Immigrant Students.* Oakland, CA: California Tomorrow.

O'Malley, J. Michael, and Lorraine Valdez Pierce. 1996. *Authentic Assessment for English Language Learners: Practical Approaches for Teachers.* Boston, MA: Addison-Wesley.

Pappamihiel, N. Eleni, and Tamara M. Walser. 2009. English Language Learners and Complexity Theory: Why Current Accountability Systems Do Not Measure Up. *The Educational Forum* 73 (2): 133–140.

Paris, Scott G., and Peter Winograd. 1990. How Metacognition Can Promote Academic Learning and Instruction. In *Dimensions of Thinking and Cognitive Instruction,* ed. B. F. Jones and L. Idol, 15–50. Hillsdale, NJ: Lawrence Erlbaum Associates.

Passel, Jeffrey. 2007. *Projections of the U.S. Population to 2050 by Age, Race, Hispanic Origin, and Nativity.* Washington, DC: PEW Hispanic Center.

Peregoy, Suzanne F., and Owen F. Boyle. 2008. *Reading, Writing and Learning in ESL: A Resource Book for K–12 Teachers.* White Plains, NY: Longman Publishers.

Pica, Teresa. 1994. Questions from the Language Classroom: Research Perspectives. *TESOL Quarterly* 28 (1): 49–79.

Pica, Teresa, Felicia Lincoln-Porter, Diana Paninos, and Julian Linell. 1996. Language Learner Interaction: How Does It Address the Input, Output, and Feedback Needs of L1 Learners? *TESOL Quarterly* 30 (1): 59–84.

Pressley, Michael. 1990. *Cognitive Strategy Instruction That Really Improves Children's Academic Performance.* Cambridge, MA: Brookline Books.

Pressley, Michael, Michael A. McDaniel, James Turnure, Eileen Wood, and Maheen Ahmad. 1987. Generation and Precision of Elaboration: Effects on Intentional and Incidental Learning. *Journal of Experimental Psychology: Learning, Memory, and Cognition* 13:291–300.

Rueda, Robert, and Hugh Mehan. 1986. Metacognition and Passing: Strategic Interactions in the Lives of Students with Disabilities. *Anthropology and Education Quarterly* 17 (3): 145–165.

Ruiz-Primo, Araceli, Min Li, and Richard Shavelson. 2002. *Looking into Science Notebooks: What Do Teachers Do with Them?* CRESST Technical Report 562. Los Angeles: CRESST.

Saunders, William, and Gisela O'Brien. 2006. Oral Language. In *Educating English Learners: A Synthesis of Research Evidence*, ed. F. Genesee, K. Lindholm-Leary, W. Saunders, and D. Christian, 14–63. New York: Cambridge University Press.

Schifini, Alfredo. 1985. *Sheltered English: Content Area Instruction for Limited English Proficiency Students.* Los Angeles: Los Angeles County Office of Education.

Shaw, Nancy E. 1997. *Sheep in a Jeep.* Boston: HMH Books.

Skutnabb-Kangas, Tove, and Jim Cummins, eds. 1988. *Minority Education: From Shame to Struggle.* New York: Taylor & Francis.

Stoddart, Trish, America Pinal, Marcia Latzke, and Dana Canaday. 2002. Integrating Inquiry Science and Language Development for English Language Learners. *Journal of Research in Science Teaching* 39 (8): 664–687.

Swain, Merrill. 1993. The Output Hypothesis: Just Speaking and Writing Aren't Enough. *The Canadian Modern Language Review* 50:150–164.

———. 1995a. Three Functions of Output in Second Language Learning. In *Principle and Practice in Applied Linguistics: Studies in Honour of H. G. Widdowson,* eds. G. Cook and B. Seidlehofer, 125–144. Oxford, UK: Oxford University Press.

———. 1995b. Communicative Competence: Some Roles of Comprehensible Input and Output in Its Development. In *Input in Second Language Acquisition,* eds. S. M. Gass and C. G. Madden, 235–253. Rowley, MA: Newbury House.

Swanson, H. Lee. 1991. Learning Disabilities and Memory. In *A Cognitive Approach to Learning Disabilities,* 2nd ed. eds. D. K. Reid, W. P. Hresko, and H. L. Swanson, 129–182. Austin, TX: Pro-Ed.

Terrell, Tracy D. 1981. The Natural Approach in Bilingual Education. In *Schooling and Language Minority Students: A Theoretical Framework,* 1st ed. Los Angeles: Evaluation, Dissemination and Assessment Center, California State University, Los Angeles.

Teachers of English to Speakers of Other Languages (TESOL). 2006. *Pre-K–12 English Language Proficiency Standards.* Alexandria, VA: Teachers of English to Speakers of Other Languages.

Tharp, Roland G. 1997. *From At-Risk to Excellence: Research, Theory, and Principles for Practice.* Research Report 1 [Online]. http://www.cal.org/crede/pubs/researchreports.html#7.

Thomas, Wayne P., and Virginia P. Collier. 1999. Accelerated Schooling for English Language Learners. *Educational Leadership* 56 (7): 46–49.

Tomlinson, Carol A. 2003. *Fulfilling the Promise of the Differentiated Classroom: Strategies and Tools for Responsive Teaching.* Alexandria, VA: Association for Supervision and Curriculum Development.

———. 2004. *How to Differentiate Instruction in Mixed Ability Classrooms,* 2nd ed. Alexandria, VA: Association for Supervision and Curriculum Development.

Tomlinson, Carol A., and Jay McTighe. 2006. *Integrating Differentiated Instruction and Understanding by Design.* Alexandria, VA: Association for Supervision and Curriculum Development.

Trumbull, Elise, Carrie Rothstein-Fisch, Patricia M. Greenfield, and Blanca Quiroz. 2001. *Bridging Cultures Between Home and School: A Guide for Teachers.* Mahwah, NJ: Lawrence Erlbaum Associates, Publishers.

U.S. Department of Education, National Center for Education Statistics (NCES). 2006. *The Condition of Education 2006.* (NCES 2006-071). Washington, DC: U.S. Government Printing Office.

U.S. Department of Education. 2010. *Elementary and Secondary Education Reauthorization Act Blueprint for Reform.* Washington, DC: Office of Planning, Evaluation and Policy Development.

Valdés, Guadalupe. 2001. *Learning and Not Learning English: Latino Students in American Schools.* New York: Teachers College Press.

Van Lier, Leo. 1996. *Interaction in the Language Curriculum: Awareness, Autonomy and Authenticity.* London: Longman.

Vialpando, Jacqueline, Caroline Linse, and Jane Yedlin. 2005. *Educating English Language Learners: Understanding and Using Assessment.* Washington, DC: National Council of La Raza and The Education Alliance at Brown University.

Vygotsky, Lev. 1978. *Mind in Society: The Development of Higher Psychological Processes.* Cambridge, MA: Harvard University Press.

———. 1986. *Thought and Language.* Cambridge, MA: Harvard University Press.

Walqui, Aida. 2003. *Conceptual Framework: Scaffolding Instruction for English Learners.* San Francisco: WestEd.

World-Class Instructional Design and Assessment. 2004. *WIDA Consortium English Language Proficiency Standards for English Language Learners in Kindergarten Through Grade 12.* Madison, WI: Board of Regents of the University of Wisconsin System.

Writing Reform Institute for Teaching Excellence. 2003. San Diego, CA: San Diego County Office of Education.

Wood, David, Jerome Bruner, and Gail Ross. 1976. The Role of Tutoring in Problem Solving. *Journal of Child Psychology and Psychiatry* 17 (2): 89–100.

Young, Jocelyn. 2003. Science Interactive Notebooks in the Classroom. *Science Scope* 26 (4): 44–47.

Zwiers, Jeff. 2008. *Building Academic Language: Essential Practices for Content Classrooms.* Newark, DE: International Reading Association.